To Steve

Thank you for your support and friendship
Enjoy your book!
"We fear naught but God"
Kind Regards
Paul Bays 654 and Annie.

SPECIALISED COOKING
THE RECCE WAY

A great meal is not remembered for the recipe – it is remembered for the occasion.

SPECIALISED COOKING
THE RECCE WAY

Volume 1

By **Justin Vermaak** and **Douw Steyn**

JONATHAN BALL PUBLISHERS
JOHANNESBURG AND CAPE TOWN

All rights reserved.
No part of this publication may be reproduced or transmitted, in any form or by any means, without prior permission from the publisher or copyright holder.

© Text, Justin Vermaak and Douw Steyn 2017
© Published edition, Jonathan Ball Publishers 2017
© Food photography, Myburgh du Plessis
© Historical images, Sasfa archive
   (also see p. 224 for photographic credits)

"Recce" is trade marked to the South African Special Forces Herirtage Foundation

Published in South Africa in 2017 by
JONATHAN BALL PUBLISHERS
A division of Media24 (Pty) Ltd
PO Box 33977
Jeppestown
2043

Standard edition ISBN 978-1-86842-788-8 (English edition)
Collectors' edition ISBN 978-1-86842-789-5
e-ISBN 978-1-86842-836-6

Every effort has been made to trace the copyright holders and to obtain their permission for the use of copyright material. The publishers apologise for any errors or omissions and would be grateful to be notified of any corrections that should be incorporated in future editions of this book.

Twitter: www.twitter.com/JonathanBallPub
Facebook: www.facebook.com/JonathanBallPublishers
Blog: http://jonathanball.bookslive.co.za/

Cover by Peter Bosman
Design and typesetting by Peter Bosman
Editing by Alfred LeMaitre
Proofreading by Kathleen Sutton
Index by Joy Clack
Maps by Peter Bosman
Printed and bound by Imago Productions (FE) Pte Ltd, Singapore
Set in Nexus Sans

COVER IMAGE Koos Moorcroft (left) and André Diedericks (right) in Angola.

CONTENTS

INTRODUCTION ... 6

Acknowledgements ... 8

A word from the South African Special Forces Association (Sasfa) ... 9

How to Use this Book ... 10

The Basics ... 11

1. TRICKS OF THE TRADE ... 16
2. IF IT SWIMS ... 36
3. IF IT FLIES ... 69
4. IF IT WALKS ... 97
5. IF IT GROWS ... 122
6. REGIONAL FLAVOURS ... 150
7. THE SWEETER SIDE ... 186
8. THE DRINKS TROLLEY ... 198
9. KILLER MEALS ... 206

Call for submissions for Volume 2 ... 218

Index ... 219

INTRODUCTION

Congratulations on acquiring your copy of *Specialised Cooking – The Recce Way*. To really enjoy this book, we suggest you pour some wine and pull up a comfortable chair. Reading through a section should take about one glass. There are nine sections, so plan your reading and drinking carefully.

Originally, this book was not intended for a broad audience; it was designated for limited distribution to a specific interest group. It came about after we were tasked, in true military style, by our colleagues at the South African Special Forces Association (Sasfa) to create a coffee-table cookbook. When their instruction came, there was no way out. We had to say 'yes'.

This book is published within a certain context. We have assumed that the reader will at least have heard of the Reconnaissance Regiments or Recces™ and have a basic idea of South African military operations between 1972 and 1997. We have observed the provisions of the Official Secrets Act and published only content that is already in the public domain.

The majority of the recipes are set in the period between the late 1970s and 1990, the time of the so-called Border War, when military activities were at their peak. However, in covering operations and events up to 1997 we want to take the history of the Reconnaissance Regiments beyond the political transition of the early 1990s. This is done to emphasise that the Special Forces soldiers are part of a formation that has served South Africa continuously for more than 40 years, regardless of the government in power.

Furthermore, in 1997, 1 Reconnaissance Regiment was disbanded – 25 years after its inception. There is no old and new formation – just the Special Forces.

Being a specialised soldier requires tremendous adaptability and the ability to stay focused on the defined outcome. It is about living in the moment. The ethos of the Special Forces is defined by these four basic qualities: persevere, focus on the moment, adapt and act. The submissions we received for this book highlight these qualities very clearly, and we trust that you will recognise this common thread running throughout the book.

While a 'normal' recipe book will contain only recipes that can hold their own in a MasterChef competition, this was not what we were after. This book is about not so normal.

Our recipes are not about simply getting some slop onto a tray. They are about creating occasions, special moments in which the people and the surroundings are very much part of the ingredients. We have limited the recipes to those that help to give broad insight into the scope of activities of the different reconnaissance units, those that are clearly about a moment created around food. Our 'living-in-the-moment' recipes are therefore recorded in an anecdotal style.

They are also funny. The Recces are a special breed of men who have adapted to excel in adverse conditions. For them, unfavourable conditions are not considered a hardship but an opportunity to perform at the highest level. Despite their status as hardened soldiers who'll stop at nothing to get the job done, almost all of them have a well-developed sense of humour. We love to tease each other, if only because it keeps you mentally relaxed and allows you to focus on the moment and the task at hand.

'Specialised cooking' is for those who find themselves in unusual places under unusual circumstances. Over the years, the Special Forces soldiers have built up a vast collective experience, with a spectrum of operations that is dazzling in its diversity, with the operational scope including places as far away as Dar es Salaam, Cabinda and Kinshasa.

This also means that soldiers must be equally comfortable wearing smart mess dress to a crayfish-and-caviar formal on a weekend and deploying deep behind enemy lines on the Monday with 'black is beautiful' cream on their faces (knowing they'll have a limited food supply for the next few weeks).

Napoleon famously said that an army marches on its stomach, so it's quite ironic that a vast number of the submissions received for this book described a lack of food. Take, for instance, this comment in one of the recipes: 'After going without food for three days you'll be given diesel-saturated dog biscuits,' or 'the stew still had the monkey hands inside when it was my chance to dish up'.

The specialised chef can prepare great food anywhere, at any time and with very little, by using his creativity to make

Special Forces instructors enjoy a Sunday lunch in the Doppies training area in northern Namibia. From left to right: Peter Lamberti, HG van Zyl, James Teitge and Ray Godbeer.

up for any lack of ingredients or cooking utensils. After spending the whole day on the back of a Russian Ural truck with 50 Unita soldiers and bouncing up and down alongside the ammo cases, it is the specialised chef who will get off to check how many eggs survived the trip in their carefully packed trays. Then it's simply a matter of whipping up a batch of flapjacks for the Tac HQ as if it were Sunday morning. These are the hallmarks of a specialised chef. Adapt, focus and perform, or get out of the kitchen!

We have also included several ingredients a Special Forces soldier may have used (or encountered) during his time as an operator. We want to remind the reader that in specialised cooking anything that is remotely nutritious can be served – nothing is taboo. For this reason, some of the meals in this book probably won't be repeated by choice. These include Diesel-dipped Dog Biscuits (a selection course treat), Omuramba Vulture Soup (a survival course special) and Roasted Mopane Worms (a local delicacy).

However, when the opportunity presents itself, you should also be able to present a formal supper to the highest cooking standards with all the pomp and ceremony required for a once-in-a-lifetime meal. It is the specialised chef who can braai even if he's on a submarine, make a three-course meal using only a dixie, and send hot steaks to the troops on the battlefront 200 km forward.

You will read many references to Fort Doppies in the former Caprivi Strip (today the Zambezi Region). It is a unique place with a unique history. At this bush base the Recce culture of brotherhood and camaraderie was instilled. It is probably the one place that every Special Forces member who served in the first 25 years since 1972 can identify with.

At Fort Doppies men from different cultures and race groups have built enduring bonds of friendship. Today the area around the former base is a beautiful game park. The tranquillity and sounds of the bush refresh body and mind. It is worth the long trip just to sit under one of many sausage trees on the banks of the Kwando River and smell the grass and listen to the crickets.

While all our recipes work and the majority actually make wonderful meals, we want to reiterate that our focus is on getting the setting and the context right, as this is the way to turn any meal into more than just the sum of its ingredients. Think about it: doesn't food always taste better when it is served in the bush under the stars while you're listening to the sounds of the night than when it is eaten in a mess hall to the sound of clattering plates?

Lastly, our lists of ingredients won't always have exact quantities because no Recce takes a measuring cup into the bush and, as we've said, adapt or die is our credo. However, we tried to be as exact as possible in our references to the facts. If memory let us down or we made a mistake, we apologise in advance and will try to rectify it.

If you're reading this book, your focus should be on creating a special occasion. So open that extraordinary bottle of wine you've been saving for years or grab an ice-cold beer and enjoy this book with us. May you be inspired and stay forever young at heart.

Justin Vermaak
Douw Steyn

Acknowledgements

Whenever the members of the Special Forces get together, we always talk about how we should write a book focusing on the lighter side of things. While we're working on *Korporaals, Cortinas and Kawasakis*, we believe this publication will help whet the appetite. After all, the main focus is on food and all the moments that go along with it.

We thank the teams from the South African Special Forces Association (Sasfa) and Recce Inc™ for their input and assistance in bringing everything together. Putting together a book like this takes a huge amount of time and effort. As when we were still operators, the greatest satisfaction is achieved when a mission is completed successfully and you can look back on a job well done.

Publishing a book is never the work of a single person. A special word of thanks to the following individuals who submitted photos or stories or helped in other ways: Roy Vermaak, Dap Maritz, Tuffy Joubert, Tim Timmerman, Spik Botha, Martin Smith, Malcolm, Johan Raath, Eugene Geyer, Blikkies Blignaut, Taffy Pelser, Willie van Deventer, Gary Yaffe, Martiens Verster, John van Heerden, Stephen Dunkley, Paul Els, Roelf du Plooy, Theo van Huysteen, Renier du Toit, Callie Roos, Flip Marx, Pierre Lundberg, Hein Vosloo, Koos Moorcroft, Marius Boonzaaier, Hannes Venter, SW Fourie, Rieme de Jager, André Bestbier, Doiby Coetzee, Barry Visser, Frans van Dyk, Johnny de Gouveia, Wally Vermaak, Roland de Vries, Div Lamprecht, Les Rudman, Olga Roos, Jakes Swart, Jakes Richter and Dewald de Beer.

The majority of photos in this book were supplied by former Special Forces members. For all those who submitted photos, whether knowingly or not, a big thank-you and please forgive us any inaccuracies or mistakes. It was often tough to manage all the incoming emails and photos without captions ... also, our memory is not always what it used to be.

While working on the book, we realised yet again that being a Recce is neither a job nor a career; it is a lifestyle. The saying 'old soldiers never die' is very true.

We would like to thank every single former or current member, regardless of whether they served for one year or 40. Our collective input has created an amazing dynamic. It is a great privilege to have served and to be still part of this dynamic – thank you for the camaraderie. The distinction of serving with such an elite organisation instils a sense of personal pride that lasts a lifetime.

A WORD FROM THE SOUTH AFRICAN SPECIAL FORCES ASSOCIATION

This book is a first of its kind and embodies all that the South African Special Forces Association (Sasfa) soldiers and Sasfa itself represents. Its publication was made possible by Sasfa members, and all income generated from the sale of the book will go directly to Sasfa.

We offer this book to readers with immense pride. The Recce units have a distinguished history covering close to 44 years and they are still regarded with the highest esteem around the world. This book acknowledges and aims to capture a part of this history.

Sasfa is a non-profit organisation for former serving members of the South African Special Forces. As an association it has three primary objectives:
1. To provide a common connection and entry point for ex-members of the Special Forces;
2. To provide and coordinate support for ex-members in times of need;
3. To maintain a strong link with the current serving structures.

To achieve these objectives, ex-members give freely of their time and resources to support their own, as with this book.

This publication will take the reader on a tongue-in-cheek journey through the first 25 years of the Special Forces, or Recce units. Even though it contains real recipes for cooking under special circumstances, it is also intended to provide a glimpse into the real world of Africa's most distinguished fighting formation ever. In these pages you will get a sense of the soldiers' lives, the operational conditions under which they worked (and work) and how they operate as a collective.

Being a Recce is about how individuals became units, and how units become an invincible adaptive force. It is this unique aspect of functioning as a collective that defines the Recce's extraordinary history. This togetherness and camaraderie is the most distinguishing aspect of the soldiers of the Reconnaissance Regiments, and it still holds strong and true to this day.

The word 'Recce' describes a soldier who has qualified as a Special Forces operator by completing the selection and all courses of the training cycle. It originates in the formation of the first unit that was called 1 Reconnaissance Commando – hence Recce. In the first 25 years after the Special Forces were established, fewer than 500 operators qualified as Recces.

As Sasfa we have decided to preserve the word 'Recce' for the sake of the members and their legacy. 'Recce' is trademarked under the banner of South African Special Forces Heritage Foundation. In doing so, we want to ensure that it is not exploited commercially without our members' consent and endorsement.

As a parting word, I want to welcome you to our specialised cookbook. When I read it, I smiled on every page. I think the compilers and contributors have executed their task exceptionally. This is a cookbook with the flavour of the Special Forces soldier interspersed throughout.

Callie Roos
Chairman, Sasfa (2014–2016)

How to Use this Book

There was much discussion on how to group the recipes in this book, and it went much like the chicken and the egg debate. Luckily, here we have both the chicken and the egg. In the end, we decided to group some of the recipes by food type and others by location or event.

For instance, in the chapters If It Swims (seafood), If It Flies (poultry), If It Walks (red meat) and If It Grows (vegetables, fruits and grains), the recipes are ordered around certain food types, whereas in Regional Flavours the recipes have been selected according to where they were made or the specific circumstances around their preparation.

So, if you're looking for a recipe for crocodile steak, to which chapter should you turn? It swims and it walks, and crocodile definitely requires specialised cooking skills. Furthermore, it bites back and is found all over Africa. In this instance, as in many others, it is probably best simply to go to the index and look it up there.

For each recipe, we have tried our best to describe the special moment created around the meal or to explain the context in which it was first made. For this reason, our recipes don't read like those you'll find in your average cookbook. Some of them don't even have a list of ingredients – even if it is all about food.

The recipes and photos of some of the dishes are also interspersed with previously unpublished or rarely seen photos submitted by former Recces. As they say, a picture tells a thousand words.

The book assumes that you are adaptable and that you will be creative enough to make certain changes to the recipes as and when required. In real life, the stage and supply line for operators was often a Cuca shop in Ovamboland or a go-down in Uganda. While we always had certain basics available (think ratpack), we could often also count on receiving some decent supplies – be it through the ratrun,[1] at an embassy or from local heavyweights. We quickly learned to build moments with whatever we could lay our hands on.

The book also assumes that you have a basic understanding of the cooking process. All the recipes list the ingredients in the order they will be used. Some of the recipes give exact measurements of ingredients; others simply list the ingredients, leaving the details for you to decide, depending on the setting and the number of guests.

You are therefore allowed to interpret the recipes as you want. So, if it says 'add curry', feel free to play around with the measurements and quantities. Every moment needs to be unique, and for this reason you should always experiment with the ingredients and explore new taste combinations.

We hope this recipe book will help you to become free when you cook. After reading it, you will be much more empowered to experiment (with new ingredients and new cooking styles). May these recipes inspire you and teach you that, no matter what you are cooking, the meal will be great if the right conditions are created around the preparation and serving of the food – that we guarantee you!

A warthog that was caught in a snare finds its way onto the coals in a true bush camp.

---

[1] The 'ratrun' was the term used to refer to incoming supplies. These usually arrived at the bases on the border by vehicle convoy or transport plane.

The Basics

Koos Verwey (holding pointer) explains the use of sand models to students on the minor tactics course.

Part 1

To qualify as a South African Special Forces operator, you need to have completed at least the following training:[2]

- Army basic training (three months)
- Army skills I course (three months)
- Pre-selection course (variable)
- Selection course (variable)

- **Dark Phase (two weeks)**
- Water orientation course (around three weeks)
- Jump course – static line (three weeks)
- Basic demolitions (three weeks)
- Weapons course (two weeks)

- **Air Orientation (three weeks)**
- Survival course (three weeks)
- Tracking and bushcraft course (three weeks)
- Minor tactics (six weeks)
- First operation

Only then are you allowed to go on your first operation as a Special Forces operator. Once deployed, you will eat almost entirely what was packed in your rucksack – meaning dry foods such as flour and maize meal as well as canned food. From a specialised cooking perspective, this means you must become skilled at packing and living out of a 35 kg rucksack.

For longer deployments, you would cache food somewhere close to your starting point. Out in the bush, you are likely to encounter 'opportunity foods' such as mushrooms, marog, thistle, bananas, fish, birds, berries, game, cassava, etc. Adding any of these fresh ingredients to your dry rations is a morale-booster like no other. It suggests that you are in control.

Opportunity foods like these must be taken without hesitation. This is vital to get fresh food and some variety into your diet. It will also make you realise how one great meal in adverse conditions can lift your morale and help you to stay focused.

---

[2] These courses varied over the 25-year period covered in this book, but this list represents as full a training cycle as one could possibly get. In the early years, passing the selection course was the most important criterion, but by the early 1980s a more formal process had been established, with the Special Forces School doing the training.

INTRODUCTION 11

A quick energy guide

During the selection and survival courses, you would've been taught and forced to eat anything and everything. You would've realised that everything is about energy. Pack for energy first, then for taste. You need a minimum of 9 600 kilojoules (kJ) per day. Table 1 gives typical energy values for a variety of ingredients.

To maintain body weight, at least 9 600 kJ must be consumed daily. This is for active deployment when you are walking four hours a day. When sitting in an observation post, you can go down to 7 600 kJ a day.

Table 1 – Energy per 100 g

	Ingredient	Energy value (kJ)		
1	cooking oil, butter, fat	3 500	2 950	3 100
2	maggots,[3] mopane worms	2 900	1 800	
3	sugar, raisins/dried fruit	1 700	1 250	
4	flour, maize, rice	1 500	1 350	1 300
5	milk, cheddar, powdered milk	279	1 600	2 050
6	chicken, meat, bacon	990	1 400	1 975
7	beer, wine, spirits	121	240	950
8	termites, grasshoppers	480	210	
9	orange, apple, banana	190	200	380
10	tomato, onion, potato	30	100	380

André Diedericks with a Small Teams rucksack for an 18-day deployment.

A basic guide to packing

The kind of deployment you are sent on will determine what you can take along. For long deployments, remember to pack treats. Ideally, you should have one for every seven days, so you have something to look forward to. It's amazing what a simple flapjack in a dixie does for you after a week of ratpack (ration pack) meals. Here are a few guidelines for different travel situations:

- When travelling on foot, your backpack should contain: Tabasco sauce, salt/pepper, lemon juice, stock cubes, raisins, sugar, coffee/tea, energy drinks, curry powder, Bisto, cooking oil.[3]
- When deployed with a vehicle – especially on Sabre-type operations[4] – add some fresh rations. These might be lower in energy value but you have the extra space: eggs, biltong, onions, potatoes, dried fruit, pickles, tinned cream, flour, maize meal, baking powder, garlic, mustard, mixed herbs, Worcestershire sauce, spice packets, parsley, cloves, oregano, dry yeast and more cooking oil.
- If you have access to a building, then add: tomatoes, veggies and other fresh things, rice, pasta, couscous, corn flour, olive oil, balsamic vinegar, bay leaves, spice packets (potato mix, fish spice, spice for rice), flavourants, vanilla essence, cinnamon.
- If you have access to a Woolworths … wake up, you are dreaming!

The outer pouches of your backpack are for water only; you need a minimum of eight litres. The bottom section is for your sleeping bag and clothes. The main pouch is for the radio, explosives, ammo, etc. The middle of the pack is your kitchen. Pack everything so that it doesn't rattle or shake. Always take 200 ml of cooking oil.

---

3 Bountiful quantities of maggots are to be found at the site of large, 'mature' animal carcasses. Scoop a few handfuls into an empty water bottle. Best served pan-fried in oil until light brown.

4 The term 'Sabre' was used for vehicles that were adapted for long-range reconnaissance, specialised raiding and ambushes. These included adaptations of the standard Land Rover and Unimog, as well as some specially built dune and desert vehicles. 'Sabre operations' thus refers to operations in which soldiers deployed with these vehicles.

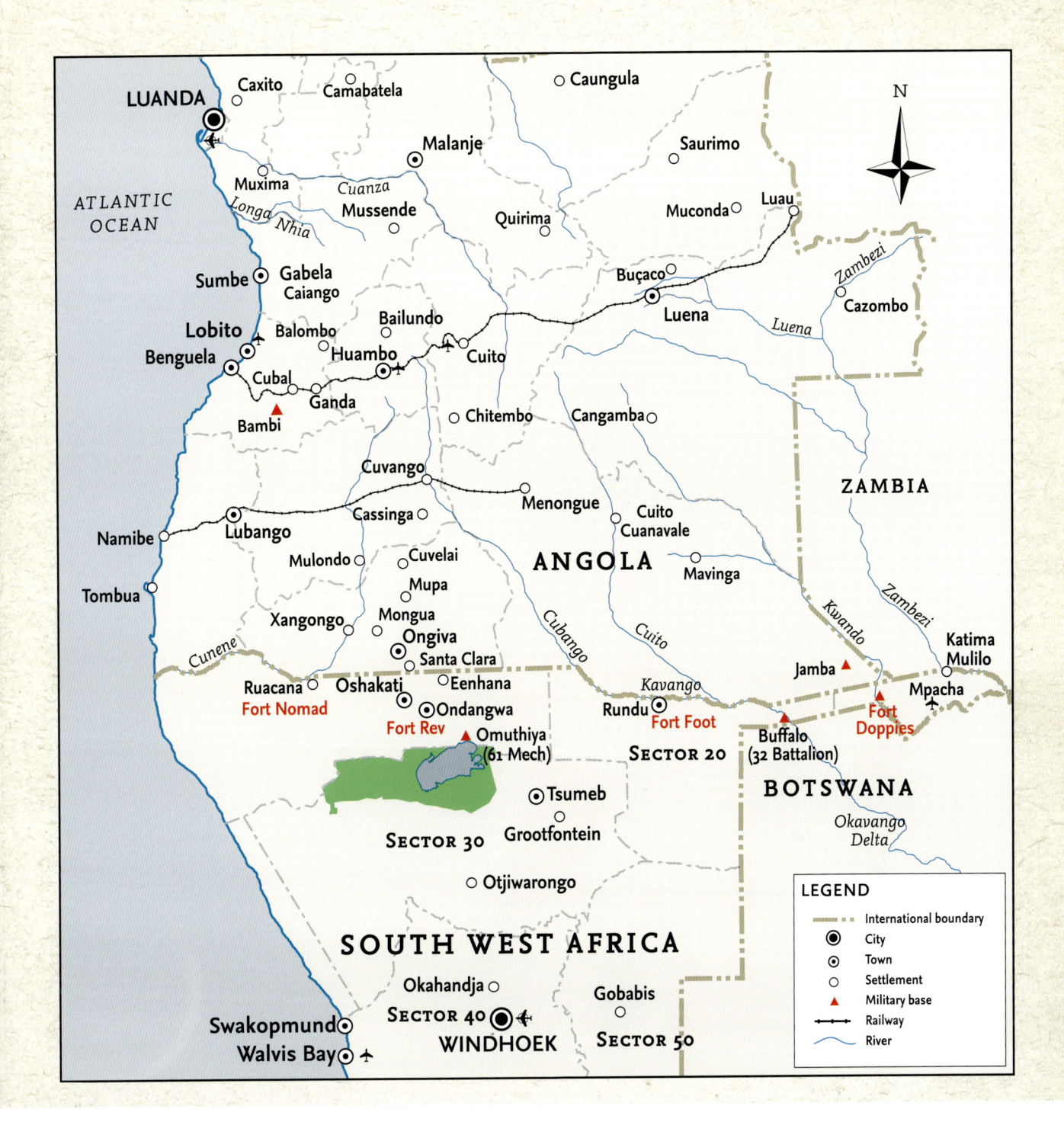

These ten food rules must be followed at all times to ensure survival:

- Your dry food should be equivalent to at least 9 600 kJ a day. If it doesn't fit into your pack, plan again.
- Eat slowly. The food won't run away.
- Tabasco sauce goes with everything.
- Pack two sizes of clothes if you'll be deployed for more than 14 days.
- Use a wooden or plastic spoon – it makes less noise. Make a wooden spoon in your spare time.
- Pack everything back into your backpack after you have eaten – stay prepared.
- Don't make a fire close to the enemy – eat during the day.
- Soup/stew is healthy and doesn't require dishwashing liquid – just wipe the dixie clean.
- Conserve water – sand is the best way to clean anything.
- Eat energy bars in private – then you won't have to share.

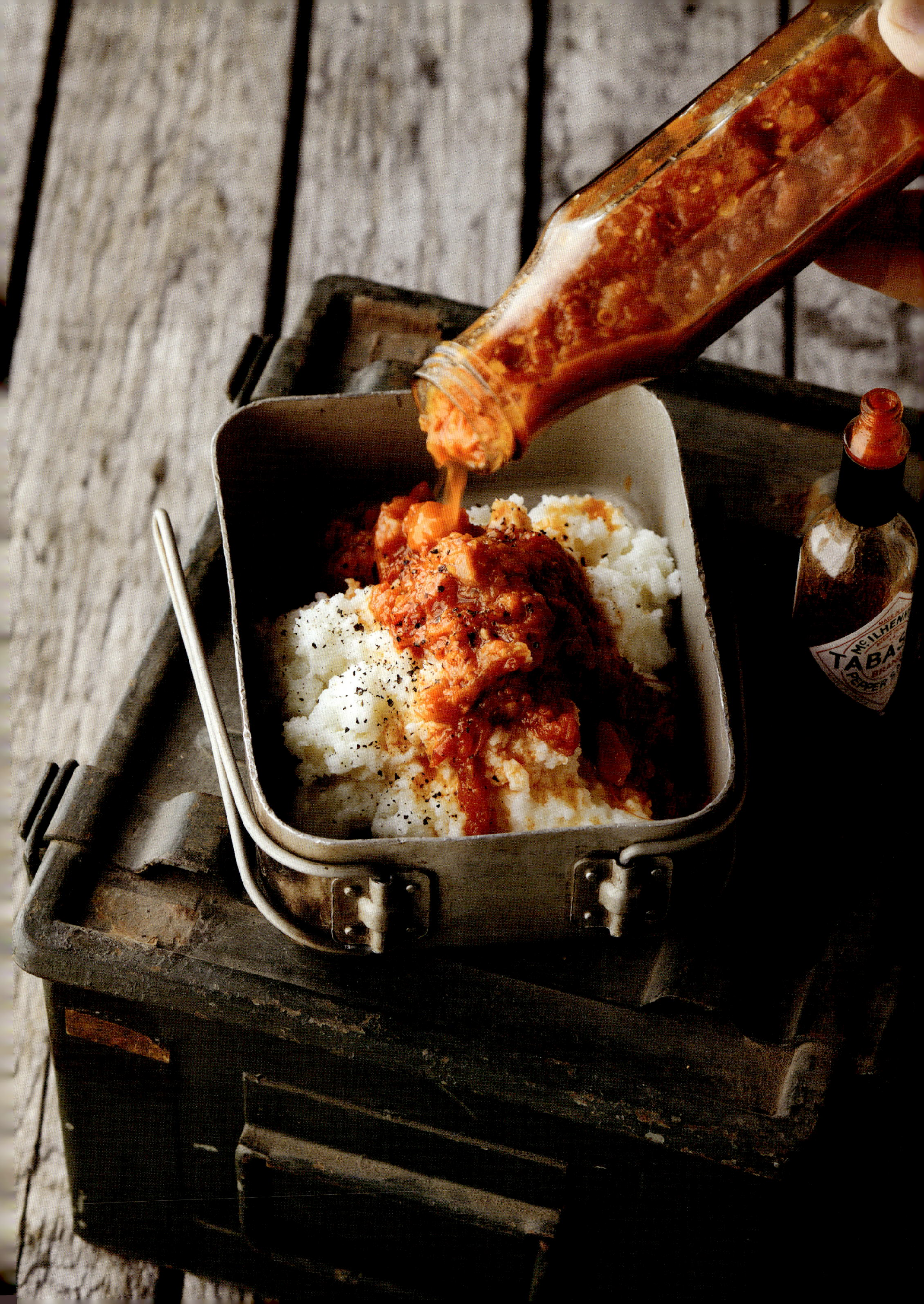

Part 2

There are a few basics every specialised chef should be able to make. The sooner you get it right, the sooner you can start creating those special occasions. You need to know at least the following: how to sauté onions, how to make a red sauce, how to make a white sauce, how to prepare a batter and how to present your food properly. You also need to have a sense of occasion and to be able to create a moment.

Sauté onions*

Nearly all cooked meals are made with onion, the world's most consumed vegetable. The smell of onion browning in a pan is your first move in creating a special atmosphere. To lightly sauté an onion in a pan:

Peel and quarter the onion, then slice and dice.

Add one teaspoon of cooking oil and two tablespoons of water per onion to the pan.

Lightly blanch the onion. It will brown once the water has evaporated.

Add salt and stir.

***Tip:** To prevent the onion from falling apart, don't cut off the leafy side on the top. Instead, follow these steps: (i) cut off the roots; (ii) peel off the skin; (iii) cut in lengths; (iv) cut across to make blocks; and (v) cut off the top.

Red sauce

After you've sautéed the onions, add finely chopped tomatoes to make a red sauce.

Add a half teaspoon of sugar for every two big tomatoes.

Cook tomatoes through.

Add salt and two shakes of Tabasco and Worcestershire sauce.

Cook large quantities at a time and store in bottles. Red sauce goes well in potato bake, kidneys, pap, potjie or even on a slice of bread.

White sauce

To make this sauce, melt two tablespoons of margarine before mixing in two tablespoons of cake flour.

Once the mixture starts to bubble, add 500 ml of milk.

While it is heating up, mix a little corn flour with cold water in a cup. Stir into the mixture as it starts to cook.

Add a teaspoon of salt, white pepper and any other spices you like.

Mushrooms and peppercorns add great flavour.

A dollop of cream will finish off your sauce perfectly.

Batter

To make a batter you need cake flour, baking powder, a bottle of beer, salt and spices.

If you have self-raising flour you just need the beer.

Mix everything together – the texture will depend on what you want to make.

For fish batter, add fish spice and make it runny.

For flapjacks, add an egg and drop the spices.

For pancakes, replace beer with milk and drop the spices.

Presentation

You will start eating with your eyes long before you taste the food. So get the colours of your meal right. Turn your rye bread toast into a spectacle with grated cheese and pickled vegetables. Just imagine the colours – green, orange, red, yellow, black. Always plate and the present the food properly, even if it's only for yourself in the bush.

A sense of occasion

For a great atmosphere and a full sensory experience, you have to get all the different elements just right: the scenery, the smells, the sounds and, of course, the taste. Even if you're only serving dog biscuits, go the extra mile: crumble and soak them in water overnight. Add a little condensed milk or milk powder the next morning, shake and serve.

The moment

Let everything build up to the final moment when the meal is served. Most people like big events, such as unit functions where you do spit braais, camo parties or formal suppers. By inviting people in time and creating some hype or buzz around the function, you'll increase their sense of anticipation. Make sure that everyone is eagerly awaiting the event – for example, a monthly big tea with lots of snacks at 10hoo on a Friday morning. It is all about getting your guests to focus.

Lastly, a defence ...

Despite your best efforts, you might not be successful in creating a moment at all meals. This happens with and without the presence of Red Heart rum (RHR). Be ready to deflect the ridicule and teasing. Blame the regimental sergeant major (RSM), the Jammies (support staff), the weather or the wood (in this order) but don't accept responsibility for the failure outright. Refer to previous instances when you got it right. Then change the topic and make sure you get it right next time.

> Never volunteer, never come first, never come last, never give up.

1

TRICKS OF THE TRADE

The hallmark of an elite Recce soldier is his resilience and ability to excel in adverse conditions. This comes from his innate ability to endure, adapt, focus and stay in the moment.

During training, these skills are tested and developed. The initial training cycle of the Special Forces is over one year long. One of the many things the soldier learns during this time is that, as far as food is concerned, nothing is taboo if you look at things from the right perspective. The courses that best impart this truth are selection, survival, dark phase and minor tactics. Each course does so in a very different way.

> You don't have to like it, you just have to do it.
> SEALS

Recce hopefuls on the pre-selection course in northern Zululand. Here the instructor (Dirk Lourens) takes them on an extended run with tar poles.

SELECTION FOOD

The Cross is one of many ways to get Recce recruits to carry awkward, heavy objects in teams to teach them the art of how to endure together.

Before you can join the Special Forces training cycle, you first have to pass a number of gruelling physical and psychological tests. After these, you join the selection course, which does exactly what it says; it selects the best of the best, and it does so by way of simple elimination. Recruits can take themselves out of the race by simply saying, 'I give up.' If you don't use these words during selection, you forever lose the right to do so afterwards.

Over the years, the selection course has evolved in different ways. In the early years, the founding members of the South African Special Forces did a Special Air Service (SAS) or SAS-type selection and this moulded the selection courses that followed immediately after. As the Border War developed, selection turned into more of a bush endurance course. These were longer courses that had no set routine and could last from four to seven weeks.

Initially, the selection course was viewed as the Alpha and Omega of all the Special Forces qualification courses, but today it is seen as only one of the many steps to becoming a Recce. The later and current courses are shorter and more intense, with added psychological testing. Despite all the changes to the course, one thing has remained consistent: breaking down the recruits and testing them to the extreme. One element that has always been used in the breakdown process is food – or the lack thereof.

The aim of whatever food is given to the recruits on the selection course is to force them to apply mind over matter. The recruits' ability to endure, adapt and do what the moment requires is also tested. They have to eat whatever is available, and edible, in order to keep going, and to keep going even if there is nothing to eat.

The following three meals have endured all selection formats and have become a permanent feature on the course: *Suurpap*, Diesel-dipped Dog Biscuits and Empty Pot Stew.

SPECIALISED COOKING – THE RECCE WAY

SUURPAP

by Callie Roos

Suurpap simply means 'sour porridge'. Pap is like porridge but made with less water so that it is stiff and bulky. Mieliepap is made with maize meal and was by far the dominant staple food in South West Africa.

During the selection course there comes a moment when you and the other recruits are presented with this big pot of food. By that time, you are desperately tired and the hunger has set in deeply. Never have a pair of eyes been more thankful than when they see the pot.

You all line up to get your scoop – be it into your bush hat, dixie or fire bucket. The instructors smile as they ladle the pap into your receptacle. You take your food and scurry off into bush to eat before it is taken away from you.

But the moment you try to eat it, your stomach starts convulsing. No matter how hard you try, you can't get it in. You try everything to improve the taste – burn it on a fire, mix it with water, cook it some more. But nothing is to be done to what you now realise is *suurpap*.

After a day or two, pap is on the menu again. You remain hopeful, but this time it's even worse; it's the same pap as before, only more rotten. Same result.

A few years after I endured the trials of *suurpap*, I happened to be an instructor on a selection course. I overheard the sergeant major tell the chef how to prepare the porridge, and that was when I realised that food preparation for the selection course is a fine art.

Big bag of maize meal
Water
6–12 tins of condensed milk

Cook a big bag of maize meal and water in a black pot until it is half-cooked.

Then add another half bag of raw maize meal and six to twelve tins of condensed milk.

Leave the mixture in the sun for two days until the porridge starts to form small bubbles.

Put the pot on the back of a Land Rover and serve when necessary.

TOP A student passes through one of many obstacles that make up the obstacle course.

LEFT A lonely recruit gets his *suurpap*. Even if you feel like you're dying of hunger, you'll still struggle to swallow *suurpap*.

TRICKS OF THE TRADE

EMPTY POT STEW

1 cast-iron pot
28 litres of imagination
Salt and pepper

This is a classic dish that almost all instructors know how to prepare. It is very easy to make.

Put a big empty cast-iron pot – number 10 or bigger – over the fire (after you've cleaned out the *suurpap*).

Get two smaller pots going on the side, usually with savoury mince in the one and pap in the other.

Once recruits arrive after walking for many days in the bush, order them to sit in groups around the fire. Watch the expression on their faces change as they smell the food.

Announce that supper is served. Let them take their hats off to receive the food and advise them they have only three minutes to line up, dish up and get out of sight.

Watch in amusement as the haggard bunch lines up. Let them come forward one by one as you open the big, *empty* pot and start dishing up with a large spoon.

Serve each recruit with a spoonful of fresh air.

Once everyone has received his portion, chase the recruits around for an hour for being too slow in queuing up.

When they are assembled for a second time, kick the pot over and watch the first recruit in line dive forward in an effort to save the food he still believes is inside.

Send them off on a long march and eat your pap and mince in peace.

It's pure agony carrying a 150 kg half-full barrel of water slung from poles.
As the drum rocks back and forth, the poles rub on raw skin.

SPECIALISED COOKING – THE RECCE WAY

Diesel-dipped Dog Biscuits

by BC Greyling

To enjoy this treat, you have to join a Special Forces selection course with guys like Peter Lamberti, Jan Greyling, Gert Nortjé, Ivan Maleta, Wynand Spies and others. First, all the recruits will assemble at 1 Reconnaissance Regiment in Durban for two weeks to do PT, complete the psychometric tests, and so on.

Thereafter you'll be sent to the Dukuduku area in northern KwaZulu-Natal for the pre-selection or water orientation course. There your numbers will be whittled down as you walk the dunes of Bhangazi with telephone poles and carry Zodiac inflatable boats around the lakes. The moment there are just over 60 recruits left, the course will come to an end.

Major Peter Schofield will be in charge, and his team will move all the recruits to the airfield at Dukuduku. Here they will make you run around the field until an aeroplane arrives. All the while, Schofield will sit in his officer's chair drinking brandy and Coke from his green Thermos and watch as you go around the airfield again, and again, and again.

If there are more than 60 recruits left by the time the plane arrives, only the first 60 who make it to the plane will get on.

You'll be flown to Omega in the Caprivi Strip where trucks will await your arrival. From there you'll drive to the training area at Fort Doppies. On the way you will get dropped on the Golden Highway in groups of four with a compass bearing, a distance and an XY coordinate to report to. It is some 25 km away, on the Botswana cutline (border).

For those who arrive there by 10h00 the next morning, the selection will begin.

After 18 days of selection exercises (including a six-day dark-phase period) you will be walking down the Botswana cutline carrying the same Second World War webbings filled with the same 25 kg of mortar cases you started out with. By now you will have walked some 260 km in the bush. At times you would have carried poles or trees, or your buddies in homemade stretchers. Sometimes it would have been cement blocks called marbles.

Either way, you would have been at it day in and day out. The instructors would have invited you to leave the course at least twice a day. By now your mind is blank and you are just hanging on.

About 25 people are left.

In front of you a few recruits – guys like Mugger Swanepoel, Sean Mullen, Theron Venter and others – walk with hunched shoulders and drag their feet in the soft white sand. You will arrive at the rendezvous (RV) point where the Botswana cutline meets the Kwando River and hope that this will be the last *opfok*.

The instructors – Karel Faber, Marius Boonzaaier, Flip Marx and others – will wait until you are all there before asking in a friendly tone who wants to quit and join them for an ice-cold beer and tender steak. You haven't had food for two days – your stomach jumps. You watch silently as six recruits get up and leave.

Adjust. Don't pay attention to the invitations or taunts of the instructors. Just wait, steal with the eyes, watch their movements and stay focused.

Walk forward when your number is called and receive your new destination, leg distance and cut-off time. Gratefully accept your packet of dog biscuits and some condensed milk (meaning a pikkie tube) and get moving before they take it from you. As soon as you are out of earshot, sit down with your little group to eat.

The anticipation of eating something solid is high. Squeeze the condensed milk into your mouth for that sweet creamy feel on the tongue …

Don't spit when the taste of diesel overwhelms you. Swallow before it is too late!

Take a closer look at the wrapper around the biscuits. On careful inspection you will notice a syringe insertion mark. You'll try another biscuit but you'll get the same diesel taste.

Try and toast them on a stick over a fire; it won't help much but you have to eat those biscuits – it's your only food. You will experience sickening diesel burps for at least the next 24 hours but at least you will have the energy to continue.

You have just been taught lesson number one.

TRICKS OF THE TRADE

BLITZ BREAKFAST

by Roelf du Plooy

2 eggs
1 packet of bacon
2 slices of bread

August 1980. On the second selection course presented by 5 Recce in the Doppies area in the Caprivi Strip. The end of the course was near and all the recruits were in a degraded state, which varied from near anorexia to the point of collapse.

One day the instructors – PW van Heerden, Pep van Zyl, Koos Moorcroft, myself and a few others – were sitting on our folding chairs around the embers of a fire. On our laps we each had a huge breakfast that had just been prepared on the coals. The smell of bacon drifted past the hungry recruits on the crisp clean morning air. We also had with us our clipboards with evaluation sheets.

PW was in charge and explained that he would be calling the recruits forward to the vehicle one by one for them to come and fill up their water bottles. As they did so, we were supposed to evaluate them. He promptly started calling them by their numbers.

When a recruit by the name of Rupert (Civvie) Burger walked forward, PW warned us that he is 'a criminal of note ... watch out that he doesn't steal anything while he is here by the vehicle. He is super sharp and wily!'

Civvie Burger stumbled over at top speed and, with a hint of bravado, clicked his heels in the sand as he announced himself.

'Samajoor!'

'Go and fill your f**king water bottle and don't waste my f**king time,' PW shouted at him.

Civvie briskly walked over to the water tank and started filling his bottle. At that stage PW winked and whispered to us, 'Look, he is letting the water run past his water bottle so he can see the layout around here. He will come to steal food from the stores tent tonight.'

Then PW shouted, 'Hey! Fill up your f**king bottle and come here.'

Civvie duly complied and presented himself at double speed.

'Are you hungry, arsehole?' PW asked.

'*Gotta, asseblief, my groot samajoor, jy weet dan hoe f*kken honger ek is.*' (Oh lordy, please, great sergeant major, you f**king know how hungry I am.)

This was exactly the reaction PW was hoping for. 'Well, OK, here is a nice plate of breakfast for you,' he said as he bent down to pick up the plate from his chair. The expression on Civvie's face was a mixture of disbelief and pain. He stretched out his hands to take the plate.

At that moment PW lifted the plate in the air before turning it over and dropping it to the ground. Civvie, however, had anticipated this move. He lunged forward and with the speed of a mamba picked out the toast, egg and bacon pieces in mid-air and pushed it into his mouth before PW could even react.

As he was gulping down the food he turned and ran back to the waiting area while PW showered him with curses. The rest of us nearly fell out of our chairs laughing.

For once, a recruit had come out on top in PW's game of Blitz Breakfast. Needless to say, Civvie breezed through selection and kept the boys at 5 Recce laughing for the next nine years.

ABOVE Some of the Recce founding members at a supper. They were instrumental in setting the tone and character of the organisation. This culture of toughness and togetherness still endures. From left to right: Koos Moorcroft, PW van Heerden, Kenaas Conradie, Dewald de Beer and Trevor Floyd.

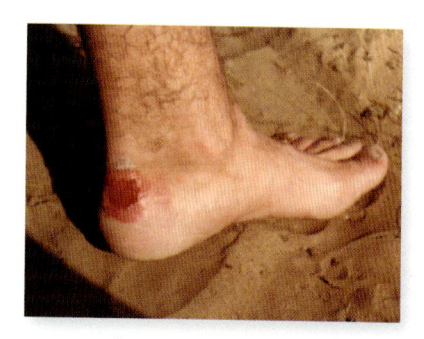

One of the consequences of signing up for the Special Forces recruitment course.

SPECIALISED COOKING – THE RECCE WAY

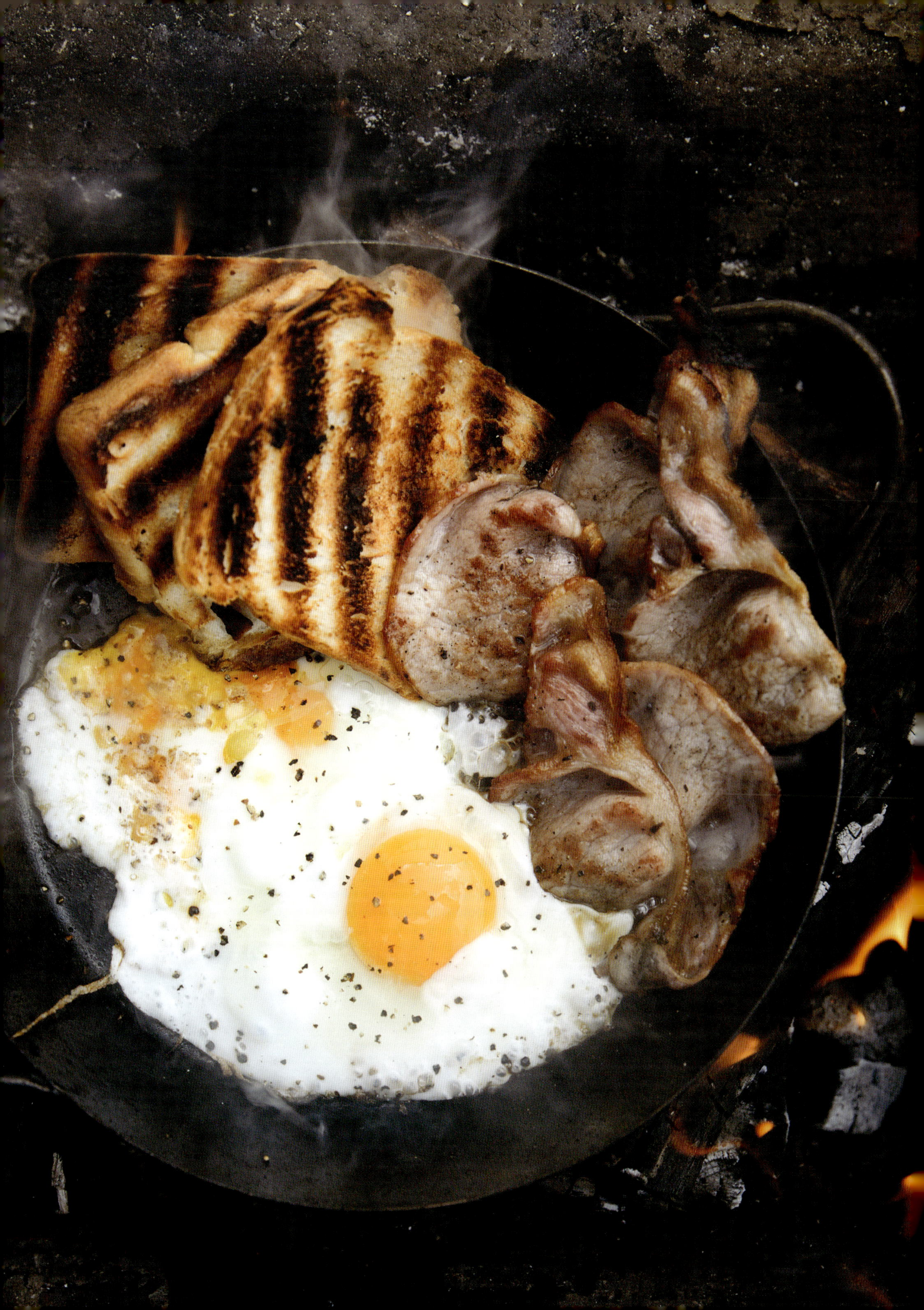

SURVIVAL FOOD

Students practise a river crossing during the minor tactics course. Their rucksacks and kit are tied up into groundsheets. These are floated across the water while a guard looks out for crocodiles.

The survival course offers by far the most singular experience in any Recce's training, and the stories about this course abound. We could easily have compiled a book only on survival food.

Survival and bushcraft is a six-week course that starts with three weeks of pure survival. There is no forced PT or anything physically intense. The focus is on learning about the bush, learning about yourself and getting to know your fellow soldiers. Because all of you get hungry, thirsty, tired and weak at the same time, an enduring sense of camaraderie develops. It gives you an opportunity to experience and respect your future comrades' ability to endure. Here you make plans that affect the entire group's ability to survive, and on these experiences lifelong friendships are built.

In addition to the survival and bushcraft course, survival courses for the sea and the city were also developed. These were done after the initial training cycle was completed. In the bush you need bushcraft and tracking skills; by the coast and on the water you need acute knowledge of tidal zone ecosystems; and in cities you need to learn how to use homeless shelters or hide in a city's stormwater system for days.

However, from a food point of view, these three survival courses have one thing in common: you eat whatever is available.

In this regard, each course is unique, as the characters, instructors, season, place and incidents differ. Each course develops in its own way, but all recruits share the same experience in the form of hunger and how this changes your view of what is acceptable. The following meals and stories should illustrate this point.

FRIED PYTHON

In 1981, the three-week survival course was presented by instructors Dewald (Dewies) de Beer, Bruce McIvor and Koos Verwey. At this time, Terry the Lion was also part of the team and a constant companion to the instructors[5] (see also 'Leeukos' later in this chapter).

By day 7 of 21, the recruits were settled into a routine. In the morning you were given lessons, be it in bird recognition, animal sounds, tracking, finding water or how to make snares. You would learn how to build shelters, make rope from baobab trees, which berries are edible and how to fish with hand lines. If you know where to look and what to look for, the bush will always provide. Between the Bushmen and the instructors, we were taught how to become one with the bush. It's an amazing experience that lasts a lifetime.

On day 9, the group was divided into three to go tracking with the Bushmen, look for honey and set a few traps away from the camp – in short, to find some food. At some point the one team, which included Leon Heiliger, Hein Vosloo, Basil Liebenberg, Klein Ian Berger and a few Bushmen, spotted a massive python. By then the constant hunger had affected their decision making. So, instead of backing off they rushed forward to try to catch it.

Just as the python reached its hole and was about to disappear, the team grabbed it by the tail and started pulling it out – all four and a half metres of it. The tug-of-war eventually started going the way of the recruits as they managed to edge the python out of the hole. With the number of blows it was taking the python was fully tenderised once extracted.

From here it was an energetic walk back to camp – six kilometres, with the snake positioned on the shoulders of the five men. When Dewies de Beer saw the snake, he lost it completely. He unleashed his impressive repertoire of swear words at the surprised team. Clearly, they had conflicting ideas of where conservation stops and survival starts.

Not one of the recruits believed him when he said he would've given them bully beef on a kilo-for-kilo basis if they had kept the snake alive. Eventually calm returned and it was agreed that at least the skin must be preserved. The snake was sent to the base in a Unimog where it was skinned with the right tools.

The vehicle returned with the skinned snake, some oil and salt. It was then cut into chunks about four fingers in width and cooked in water for an hour before it was fried in oil with some salt. The meat tasted amazing, and the carcass yielded an impressive amount of food. Each of the 14 recruits got over 500 g of protein, and for most it was the only big meal they had during the entire 21-day course.

---

[5] Teddy arrived in Doppies as a cub in 1978. He was raised by Dewald de Beer in unique circumstances: the lion was fed and was never locked up, so it could roam the surrounding bush. Over time, his name changed to Terry – short for 'terrorist', as he terrorised the visitors to Doppies. It is difficult to say whether Terry was half-tame or half-wild. He would often stay away for days but always return.

---

1 group of starving recruits
1 Namibian python
Cooking oil
Salt
Water

Just like the Recces, this leopard has also learned that anything in the bush can be food. If you can catch it, you can eat it.

TRICKS OF THE TRADE

OMURAMBA VULTURE SOUP

à la Roy Vermaak

One morning in 1977 on the survival course, someone said, 'I am so hungry I will even eat my grandmother's sh**ty chicken soup.'

Little did we know what this comment would lead to later that day. That afternoon, as we were driving back to camp (that is, our self-made grass structures under the trees) in the Unimog, Dewies the instructor (Dewald de Beer) stopped close to a carcass in an omuramba (dry river bed) that was surrounded by numerous vultures. 'That's food,' he said. 'You said you would eat anything, so go catch them!'

His words hadn't left his mouth when seven or so *masbieker*[6] type figures leapt off the back of the Unimog. Within the first few metres we zoomed in on a vulture that was struggling to get airborne. It looked just like an overloaded C-130 on a short runway on a boiling-hot summer's day in Phalaborwa – it just couldn't get lift-off.

The other *masbiekers* who were still on the Unimog were cheering like men possessed – they were doing the Mexican wave so intensely it looked like the Unimog would tip over. As the vulture's feet touched for his third hop there were two *masbiekers* on either side of him to grab the wings, while another went for the neck, one for the head, and one for the beak, to limit the biting.

In a flash a Puma hunting knife appeared and the neck was cut just behind the head. We lifted our trophies (bird body and head) proudly to the rowdy crowd on the Mog, as if to say: 'We have food, boys – we have food!'

On the way back there was wide debate on how to prepare our meal. Should we smoke it or put it on the spit? Braai sticks? Or perhaps use granny's chicken soup recipe. Our vulture had suddenly become cuisine.

As we started skinning the bird, we noticed a piece of wire that had gotten stuck in its throat, probably from stealing biltong meat. The slaughter team dwindled as the feathers flew and the stomach was opened. An awful smell hung over the campsite, and it was decided which recipe would be used … Granny's sh**ty chicken soup. It could only get better.

---

[6] According to the dictionary, the word 'masbieker' refers to a Mozambican slave. In our context, it was often used to describe the scrawny appearance of recruits after a few weeks on the course.

SPECIALISED COOKING – THE RECCE WAY

Pluck off all the feathers with whoever you can force to help you.

Breathe in deeply, close your nose and open the abdomen. Properly clear out the chest cavity, that is, the rest of the stomach, gut, all the innards, neck, etc.

Walk briskly towards fresh air, take a few gulps and return to cut the bird into chunks.

Make a fire and put a cast-iron pot with some water on the coals.

Add chunks of vulture, stir and start praying.

Once the water boils, add salt and stolen ingredients from the instructors' section according to your gut feel and cook, cook, cook, cook …

With comments that the vulture had better taste better than it smells, the rest of the recruits should have fled to their bivvies (temporary bush shelter) under the trees by now.

After an hour move back five metres away from the smell. After another three hours, retreat entirely from the area around the pots and find a hiding place to avoid the backlash from the other recruits. If they find you, the consequences will be dire.

Stay focused and go back to add more water. Keep the coals going during the night.

The next morning you can hand over the pot with instructions to the next *masbieker* on duty. Share your tips on how to acquire spices from the instructors' section.

By last light that day, it will be safe to return to the pot area. Assemble all the *masbiekers* and serve the vulture soup.

Let me tell you, sh**ty or not, there was nothing left in that pot. We didn't even have to wash it before we used it again.

1 overweight vulture with poor flying skills
15 litres of water from the Kwando River
1 handful of stolen salt
Whatever number of potatoes and onions you can steal

On the survival course at Doppies. All students learn the skills of building basic temporary shelter from natural materials.

You learn all about being in harmony with nature while on the survival course. Once you understand the concept that the bush is neutral, then living in it becomes easy.

TRICKS OF THE TRADE

'Leeukos'

Terry, the (sort of tame) lion of Doppies, feeding on a carcass.

INGREDIENTS
1 lion called Terry
1 carcass
Salt, when available

Out in the wild, it is the lion who does the hunting. But the hunter can become the hunted.

On this particular survival course, it was about day 16 when the following events happened. By then the recruits had nearly no fat left on their bodies; their tummies were flat like six-packs.

For the previous two weeks, Terry the Lion had been a constant companion, lazing about our survival camp and even swimming with us. While we had to survive without any food, Terry regularly got some meat from the base. So it happened that the service Land Rover passed by one Saturday afternoon with a big chunk of a buck carcass on the back.

The vehicle was heading in a southerly direction, meaning away from the campsite and the base and therefore into neutral territory. It returned some 30 minutes later. The group stopped the driver (a national serviceman) and eventually he admitted that he had dropped the carcass about three kilometres away.

Our ears pricked up. This was less than a 45-minute walk away. Immediately a plan was concocted, and shortly afterwards a raiding party set off in the fading light. Once we got to where a lion was feeding on a carcass, we first confirmed that it was indeed our lion – Terry – and not a wild one. Lion attacks in the area were not uncommon and many a recruit on course had had skirmishes with lions before.

We spread out – sucked our lungs full of air and then the 'attack' began! With a concerted high shrill and wild waving of branches and our little okapi knives we stormed. Poor Terry got such a fright he jumped up and scuttled off. The carcass was now clear. As the military strategist and philosopher Sun Tzu once explained, 'The wise general will make it easy for a desperate enemy to withdraw, this prevents him from having to fight to the death.' Even Terry the Lion had to learn this.

Flashing blades sliced off chunks of meat while the lion growled at us in the dim light, but for now it was our carcass. Minutes later we withdrew with enough meat to survive a few days longer. For once the lion did not come out on top. Or did he?

SPECIALISED COOKING – THE RECCE WAY

Early the next morning, even before we had boiled the water for our sweet coffee, instructors Dewald (Dewies) de Beer and Bruce McIvor drove past in the Landy. Direction south. A short while later they were back and joined us for coffee. They started talking about Terry and his apparent inability to hunt. The next moment they asked us whether we had gone to see how much he had eaten.

Alarm bells went off. Were we being led into the proverbial lion's den?

Our minds raced. If we said no, they might've seen tracks left behind despite our best anti-tracking techniques. If we said yes, we were closer to the truth but also closer to trouble. We decided to admit that we had gone to the carcass.

'So, looking at the carcass, did you think the lion was hungry? Does he ever catch his own food?' De Beer asked.

'Umm, that's difficult to say, Sergeant Major,' we answered in chorus.

At this point he broke into his famous repertoire: 'One thing is f**king certain and that is that he eats less that the f**king troops who are stealing his f**king food. This is the first time in my life that I have seen a lion bite off meat in such f**king straight lines. You would think the f**king lion had attended officers' course to be able to eat so f**king properly.'

Needless to say, all of those involved joined the Sunday Express to the Botswana cutline with mortar cases filled with cement on our shoulders. As we were sweating away, we told ourselves that next time we wouldn't leave anything behind for the lion. If only he had eaten his food – as a real lion would!

Having a playful, free-roaming lion as constant companion on the survival course adds a whole new dimension to the experience.

Mince and Sand

by Ray Godbeer

On the survival courses each buddy pair of recruits got an opportunity to clean the pots that we, as the instructors, cooked our food in. One night, when recruits Rob Jennings and Gary Yaffe were on duty, we had savoury mince for dinner.

When we were finished I mixed some fine river sand into the remaining mince (ratio 5:1) so that they would not be able to see the sand. When Rob and Gary arrived, they could not believe their eyes; there was actually leftover mince and gravy in the pot. You could see their faces light up.

They briskly carried away the big cast-iron pot. Their hands were digging into the pot the moment they reached the edge of the firelight. We were, of course, watching them. The next moment their faces scrunched up as they bit down on the sandy mixture.

Did they spit it out? No! They just carried on eating.

On a survival course, food is food. But you can imagine the bricks that came out the other end the next day.

TRICKS OF THE TRADE

Dirties à la Lunch Bar and Bar One

In the Special Forces context, the word 'dirty' is used to describe any type of punishment handed out by an instructor. If you haven't received a dirty by the time you're done with the survival course, you probably have very limited testosterone or lack creativity.

On survival, the lure of 'free' food (read stolen) gets stronger by the day and hunger plays an increasing role in decision-making. By day 7 the mind is free and the risk of being caught moves lower on the list of things to concern yourself with. FOOD – that is all you can think about.

Discussions at night also start to include plans to make contact with the national servicemen drivers about bringing in food. Of course the instructors know this and have good plans in place to check that this doesn't happen. They are skilled at setting traps and finding evidence of such infractions.

One fine morning in 1985, instructor Ray Godbeer acted on information and decided to search the survival camp area after morning coffee. He discovered a Bar One and a Lunch Bar wrapper in the shallow sand. An ominous silence followed. This was a mortal sin. Commandment 11 – don't get caught – had been broken.

As per Commandment 12, the two recruits, MP and Shane,[7] owned up. This wasn't something you could allow everybody to get punished for. They should have shared!

It was decided that Sunday would be dirty time for them.

---

[7] MP Viljoen and Shane Sclanders.

During the week, the discussions were about what their punishment would be, whether they would get kicked off the course, and whether there would be only physical repercussions.

Sunday came and so did Ray. Two hefty logs lay on the back of a Unimog. The two recruits were called forward and Ray announced the punishment: 'OK guys, meet Lunch Bar and Bar One. Botswana cutline it is. I will see you back here at five.'

An hour later, the Unimog dropped them off on the Botswana cutline with Lunch Bar and Bar One. The distance back was just over 19 km. It would take them five hours to get back, with not much time to spare.

After two hours their necks were red and blood was oozing from the chafing on their shoulders. The flies kept landing on the wounds and it was impossible to swat them away. Also, having been without food for a week, the guys were weak. As we know, desperate times call for desperate measures. Adapt, adjust and stay in the moment.

They walked into the treeline and ditched the logs, with the idea of replacing them with similar-sized ones when they got close to camp. It was close to 15h00 when they approached the camp, but wily Ray was already waiting for them. As if from nowhere, he appeared out of the bush.

'So, where the f**k is Lunch Bar One and Bar One?'

MP and Shane turned in surprise but stayed in the moment.

'Sorry, Staff, we got so hungry we had to eat them,' MP answered with a straight face.

Dark-phase Baboon

During the year-long Special Forces instruction you underwent a training course called 'dark phase'. This involved recruits living and operating for almost a week under captured conditions – not in a cell but in a remote location – as part of a guerrilla-type operation.

The period started with a simulated capture and some proper roughing-up, whereafter you were transported to an isolated site. By day you had to work – chop wood, dig pits in the sand to serve as cells for troublemakers, undergo guerrilla training, and so on, with any minor transgression offering enough reason for a quick *opfok*.

The white students wore 'black is beautiful' camouflage cream on their faces to look like their black captors. The black recruits on course also had to put it on – in sympathy with their white counterparts. (Use of 'black is beautiful' on a deployment meant that you would be dirty by default for the entire time, as the cream sweated down your body and seeped into your clothes.)

By night you had to sing the revolutionary songs of your captors for hours and hours on end. After the training, the songs were burned into your memory. This was how you learned to think and work like the enemy and better understand their ways.

During this time you had to share everything: two guys (one black, one white) would sleep in a shallow trench and share a blanket. Mornings were haggard affairs as shuffling troops who hadn't seen a bath for two weeks lined up with blackened hands to receive their food. Meals could be anything from a Weet-Bix with jam or a simple scoop of pap. Together, you and your black buddy would eat your food with your dirty hands from dirty, sweaty hats.

The course might not be that demanding physically, but mentally it tested your ability to live in the moment and stay sharp. Your buddy – no matter his colour, creed or capacity – was your ticket to survival.

Then one day you got the good news: the 'camp commander' announced that he was happy with your progress and that his hunters had managed to get some fresh food. 'Tonight we will have a feast, so let's get the right energy levels,' he said.

So, all day long the marching in the camp was done with extra vigour and the songs were sung just a bit louder. The

The dark phase course is called this because it involves a continuous attack on your mental capacity and takes your mind to dark places. The trademark food item on the course is half-rotten baboon.

'feast' was served after dark. The smell of real food drove everyone crazy.

You started eating, thinking the game was fairly edible, albeit somewhat tough and sinewy. As you dug out more pieces of meat from the slosh you realised the taste was rather strange and didn't settle.

Moments later, a baboon hand made its appearance. And yes, it had been 'matured' in the sun for a few days before it was cooked.

But this was not a time for sissies, so you were first in line when they offered seconds. It was food and it was good!

Living from a Rucksack

by Sybie van der Spuy

Unlike James Bond, who works for MI6 and drives around in fancy cars, the Recces are infantry soldiers who work for the Army, and we have to carry everything we need in our rucksacks. The saying goes that the bush is neutral because it treats all parties to a conflict in the same way. In respect of food the bush rules very clearly state: what you don't pack, you won't have.

For this reason, any Recce will tell you that a big part of his life is spent preparing and packing his rucksack before deployment. Once deployed, you operate independently and in isolation, with zero support – no vehicles, no access to bases. It is you, your team members and your rucksack. So everything has to fit into your rucksack – radios, medical requirements, weapons, a bivvy for shelter, and, of course, water and food.[8] For really long deployments into the bush, you deploy with a cache during the infiltration phase and return to it later.

Preparing for deployment takes meticulous planning and preparation; many, many days are spent trying to work out what must go into the pack and where exactly. It is all about getting the calculations right, weighing kilojoules up against space and weight. When operating clandestinely, you also have to remove all labels, packaging or anything that can point to the origin of the contents of your pack so you remain untraceable.

It is all about being organised in the veld and knowing where to find anything in your pack without making a noise, as well as being able to put something back into the same place. When you are walking long distances every day and you have only 30 minutes to rest, you don't want to spend 25 minutes finding what you need and packing it all away again. This is quite an art. Guys like Jack Greeff and Rieme de Jager were master tutors and their advice helped many an operator to organise and pack their backpacks in masterful ways.

TOP **During the Border War, Recce soldiers walked hundreds of kilometres in the bush carrying all their supplies with them.**

ABOVE **This rucksack was used by the Special Forces until the mid-1980s. Thereafter it was replaced by a custom-designed and larger, yet more lightweight, version.**

---

8 During the Border War, Special Forces teams were often dropped by Puma helicopter and lived from their backpacks for several weeks. Making a cache was necessary for deployments that exceeded six weeks.

32 SPECIALISED COOKING – THE RECCE WAY

Rucksack Food

The ratpack (ration pack) is the product of some of the best brains in the world. Just like a mother marks a lunchbox when she sends her child off to school, so the military machine marks the ratpacks for each day. This way, even the 'doffest' soldier gets his daily nourishment.

While the simplicity of it makes sense, it's helluva tough to eat 180 packs a year. You will need to use your specialised skills, meaning thorough planning and preparation, to ensure that you pack something extra and unusual to make the mission a true (food) adventure. For example, add some bully beef, irradiated (zapped) meats, soya mince and self-raising flour. It doesn't matter if you pack only one 100 g measure in a ratpack sachet for that one day when you need it. Just do it – it is what defines you as a soldier.

Always take along a water bottle filled with cooking oil. Invariably, you will secure some 'opportunity food' from the area you'll be operating in that you can then use to make a proper meal. At least you'll have all the ingredients needed to create an occasion – food, friends and a great setting.

In fact, the more you think back, during most deployments you'll have lots of spare time during which you can start experimenting. Working with local forces, such as Unita/Renamo, creates much spare time … as does waiting in a temporary base while the Small Teams guys complete their reconnaissance, or waiting with an SA-7[9] for aeroplanes to appear.

You may even have whole days of being static, so use the time to stay mentally alert. The recipes that follow will show you how the basic old ratpack can be zhooshed up to create some magic.

ABOVE The traditional ratpack meal of bully beef and beans with a dash of Tabasco sauce is as good a meal as any five-star hotel can serve.

LEFT Freeze-dried rations are nutritious and offer a variety of tastes without your having to carry the liquid component. For a soldier, this is gourmet food.

RIGHT The trusted fire bucket and water bottle.

9 The SA-7 (Strela) is a surface-to-air missile of Soviet origin that was often used by the South African Defence Force during the Border War. Typical targets would be Mi-24 and Mi-8 helicopters, Antonov-26 cargo planes and MiG fighters.

TRICKS OF THE TRADE

Ratpack Magic

To unlock the ratpack's 'magic' you need to innovate. Try boiling one or two things and fuse a few flavours. A small gas stove is essential, as well as some of the extras you should've packed. If you haven't read the panel on the preceding page, this includes freeze-dried packs, zapped meats, bully beef and oil. Now you can prepare vetkoek and mince just as easily as strawberries and cream!

Energy Bar and Raisin Muffins

The stalwart of the ratpack is the energy bar. At 2 800 kJ per 100 g, this is enough to keep you going for hours, whether you like rum and raisin, chocolate or strawberry flavour. You can use an energy bar and some flour to create a decent occasion while you wait for that plane:

Use your knife to cut thin shavings from the energy bar.

Mix the shavings and raisins, and milkshake powder from the ratpack, with a premixed muffin mix.[10]

Bake in a closed pot/container (or oven if you're at home and feeling nostalgic).

ABOVE **A rum and raisin energy bar.**

TOP RIGHT **An Esbit stove.**

LEFT **The breakfast porridge/milkshake mix.**

Milkshake Doughnuts

Milkshake powder
Premixed vetkoek mix
Oil
Sugar

Add the milkshake powder from the ratpack to a premixed vetkoek mix.[11]

Fry the milkshake doughnuts in some oil in the dixie.

Serve with caramelised sugar.*

If you don't have any oil, make dumpling balls in boiling water with this mix.

* Caramelised sugar
Heat sugar over a very low and even flame and stir gently until it caramelises (turns runny and brown). Drip over milkshake doughnuts, muffins, flapjacks or fried plantains and banana, when available.

If you have nothing but the contents of your ratpack available it means you have been sitting in one place for a very, very long time. In this instance, caramelise your sugar in a tablespoon over the gas flame and drip it over your breakfast cereal. This can be done with every ratpack and you'll still have sugar left over for your coffee. After the third session, sit back, smile ironically and then remind yourself to plan better next time so you don't run out of interesting things to cook.

---

10 See the section on basic bakes in Chapter 5 (If It Grows). These are easy and simple to make if the ingredients are premixed and packed in containers. Always be prepared!

11 When you pack the ration boxes for the cache, resupply or vehicles, you need to plan your moments in advance. For shorter trips, pack one or two into the rucksack. Premix as many meals as possible so that you only need to add water and mix.

SPECIALISED COOKING – THE RECCE WAY

A Dog Biscuit Treat

Dog biscuits
Milkshake powder
Raisins
Cinnamon

RIGHT Army dixie.

Crumb two dog biscuits finely and place in a plastic sachet.

Add the milkshake powder and shake to mix (no water).

Empty into a dixie, add a few raisins and press flat with your spoon.

Drip water evenly onto the crumbs to bind them.

Gently roast over a small flame.

Adding a dash of cinnamon will make all the difference.

VARIATION
If you have any fresh fruit around, purée the flesh and use it instead of the water to bind the crumbs.

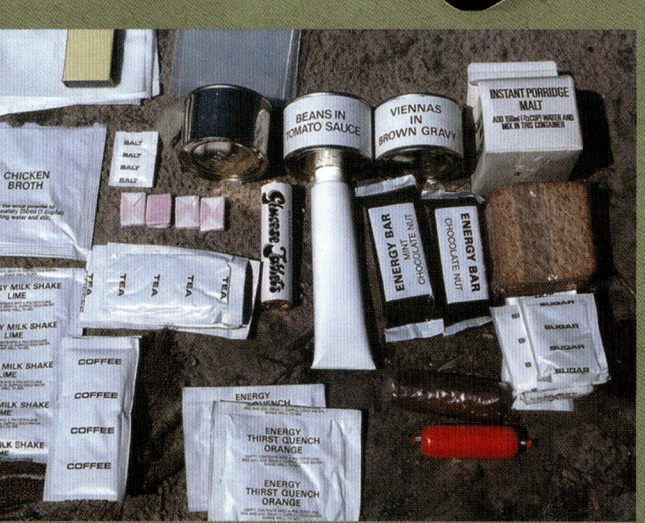

ABOVE The full contents of the ratpack distributed during the Border War amounted to a full 6 200 kilojoules. There was porridge for breakfast, energy bars and sweets for the day and tinned foods for dinner. Coffee, tea, sugar and energy drinks completed the pack.

RIGHT The full set of utensils available to soldiers, with Esbit fuel tablets to make coffee and heat food. Soldiers would only pack their preferred items.

Mixed Fruit

For this popular meal, which is obtainable nearly anywhere in the world, you need only open a tin. However, there are guys like Mac McCabe who don't like mixed fruit and will swap their tin for your can of viennas in brine. Grab the opportunity. The mixed fruit has more kilojoules and the taste will definitely lift your spirits.

If you have a few tins, you can drain the juice for a lovely drink.

VARIATION
Make a fresh fruit salad by chopping up all your favourite fruits, such as apple, paw-paw, grape, orange and banana. Squeeze over lemon juice.

TRICKS OF THE TRADE

> He who knows when he can fight and when he cannot, will be victorious.
> SUN TZU

2

IF IT SWIMS

Fish or meat – which is best? This question has led to many late-night debates, and is much like the argument among Recce units about the superiority of waterborne versus airborne operations. We won't even try to offer an answer to this tricky question, except to say that if it swims, it produces an amazingly wide variety of tastes. Also, most seafood dishes can be enhanced by a great sauce while steaks and chops need only a sprinkling of salt and pepper.

The history of the Recces is intertwined with all major water features in the region, from Zanzibar on the east coast and the Democratic Republic of Congo in central Africa to Angola on the west coast. If you cross from Dar es Salaam to Kinshasa overland, you will cross the region's major rivers and, of course, the great lakes.

It is very likely that a serving Recce would, in his time, have swum in the Kwando River, crossed the Cunene and Kavango rivers and navigated or operated in the waters of the Cuito and the Zambezi, as well as on Lake Kariba.

And in the waters of Africa the playing field is neutral. Even during training you don't need an enemy with a gun; the crocodiles, hippos and sharks prove formidable adversaries.

Locally there are the coastal towns of Durban (home to 1 Reconnaissance Regiment), Simon's Town (Navy headquarters) and Langebaan (home to 4 Reconnaissance Regiment), where many a soldier spent countless hours honing their diving skills or interacting with the navy. For the open seas you would be exposed to the humble 4 Recce yacht called the *Compass Rose*, or to strike craft such as the SAS *Oswald Pirow* or to the stately SAS *Tafelberg*.

If you were around for long enough, a mission or two that included a voyage on the submarine SAS *Maria van Riebeeck* would complete your seafaring experience.

Special Forces seaborne operators train to clandestinely infiltrate a ship from the sea.

DORADO FILLETS
Whaling Station style

Dorado, fresh from the sea
Beer (one bottle to cook with and five to drink)
Flour
Spice for fish
Parsley
Garlic
Oil
Lemon

The Old Whaling Station on the Bluff in Durban was the centre for urban training while 1 Reconnaissance Regiment was stationed there.

---

12 The Bluff Military Area was the base for 1 Recce from 1978 until 1997. The Old Whaling Station buildings provided the base for all types of training, as well as a space to rehearse for urban operations.

13 Refuelling was an intricate manoeuvre during which the supply vessel would tow the strike craft at about four knots for nearly two hours as it was being refuelled.

Nothing tastes better than fresh game fish. The meat is firm and the taste is not that strong. A perfect place to get it is the stretch of coast by the Old Whaling Station on the Bluff in Durban.[12] This is a restricted area, so the only people who have access to it are the base personnel of 1 Reconnaissance Regiment (1 Recce). Here you can catch good game fish – just go out and get them.

Get up early on a Saturday or a Sunday and grab a speargun. Drive down to the Whaling Station area. If you find Oom Gellie (from the parachute store) or Rose dalla Pria (signals) on the beach fishing for shad, you know there are fish around. Also check to see whether Nick Wilson, Japie (Kloppies) Kloppers or any other guys are out there with spearguns; they will point you in the direction of the fish. Swim out to the reef and go and shoot your fish.

Fillet the fish and then cut it into smaller discs.

Mix the beer and flour to make the batter. Stir until smooth and runny.

Add the spices and garlic and finish the remaining beer; only about two sips should be left.

Dip the fish in the batter and cook slowly on medium heat in a lightly oiled pan. Turn over when brown.

Fry all the fish pieces so each person has about six pieces. The rest will make excellent leftovers. Add a squeeze of lemon and serve.

If you are not any good at spear fishing, you can always catch fish the old-fashioned way. This is best done at night from the back of a strike craft as it refuels from the SAS *Tafelberg*, as once happened during a training exercise for Operation Kerslig in 1981.[13]

If General Kat Liebenberg, general officer commanding Special Forces, is in attendance on the boat, you may have to give up your spot to him.

Ask Corporal Chris (Kolle) Olivier to teach the General the ropes. He will break a Lumistick and put it on the line with a hook and some meat from the galley and let it trawl behind the slow-moving craft. Double check that Kolle explains to the General how the light will attract the fish to the bait and that the General should stand ready to strike. Keep this going for at least an hour.

Just make very sure the General doesn't see or hear you laugh at this practical joke.

VARIATION
Barracuda, tuna or any other sizable game fish also works for this recipe, although tuna can be rather dry. A good rule of thumb is that it should be a long and thin type of fish.

38 SPECIALISED COOKING – THE RECCE WAY

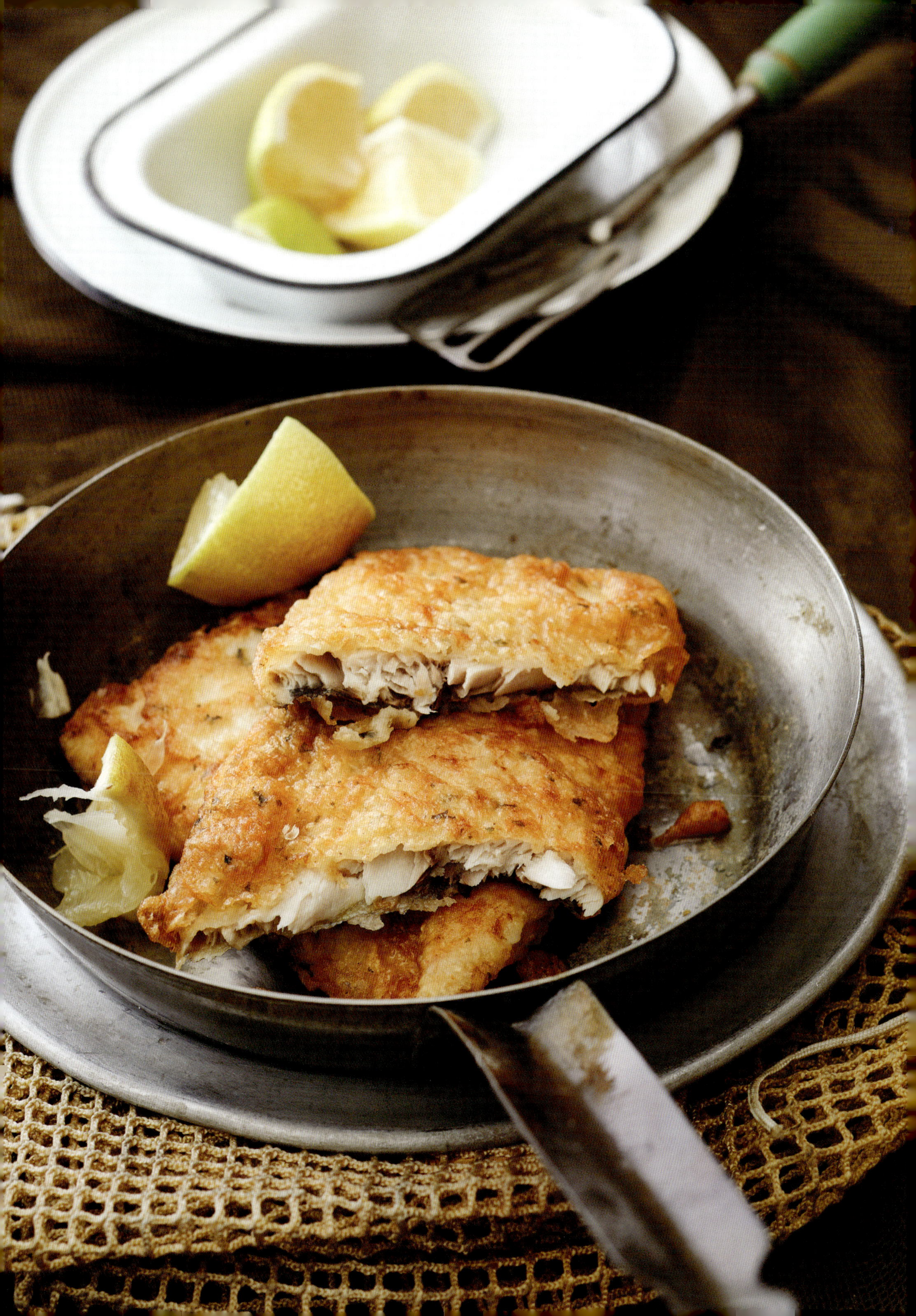

Survival Seafood Ensemble with Beach Spices

by Fred Wilke

All seaborne operators do seaborne courses in addition to their normal training. This includes a sea survival course. Now, most guys from 1 or 5 Recce will tell you in their curriculum it is called 'fishing' or 'weekend sport', but the guys from 4 Recce take their survival courses seriously; some even do them every weekend!

Anyway, to demonstrate your ability to sit on a beach and do nothing, the course requires you to live off the sea life on the shoreline where there is food in abundance but spices are generally lacking.

If you happened to be on the survival course in mid-1984 with Wilco Meyer, Dirk Steenkamp, Henk Liebenberg, Johan Oetle, Billy Faul and a few others, you would be hanging around the Langebaan Peninsula. By day two you will be bored but not yet hungry. This boredom will inspire the idea to go and 'release' some of the spices from the few isolated holiday cottages just outside the military area fence, some 15 km away.

On arrival, scout for people, appoint a few guards and assign the break-in party – Wilco and Dirk.

Just as the team enters the first house, the impossible happens – the lady of the manor arrives. As luck would have it, she is the wife of some Cabinet minister. The team hide behind the curtains and, thanking their lucky stars they weren't spotted, listen to her scold and threaten the 'guards' outside.

They procure the spices in any case. However, on the way back they work out that the risk of getting caught is too great and they bury the spices a bit closer to the camp.

The next day, the news filters through that the OC (officer commanding), Colonel Hannes Venter, has received a ministerial call and has gone ballistic. Waiting for the axe to fall is like a jail sentence.

A few days later the course ends and the team members are advised that they should prepare an end-of-course meal, to be attended by Colonel Venter. The team splits into groups, with one scouring the shores for 'washed-up' spices, lemons and wine. The other groups look for crayfish, perlemoen and mussels.

After the catch is cleaned and deshelled, the team cuts off the tops of some kelp gathered from the shore, and places the seafood inside with some 'beach spices' – meaning the garlic, tomato sauce and a dash of white wine! The ends of the kelp are plugged before the kelp parcel is cooked on a fire in the rocks for an hour.

Just about then Colonel Venter arrives and the team presents their dish. The slow-cooked meat is tender and has released its flavours fully – it is out of this world. After the meal Colonel Venter advises us that he would inform the minister that he stocks good spices at his holiday home.

Cooking seafood in kelp requires you to gather dried kelp that has already released its iodine. Once you add the mussels, fish and/or crayfish, it works just as well as any oven. Keep the parcel tilted upwards to keep the moisture inside.

SPECIALISED COOKING – THE RECCE WAY

ABOVE A recruit on the selection course on a lonely walk on the West Coast with two ballast balls slung over his backpack. At this point, there are no thoughts of bountiful crayfish or other seafood.

BELOW An SA-9 mounted on a BRDM.

Sushi

SA-9 style

If you attended the SA-9 (surface-to-air missile) course with Spik Botha, Abel Erasmus, warrant officer Peet (Oom Pote) Coetzee[14] and a few others you would've stayed at the South African Air Force (SAAF) headquarters in Pretoria. There you'd eat in a normal army mess and also meet real life Permanent Force members, or PFs, as they were called.

This could be a bit of a revelation as these soldiers seemed to come from a different world. They would look at you with big eyes and ask the most idiotic questions. The most common were: 'Did you have to shoot your mother's dog?' or 'Did you really eat fried maggots on the survival course?'

You would also have to contend with the tougher PFs, who rather rated themselves and always wanted to test and challenge the Special Forces guys. We had a number of ways of dealing with them.

The easiest and most diplomatic way of dealing with the stares and the challenges was to laugh them off. If that didn't work, you could place a little bet with the PF concerning a goldfish …

For maximum effect, put your drink down immediately after placing the bet and walk calmly to the fishpond in the foyer of the SAAF headquarters, without saying a word. There you would grab the biggest goldfish you could find, ideally one with really big bulging eyes. If you ever try this, be sure to check that it will fit into your mouth.

You would then walk back to the bar and bite off the back half of the fish in one go and swallow on the spot, then hand over the front half to the one who challenged you, with those bulging fish eyes staring at him and blood dripping in your hand. Challenge over. Special Forces 1: PFs 0.

Order the double Red Heart rum and Coke you have just won and carry on talking to your friends. For the next ten days on the course nobody will give you any trouble and they'll walk circles around you in the bar.

---

[14] Warrant Officer Peet Coetzee (SAAF), a specialist in aerial photography interpretation, was attached to the Recces for a very long time as the Chief Intelligence Officer. He is the author of three books on the Special Forces: *Special Forces "Jam Stealer"*, *Point of the Dagger/Punt van die Dolk* and *Ons Vergeet Nie*.

SMOKED SNOEK
Langebaan style

4 x 500g filleted snoek (this will serve at least eight people)
Apricot jam
Garlic, crushed
Olive oil
Salt and pepper
Lemon

> If it's stupid, but it works, it ain't stupid. (worth repeating)

The word 'snoek' conjures up images of Table Mountain, the Cape West Coast, crisp white wine and a gentle braai. As all the Kapenaars will tell you, snoek has a strong and distinct taste. While it might be a firm favourite on the West Coast, you should perhaps just be mindful of this when you prepare snoek for people who haven't eaten it before or not very often. Try a few of the variations below for a slow introduction to snoek's unique taste.

Make friends with someone who owns a boat and hint strongly that you'd like to go along when next they go fishing. If you are the guy with the boat, then get up early and set out to sea with hand reels and rods.

Try your best, but don't worry too much if you don't catch any fish. If your fish got away, stop at the local harbour on your way home; there's bound to be a toothless guy with a bakkie-load of fish who'll sell you some snoek.

Once you have the fish, pick a decent spot to braai. Start the fire.

While the wood turns to coals, take the filleted snoek and dry it off with kitchen paper. Open some cold white wine so long to make sure you don't go dry yourself.

When the coals have lost most of their intensity, braai the snoek slowly and baste it regularly with a sauce made of apricot jam, garlic and olive oil.

Fish doesn't take long to cook through; it takes a maximum of 15 minutes. Keep it on just long enough to get that smoky flavour and to firm up the flesh. Once again, be careful not to dry out the fish; if needed, drip on extra olive oil.

Serve directly from the grill with a little salt, pepper and lemon juice.

VARIATIONS
Make a pâté with the fish by flaking it and then puréeing it with cream cheese, mayonnaise, parsley and chives. Serve on lightly toasted rye bread with butter.
For snoek balls, follow the instructions for pâté and fry lightly in oil.

The soldiers from 4 Recce are taken from Langebaan to the Donkergat base every day from the jetty in the foreground. The buildings in the background are the old Flamingo Hotel.

SPECIALISED COOKING – THE RECCE WAY

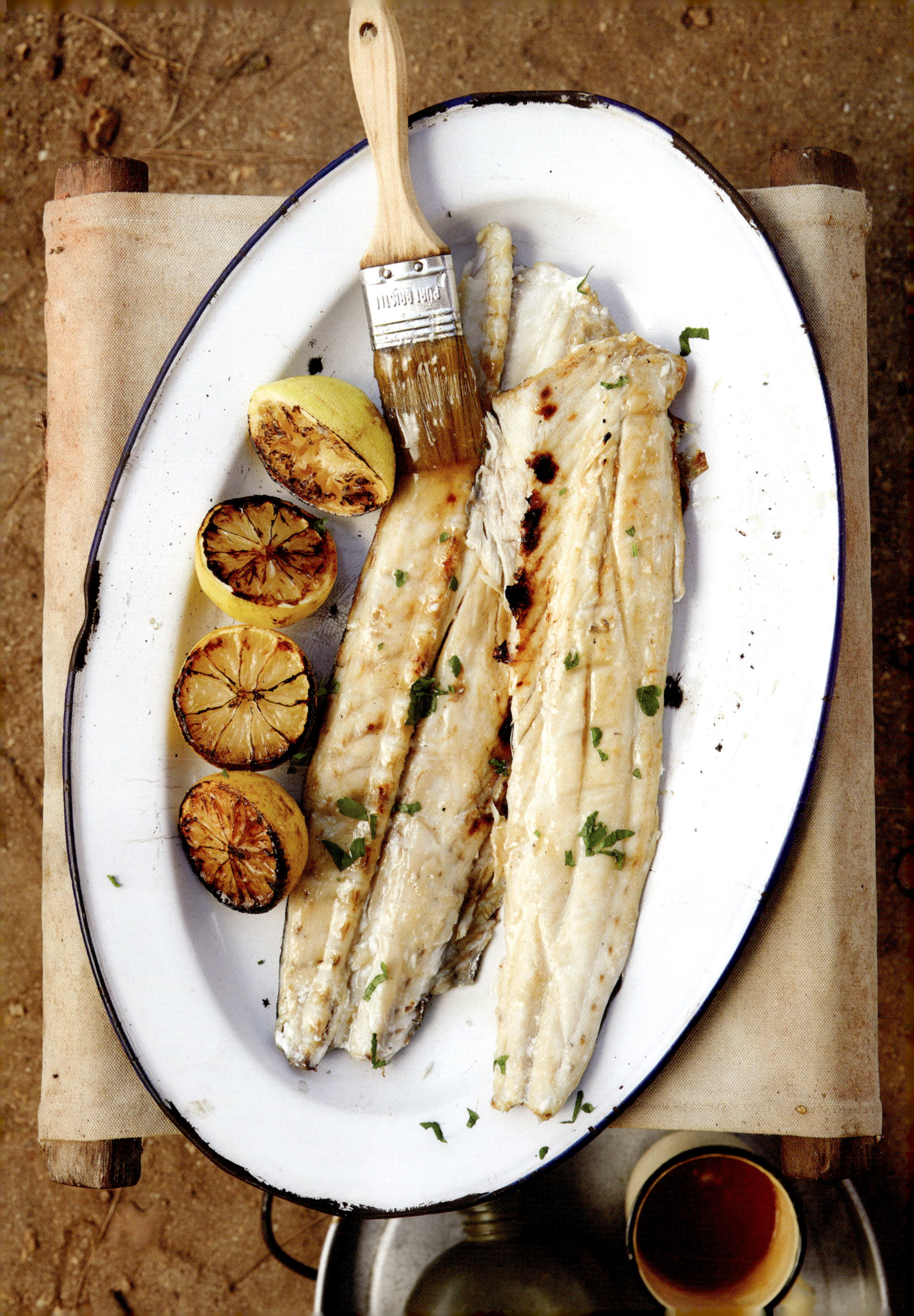
PURE BRISTLE

CRAYFISH
à la Donkergat

Fresh crayfish of a decent size
Lemon
Butter
Garlic
A side dish that smells good (savoury rice or something)

For many centuries the West Coast has offered crayfish as a delicacy to its inhabitants. Crayfish grow really big in places, especially in restricted areas such as Donkergat, the seaborne base of 4 Reconnaissance Regiment (4 Recce).

Donkergat is situated across Langebaan Lagoon from the town of Langebaan but is out of sight to the public. The only way to get access to it is by ferry or a two-hour drive around the lagoon.

As Regimental Sergeant Major GD (Maddies) Adam would say, 'The crayfish get so big at Donkergat that you never know who is trying to catch who when you see them under the water. Some say smaller crayfish taste better, but that's probably because they simply can't catch the really big ones.'

Crayfish is best when served fresh from the sea, and an early-morning swim is just the right way to kick-start the day. To ensure maximum freshness, take a mask and snorkel, a crayfish bag and put on a very thick wetsuit before you go in search of your crayfish on a Saturday morning.

Hugos Pos, a small bay next to Donkergat military area, is a great place to start your search. On finding the crayfish, take out a few extra ones for friends; in this way you will save on your bar bill at the end of the day.

To prepare the crayfish, cut through the stomach plate with kitchen scissors and remove the black things (intestines). Then rinse away the little pieces that didn't come out cleanly.

Cut almost all the way through and force the crayfish open so that you can spread it on the grill and get decent amounts of lemon, butter and garlic in there.

To make garlic butter, just soften/melt some butter and mix in minced or crushed garlic. Keep the lemon aside to drizzle over the crayfish every now and again and before serving.

Grill on the fire over low heat to ensure the crayfish cooks through without drying out. Cook on the shell mostly and keep basting with the garlic butter.

Once the meat turns white all over it should be ready. Remember, you can always put it back on if it's not cooked through, but you can't 'undry' a crayfish.

VARIATION
Place a pot on the fire/stove and boil the crayfish. Break off the crayfish tails when done and serve with garlic butter.

Learning how to catch crayfish is a tough job, but someone has to do it. James Teitge is shown in the foreground, with Julius Kratz ready to cover him in crayfish.

Special Forces operators trained and worked at Donkergat base, on the Langebaan Peninsula (across the bay). This boat (an old whaling boat) originally served as the jetty. Donkergat was once a whaling station.

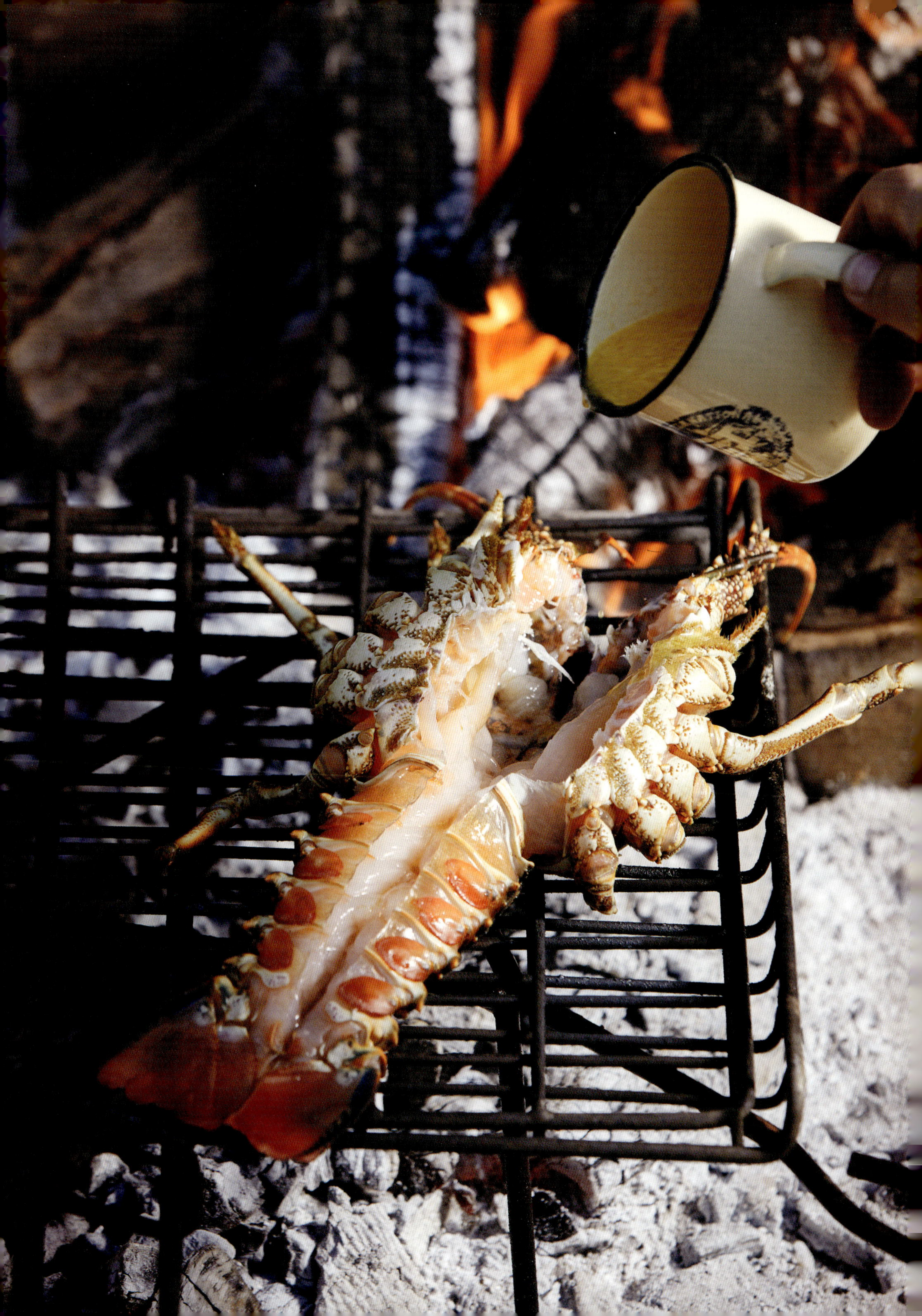

FRESHWATER MUSSELS
Kwando style

Mussels
Students on the Recce survival course
Instructors
One young lion

While the majority of recipes that you find call for sea mussels, this one requires freshwater mussels. You can have a lot of fun collecting them in the sandy bed of the Kwando River[15] in northern Namibia ... For that, though, you'll have to sign up for the Recce selection course – and pass it! You then proceed to the survival course at Fort Doppies (see opposite page), where you'll soon learn how to live and survive in the bush.

Equipped with these skills, you will now know how to find edible mussels on a sandy river floor. To harvest them, you need to walk in a shuffling motion while half-submerged in the water until your feet encounter something hard. Use your toes to dig out the mussel from the sand. Try to pick the mussels out with your toes.

If you can't lift them with your toes, just sink down and scratch them out with your hands. Throw them onto the river bank until you've got enough – meaning whatever you can find in an afternoon – hopefully about 15. It looks like a lot but there is very little inside, so try to get enough for a proper meal. Do this for a week and cover a different section of the river every day until there are no more mussels in your area.

While doing this, post a sentry to watch out for crocs; they are always around. Also make way for hippos; they don't negotiate. If Terry the Lion is on your course, watch out for him too; he loves the water.

Cook the mussels over the coals until they open. Pull off the stringy parts and eat.

VARIATION
Cook in a pot with fresh cream, garlic, lemon, salt and pepper until the mussels open. Serve hot in the sauce.

The welcome sign just past the old baobab tree at the entrance to the Doppies training area.

[15] The Kwando River rises in central Angola and runs south through the Caprivi Strip (today the Zambezi Region) and divides western and eastern Caprivi. It then flows into the Chobe, eventually joining the Zambezi.

> We cannot enter into alliances until we are acquainted with the designs of our neighbours.
> — SUN TZU

SPECIALISED COOKING – THE RECCE WAY

Doppies

The contemporary traveller who ventures into Bwabwata National Park in the central part of the Caprivi Strip (Zambezi Region) may not be aware of its early history. What is today a stunning outdoor destination with amazing birdlife and a number of lodges on the eastern bank of the Kwando River was a military area known as Doppies during the Border War.

This area and the base, called Fort Doppies, were used by all the Special Forces units as a training and staging area for a multitude of applications. The selection, survival and minor tactics courses were presented here, preparing operators for operations on both land and water.

From time to time, Fort Doppies also hosted the leadership of Unita. The military area included the St Michelle training area to the north of the Trans-Caprivi road, with a second base to deal specifically with the training and support of Unita.

The old baobab tree that marked the entrance to Fort Doppies fell over sometime in 1998, so the base area is no longer that easy to find. However, when you drive up to the lookout point on the river and spot a cement slab on your left, you are standing at the site of the base. If you carry on past the old base down the dune and travel for another eight kilometres on the river road, you will arrive at the park's designated camping site. Go and sit under the old sausage tree and listen to the stories it has to share. You'll hear about the history of Old Doppies, the old survival camp and other landmarks. In these stories, roads will be referred to either as *duinpad* (dune road) or *rivierpad* (river road). Expect other area-specific terminology such as *spring omuramba*, *eerste elmboog*, *tweede elmboog*, *Immelman airstrip*, *Boesman-kamp* (Bushmen camp) and St Michelle.

The old sausage tree will share anecdotes of lion attacks on students and instructors alike, and will tell you of the hippo charges and elephants, of crocodile bites, and snakes. You'll hear about full-kit water crossings and how the members of the Special Forces often got lost as they traversed the floodplains and waterways in tin boats.

Together you'll recall memories of extreme hardship, endurance and grit, and of friendships forged and characters built. The night will be too short but you will never forget the place where boys became men and men were forged for battle.

Sundays at Doppies is river time. The clear water washes off the week's sweat and grime and refreshes the body for the next week's efforts. Inflatable boats and canoes help to make it fun.

Crocodile Stew

In a chapter dealing with everything that swims (and is edible), as well as with specialised cooking, it is important to mention crocodiles. However, before trying your hand at cooking crocodile meat, it is useful to remember that the water is their territory and they are a real and serious threat. While hippos actually kill more people than crocodiles, the crocs are equally dangerous. Good practice requires posting an armed lookout whenever you enter a hostile African waterway. But, this will only help by day. When you do a river crossing at night, with the intention to go unsighted, and you don't have the luxury of a sentry with a spotlight, the crocs rule – no matter how tough you are.

Sadly, the Special Forces units have a poor record when it comes to crocodiles. We have lost to them on more than one occasion. Gert Nortjé (5 Reconnaissance Regiment) was killed by a crocodile in the Cuito River in 1986. Then there was the well-known incident that took place in 1988, during Operation Coolidge, near the bridge over the Cuito at Cuito Cuanavale. A group of 12 divers from 4 Recce set out to blow up the bridge. Guards on the bridge spotted them and started shooting. On top of that, the crocodiles attacked them as they were escaping.

So, for now we will leave out the croc stew and rather acknowledge crocodiles as serious adversaries. For a crocodile recipe, see Chapter 6 (Regional Flavours).

RIGHT **The 'trophy' given to Anton Beukman after he was attacked by a crocodile during an operation and pulled to the bottom of the Cuito River near Cuito Cuanavale. His training and the fact the he remained calm saved him that day.**

BELOW **Heed this warning sign!**

TIGER FISH CURRY
Caprivi style

Since most fish cooks quite quickly, it makes for an easy, tasty meal. However, 'quick' is not the operative word if you first have to catch your tiger fish in the rivers (the Okavango, Kwando or Zambezi) of the Caprivi Strip (now the Zambezi Region).

The simplest way of catching a tiger fish is by drifting down the river in a tin boat with an ice box and getting lost in the multitude of reed-lined channels. You can spin for tiger fish or use drift bait.

When fishing on the Kwando River on your weekend off, you will have the luxury of an engine. You can go upstream from Fort Doppies to the main stream and then all the way down to the Botswana border. This will take almost an entire day as first you pass by the hippo pools, the survival camps and then the horseshoe. Enjoy the abundant birdlife.

Don't be too disappointed if you don't catch lots of tiger fish, since there aren't that many in the river. As late afternoon approaches, steer back to camp. Just remember that you'll have to walk back up the steep dune to Fort Doppies with the engine on your shoulder, so don't overdo the cold ones.

Tiger fish curry must be prepared to the call of the fish eagle and the sounds of the bush. Fish until late and don't forget the sundowners. (A reminder for the uninitiated: technically, sundowners start just after noon.) Clean and scale the fish.

Start a fire or get your gas braai going on a river bank. Since the fish don't take long to cook, stretch out the prelude to dinner by arguing with your companions about who actually caught the biggest fish.

Heat the oil in a deep pot over slow coals or gas. Fry the cut onions until softened and stir in the spices until you get a paste.

Let the mix simmer for a short while before adding the fish, tomatoes and cubes of parboiled potatoes. Simmer until the potatoes are cooked through (15–20 minutes). Add salt and pepper.

Inflatable boats were used to navigate the vast waterways and deltas of Africa. Once at the destination, they could be folded and hidden until the soldiers returned.

- Cubed tiger fish
- Oil
- Onions, chopped
- Curry spice mix (coriander, garam masala, chilli, ginger, garlic, turmeric)
- Tamarind
- Bay leaves
- Tomatoes
- Potatoes, cut into small cubes and parboiled
- Salt and pepper

> We make war that we can live in peace.
> — ARISTOTLE

FISH CURRY ON THE BEACH

Fresh fish

Tamarind juice

1 onion, chopped

2 tomatoes, chopped

Ground coconut

2 green chillies

Turmeric powder

2 teaspoons red chilli powder

Curry leaves

Ginger, finely chopped

Salt and pepper

The next time you go fishing off the rocks, try this. All you need is to mix some spices in a container and add it to the fishing tackle box. Then put the braai grid, charcoal and a small pot in the back of the boot so you can do anything with the fish you catch. Once you have caught and cleaned the fish, make this quick curry on the beach while listening to the waves and enjoying the smell of the sea.

Put the chopped fish in the pot, add the fresh tamarind juice and let it soak for 2–3 minutes.

Place the pot on the fire and bring the fish pieces to a boil.

Add the chopped onion and tomatoes and stir.

Once this pot is simmering, add the coconut, chillies and all the other spices and stir.

Taste and add salt if needed. Simmer for 12 minutes.

PAN-SEARED TUNA/MARLIN

Marlin or tuna fillets

Garlic powder

Ginger powder

Spice for fish

Oil

Spring onions

Lemon juice

Salt and pepper

This dish should be made only if you have caught the fish yourself. Be careful to manage your expectations: even though the ocean is vast, contrary to popular belief there are not that many big fish in it. This is not only a Mauritian phenomenon but also prevails throughout the seas. We fishermen just don't want to admit it.

Tuna, of course, is much easier to catch than marlin, but pulling out a marlin puts a completely different spin on the whole experience. It may take you about nine years longer to catch a marlin, but keep at it – you will succeed at some point.

Remember, catching marlin is best done with the right type of tackle. Try to avoid catching one on a Scarborough reel[16] just as you leave Durban harbour on a boat. If you insist on doing this, speak to Struis Strydom and JC Erasmus from 1 Recce, who have first-hand experience.

Go out and catch the tuna or marlin from a ski-boat.

Fillet the fish. The fillets should be about as thick as your finger and the size of the palm of your hand.

Mix all the spices in a bowl, add the oil and stir.

Empty the oily spice mix onto a plate and lay the fillets on top. Rub the mix into the fish so that the fillets are completely coated or else the seared fish will be dry.

Heat up the pan and sear the fillets for about 45 seconds on each side. Garnish with spring onions and lemon juice and serve directly off the stove with some salt and pepper.

---

[16] A Scarborough reel is designed for casting long distances from the beach or for bottom-fishing off a boat. It has no brakes or fancy gears, which makes for interesting antics on a boat if, by some fluke, you hook a marlin.

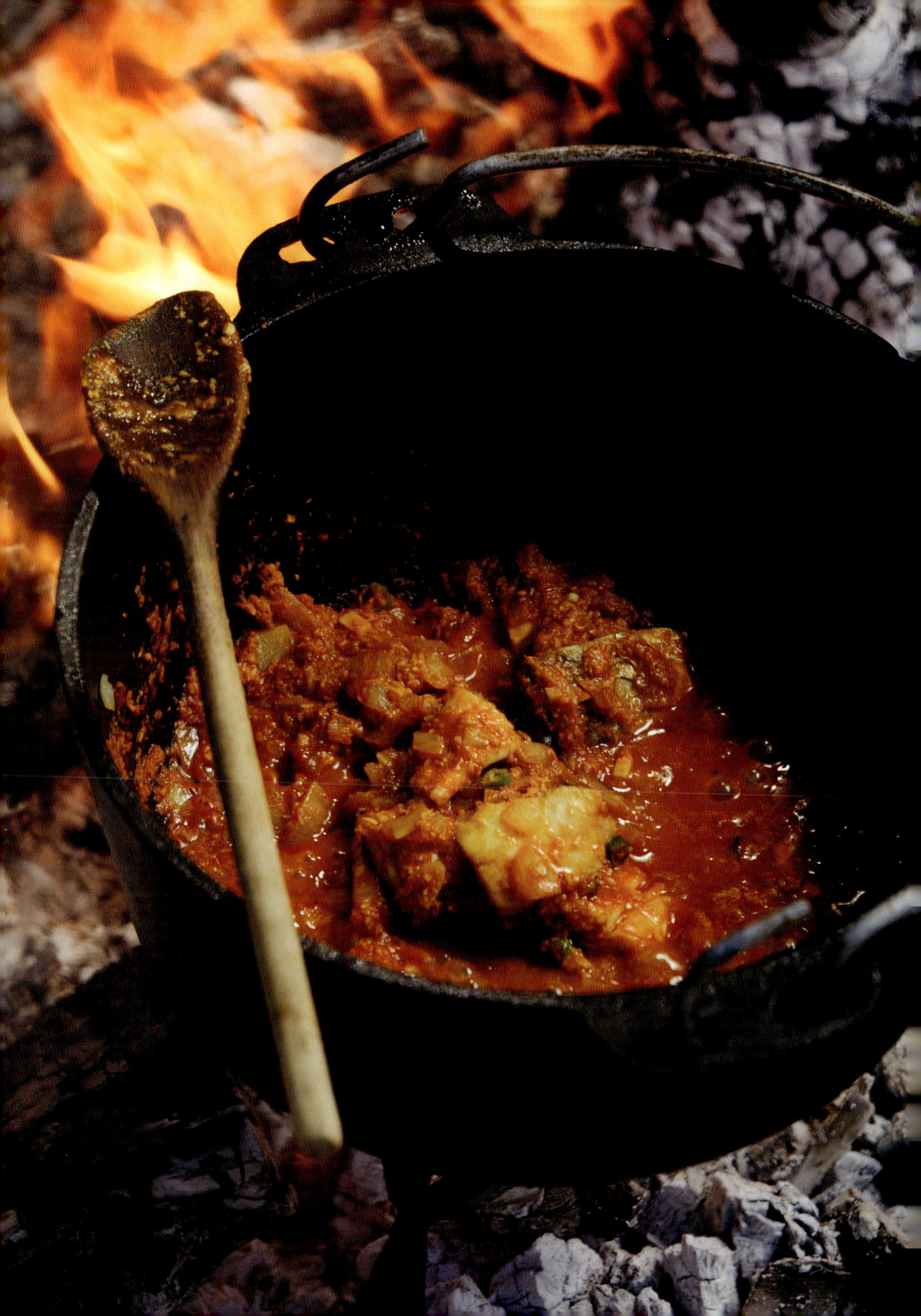

PRAWN COCKTAIL
à la Porthole Grill[17]

Prawns or shrimps

Splash of white wine

Cooking oil

Salt

Mixture of mayonnaise, tomato sauce, Tabasco sauce, lemon juice, pepper

Onion, finely chopped

Lettuce

Parsley, chopped (for garnish)

VARIATION
This dish is all about the sauce and the presentation. You can add chutney or horseradish as well as sour cream. A touch of chilli powder is a great substitute for Tabasco sauce, but be careful not to use too much chilli. Even a bit of chopped jalapeno can work.

No seafood menu is complete without prawn cocktail. It always impresses your guests and puts everyone in the mood for a party, so don't screw it up! The sauce must be balanced, with just a hint of chilli, and the presentation should be perfect.

This dish works especially well if you forgot to light the braai fire at half-time and need a diversion while you play for time.

Deshell and clean the prawns (none of the black veins should be left). As the prawns will be used in a cocktail, the smaller-sized prawns or shrimps are fine.

Prawns are best cooked in a skottel braai or a pan, because you need slow, consistent heat.

Add an 80:20 mix of white wine and oil to the skottel – just enough to cover one-third of the prawns to allow them to simmer. Add the prawns.

By the time the liquid has reduced to a thick gravy-like consistency, the prawns will be ready and won't be dry. Sprinkle with salt and take off the heat.

Mix together the mayonnaise, tomato sauce, Tabasco sauce, lemon juice and pepper. Add the prawns to the mix while hot and stir. Mix in very finely chopped onion. Leave to set.

Chop the lettuce.

Line a glass with lettuce before scooping the prawn mixture on top, and then garnish with some chopped parsley. A wine glass will do but a wider cocktail glass is even better. On second thought, don't skimp: go and buy some proper wide glasses; these can also be used for other treats such as ice cream and cocktails.

SHANGHAI PRAWNS

Groundnut oil

Green chillies, chopped

Garlic, minced

Spring onion, white parts only (greens reserved), chopped

Large deshelled prawns

Tomato sauce

Vinegar (white)

Soy sauce (light)

Corn flour

Spring onion greens, chopped

Bean sprouts

Sesame oil

Heat the groundnut oil in a wok and sauté the green chillies and garlic for a while. Chop the spring onion whites and stir in.

Add the prawns and continue stirring.

Add the tomato sauce, white vinegar and light soy sauce.

Mix in the corn flour.

Then toss in the spring onion greens and bean sprouts.

Drizzle the sesame oil over it, stirring all the while.

Simmer and serve.

---

[17] The Porthole Grill restaurant in Langebaan was owned by the late Gavin Christie, a member of 4 Recce and a recipient of the Honoris Crux. He was also the head chef at the restaurant.

LM PRAWNS

From Pemba in the north all along the coast to Beira, Vilankulos, Inhambane, Xai-Xai, Maputo and Ponta Malongane in the south, our neighbour Mozambique is famous for its prawns. You can almost always get prawns there (whether fresh or not).

For traditional LM prawns you obviously have to go to the capital, Maputo – formerly known as Lourenço Marques (hence LM). The city's northern beaches have a wide variety of eateries, including landmarks such as the Polana Hotel, the Clube Naval and even the bar next to the mini-golf course. Regardless of whether you are looking for high-end cuisine or beach-style *pili pili* (or *piri piri*) prawns, you will find it on this strip.

Best enjoyed after sunset.

Drive to Maputo in a brand-new minibus and book yourself into self-catering accommodation.

On your way there, buy the *pili pili* sauce, which is usually sold in old whisky bottles at roadside stalls. You can make your own but it won't taste the same.

Buy Mozambican prawns, devein and butterfly.

Brush with *pili pili* sauce in a pan or skottel. Don't be afraid; be liberal with the sauce. Fry in butter and garlic.

Once the prawns are done (don't overcook), squeeze fresh lemon juice over them and serve with rice or chips.

Put your toilet paper in the fridge for the next morning.

Mozambican prawns
 (enough for hungry men)
Mozambican *pili pili* sauce
Butter
Garlic
Lemon

Strategic points such as Maputo harbour (pictured) were targets during the Border War.

VARIATION

Arrive in Maputo Bay as part of a raiding party of 11 operators taking part in Operation Vine in October 1983.[18] You'll be transferred to the coast by 4 Recce boat teams before being collected by your agent. Pile into a waiting minibus and set off for your destination ... only to have the minibus break down a short distance further because the battery gives in.

Captain Daan van Zyl, who is leading the raid, will then give the instruction to abandon the operation but the team comes back to complete it two weeks later. By then, however, the tides have changed. You will have to walk a long way over a very flat beach to make it to the treeline.

This time the minibus will work and take you to your target destination. Ask for Gloria. If she is not home, climb onto the roof and place your prepared bags in a strategic position. Return to the boats.

No chance to get any *pili pili* sauce that late at night, though. All the shops are closed.

BELOW The bus in the picture was replaced after an M72 fired during rehearsals damaged the front. The brand-new bus collected the party but the vehicle's battery failed on the night. Once again, a lesson in not using untested equipment.

---

[18] According to the book *Iron Fist from the Sea*, the aim of the operation was to capture important documentation at an ANC administrative centre located at 370 Rua General Pereira d'Eça in Maputo and then to destroy the centre. It had been established that Umkhonto we Sizwe (MK) recruits and trained guerrillas were processed at this centre when transiting through Maputo: 'Here their South African identity was exchanged for a nom de guerre and new documentation and then filed. These files with personal data and movements would provide unique intelligence ...'

IF IT SWIMS

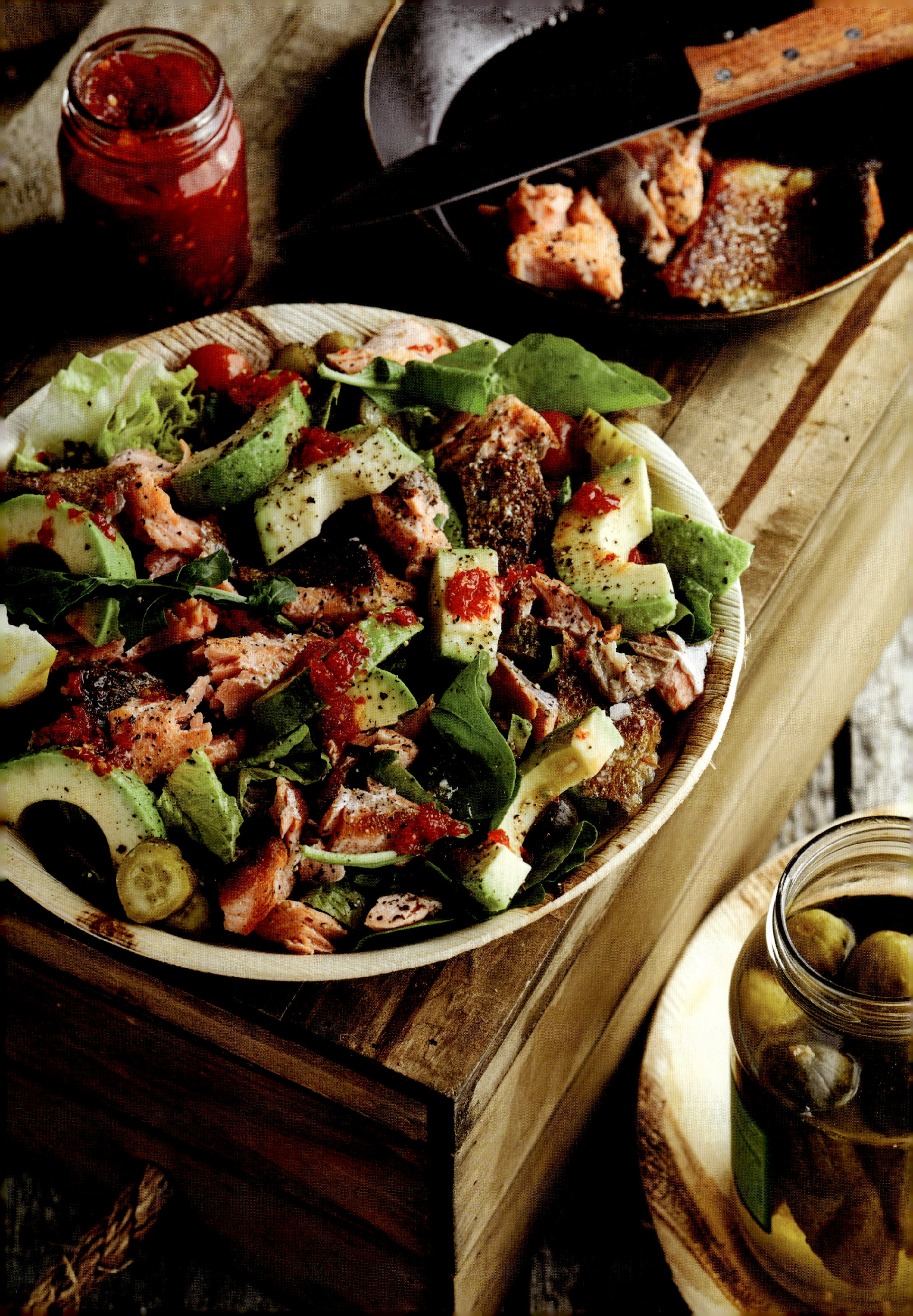

TROUT SALAD
Drakensberg Style

Trout is often referred to as a rich man's food – and with good reason. The meat is delicate and sweet and comes clean off the bone. It is versatile and goes well with a range of condiments.

Discerning gentlemen, such as Major Peter Schofield,[19] who loves fly-fishing, will catch the trout themselves and prepare this dish in the old-school way: by steaming the fish in tin foil over hot coals.

For the rest of us, there are simpler ways of laying our hands on this wonderful fish: stop at the Trout and Toad at Sterkfontein near Harrismith on your way to the Berg or simply pop into your nearest Woolworths and get a packet of Woolworths trout.

Lettuce
Rocket
Cherry tomatoes
Gherkins
Balsamic vinegar
Olive oil
Woolworths smoked trout
Avocado
Sweet chilli sauce

FOR THE WINE MIX
Splash of white wine
Olive oil
Juice of half a lemon
Garlic
Parsley
Salt and pepper

SALAD PREPARATION

Prepare a bed of lettuce and rocket by chopping up the leaves. Add cherry tomatoes and gherkins.

Sprinkle with balsamic vinegar and olive oil.

In a separate bowl, mix the wine, olive oil, lemon juice and seasoning.

Break the smoked trout in small pieces and dip it in the wine mix.

Layer the pieces in a circle on top of the salad bed.

Peel and cut the avocado into slices and place in the centre.

Fill the avocado with sweet chilli sauce.

Grind some black pepper over the salad before serving.

VARIATION

Soy sauce brings out deeper flavours and pickled ginger offers a great alternative to sweet chilli sauce.

The trout can be replaced with tuna; for this salad, just add some mayonnaise to the wine mix.

CRUSTED FISH FINGERS

Marinate the fish for about 15 minutes in a mixture of lemon juice, Worcestershire sauce, salt and pepper.

Roll the fish fingers in flour and dip in egg white to moisten.

Dip in the bread crumbs.

Fry in medium heated oil until golden brown.

Any fish, cut into fingers
Lemon juice
Worcestershire sauce
Salt and pepper
Flour
Eggs, whites separated
Bread crumbs
Cooking oil

---

[19] Peter Schofield is a former British parabat who did the Recce selection course in 1977. At the time he was 41 years old and held the rank of captain. He is the oldest person to have passed the Recce selection course. He served in the Training Wing of 1 Recce.

Watch Your Step

We were busy with a night diving exercise, this time training to swim on our backs all along the jetty at Donkergat, looking out for sentries on the jetty. On this night Commandant Malcolm Kinghorn was acting as a sentry.

He was all dressed up in his uniform, his well-known *kromkierie* in hand, as well as the Dictaphone with which he recorded things he had to remember for the next day and to debrief the divers after the exercise. The divers could follow his every step as he marched up and down the jetty, because every time he pressed the Dictaphone's record button a little red light went on.

Then suddenly he disappeared. Was he trying to trick us, as he often did?

But the next moment, to our amazement, we saw a guy swimming around the point of the jetty towards us. It was the Commandant.

After we had helped him to get onto the slipway we heard the story. He had been walking to the end of the jetty when he looked up at the sky, not realising how close he was to the edge. He then simple walked off the jetty with all his kit.

Of course, we were not allowed to laugh, but it was *the* joke at Donkergat for a long time.

TOP Commandant Malcolm Kinghorn (second from right) addresses the staff at Donkergat. This photo was taken before the 4 Recce base at Langebaan was built. At this time, all staff, including civilian workers, were ferried across the lagoon to the base in the military area.

BOTTOM 4 Recce soldiers have fun at tea time. Fred Wilke (in the centre with mug) is busy with antics while SW Roland (second from left), Dap Maritz (third from left) and Otch Otto (fifth from left) look on.

Seafood Leftovers

by Uil Trauernicht

It was a rainy day in Langebaan, sometime in the early 1980s, and we were expecting the GOC Special Forces, General Kat Liebenberg, for a visit to 4 Recce. As always, the General's visit was a serious affair and no effort had been spared to prepare. We had gone especially big with the food – in both variety and quantity.

As per protocol, our officer commanding (OC), then Commandant Hannes Venter, went to collect Liebenberg in Cape Town, a drive of about 90 minutes. Since the general was only due on the midday flight, Hannes decided to visit the naval headquarters in Simon's Town first, but unbeknown to him the General had taken an earlier flight that morning.

At Cape Town airport (then DF Malan Airport), General Liebenberg apparently smoked two Lexington cigarettes before he started looking around for a payphone. He got through to Ursula van Basson, who was manning the switchboard at the time. Now Ursula was infamous for her sharp tongue and was also a veteran of many a prank.

Hannes Venter with a big smile on his face after completing his selection course.

When the caller identified himself, she duly informed him, 'If you are General Liebenberg, then I'm f**king Doris Day!'

It was only after the third call that she realised it really was Liebenberg, but by then there was hell to pay. She put him through to me. I apologised profusely on behalf of everyone involved and offered to come and fetch him immediately. All he said was, 'Uil, you tell Hannes Venter that if he is not here in 30 minutes I will get back on a plane to the Transvaal and he can go and get stuffed.'

Since this was in the days before cellphones, attempts to reach Hannes were futile and the General departed. What could we do but feast on all the seafood leftovers?

CALAMARI PIECES
for corporals

- Freshly caught squid (calamari)
- Tabasco sauce
- Lemon juice
- Cooking oil
- Garlic, crushed
- Milk
- Salt and pepper

Work until late at night at Donkergat and then take the ferry back to Langebaan. On the ferry, hide behind the tall and straight figure of Commandant Malcolm Kinghorn (OC of 4 Recce from 1978 to 1982), since he will stand steadfast at the bow in his 'weathersuit' and take the spray over the side as true captain of the ship.

Once you get to Langebaan, avoid Kinghorn's gaze, for he is a true officer and his penetrating look of disapproval will make you want to cringe. Run to the base and grab the jigging rods and a spotlight, then return to the jetty to catch some squid.

When you have as many of the hand-sized squid as is needed for a decent meal, make your way back to the living quarters. While some members of the team clean the squid in the hand basin, the others can go to the mess to 'borrow' some salt and pepper and cutlery from the set tables, also some milk if the kitchen door was left open.

Put the squid in a cloth and tenderise with the heel of an army boot.

Take your little gas stove, Tabasco sauce and lemon juice out of your backpack. Heat some oil in your dixie.

Fry the calamari and crushed garlic lightly in the dixie. Add a little milk to the oil so that it bubbles off before it gets really hot.

Sprinkle lemon juice and Tabasco, together with salt and pepper, on the calamari and serve.

> There is no harm in repeating a good thing.
> — PLATO

CALAMARI IN CURRY YOGHURT

- 1.5 kg calamari
- Water
- Curry powder mix
- Tomato sauce
- Light soy sauce
- 250 ml yoghurt
- Mustard
- Chilli
- Salt and pepper
- Dill (for garnish)

Tenderise the calamari by chopping a fine edge on it — the edge of a plate, the handle of a hunting knife, the heel of a boot or even the bottom of a wine bottle held at an angle all work equally well.

Add the tenderised calamari to boiling water for 4 minutes, then remove.

Stir in the curry powder mix with the tomato sauce, and light soy sauce with the yoghurt.

Add mustard, chilli, salt and pepper to taste.

Place calamari in a bowl. Add the yoghurt mixture and stir.

Garnish with dill.

FISH HEAD SOUP
à la Valerie

Catch a biggish fish. You will need about 200 g of offcuts to make a soup. Scale, clean and gut the fish before cutting it into fillets. Put fillets aside for another meal.

Place all the offcuts, including the head, in a pot and add water, salt, stock cubes and vinegar.

Boil on high for 30 minutes.

Remove all the bones by straining the soup through a sieve.

Add the finely cubed potato, chopped leek or onion and boil for 10 minutes. Add bay leaves for taste.

Serve with noodles and a dollop of sour cream.

1 fish
Water
Salt
Stock cubes
1 tablespoon vinegar
Potato, finely cubed
2 leeks (or an onion), chopped
Bay leaves
Noodles
Sour cream

PERLEMOEN
à la Dirk Steenkamp[20]

Secure the perlemoen, but don't tell anyone where or how you got this rare treat. No matter the quantity – just get some and prepare it.

Cut into thin slices and tenderise with the edge of a saucer/plate.

Fry in a hot pan in a butter and lemon mix as you would for an underdone steak.

Mix garlic, chillies and cream together to make a sauce and simmer for a few minutes.

Eat in private; this delicacy is not for sharing.

Perlemoen (abalone)
Butter
Lemon juice
Garlic
Chillies
Cream
Salt and pepper

The daily ferry leaves Donkergat to take the staff back to Langebaan.

---

[20] Staff Sergeant Dirk Steenkamp, or the 'Ou Man' of 4 Recce, was renowned for his perlemoen poaching abilities, but fortunately he didn't mind sharing.

IF IT SWIMS

SEAFOOD PAELLA
with pasta

Onion
Tomato
Red pepper
Green pepper
Fish
Tinned mussels
Shelled crayfish
Garlic
Tabasco sauce
Dried parsley
Salt and pepper
Penne pasta

[21] A bola is a traditional African stove. Normally, it is made from a tin with a few holes punched in it and flared at the top and the bottom. The coals are placed at the bottom, with the pot placed on top.

Making a paella on the beach is all about being calm and in sync with your surroundings. This kind of cooking, where you are immersed in the moment and enjoying the company of friends, is really the essence of specialised cooking.

Paella is easy to prepare and a variety of ingredients can be used. Normally, paella is made with rice but pasta works just as well.

Any budding army chef should be able to make it since it can be prepared in a dixie, on the beach in a wok or as a signature dish for special occasions.

Wait for the sun to start setting and serve G&Ts all around. Making your paella on the beach is first prize; then it's easier to hide any G&T-induced instability.

Make a small fire and transfer a few coals to the bola.[21]

Sauté the onion and veggies in a wok using a bit of butter/oil.

Once sautéed, add the seafood portions in any order.

Add garlic and Tabasco sauce, plus the dried parsley and salt and pepper.

Cook the pasta for 5 minutes in a separate pot.

Just before it is *al dente* add the pasta to the seafood and let it soak up the juices.

Serve your paella in the big wok as it makes for a beautiful presentation.

BAKED BARBEL
Khud style

Cumin seeds
Coriander seeds
Fennel seeds
Garlic
Salt
Dry red chilli paste
Turmeric powder
Salt and pepper
Lime juice
Buttermilk
Ghee
Handful of fresh coriander, chopped
Fresh barbel, skinned and filleted
Banana leaves
Rice

By now you may be asking about portion sizes, how much of what, for how many people, and so on. In specialised cooking, you work with what you have. If all you caught was an undersized rock barbel in the Okavango River, then adjust it to be a starter and don't tell anyone you can't really fish. If you caught a monster Cornish Jack (barbel) barehanded on Lake Kariba, then serve it as the main meal while you boast about your incredible skills. You are a specialised chef; you can work out the portion sizes. Just stay in the moment.

Dry roast the cumin, coriander and fennel seeds, and grind to a powder.

Char the garlic and grind to a paste with a pinch of salt.

Combine the ground spices and garlic paste with the dry red chilli paste, turmeric powder, salt and pepper, lime juice, buttermilk and ghee. Mix well before adding chopped coriander. Coat the fish fillets with the marinade paste.

Layer a banana leaf with kitchen foil, make a bed of rice on it, and place the fish carefully on the rice. Fold the banana leaf over to make a parcel and tie with string.

Place the fish parcel in an oven on medium heat (or on the embers of firewood/dry cow dung) for 20 minutes.

Unwrap the banana leaf parcel, and serve as is.

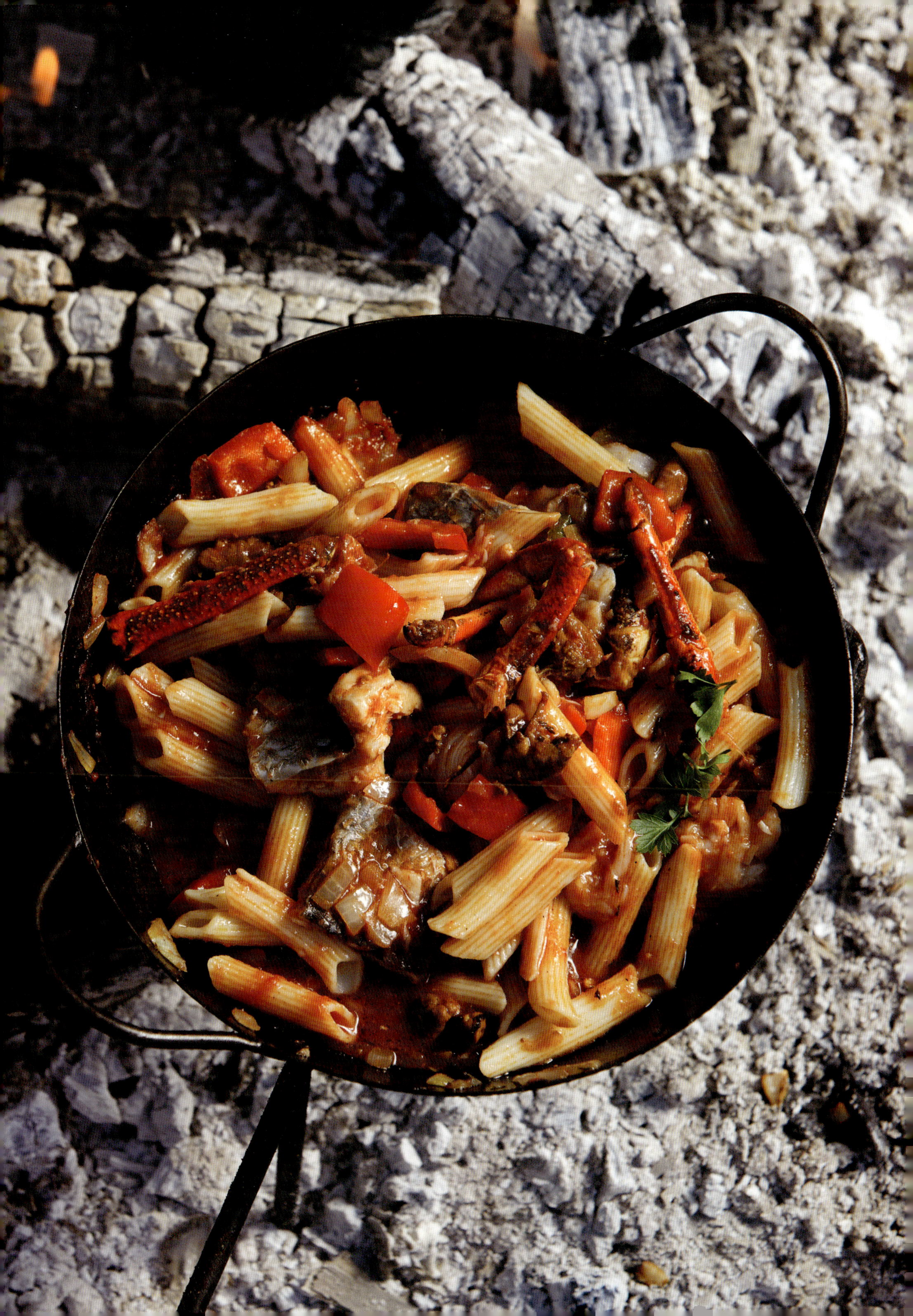

DEEP-FRIED FLYING FISH
Oswald Pirow *style*[22]

One flying fish
Parsley, chopped
Half a lemon, cut into thin slices
Garlic
White flour
Milk
Salt and pepper
Cooking oil (for deep frying)

Most people are caught by surprise the first time they see a flying fish, mostly because so few people are aware such an animal actually exists. To catch them is rather tricky as they don't really take to standard fishing gear.

An ingenious way of catching flying fish is to let them catch themselves, so to speak. Get a bunk on a strike craft going out to sea. Leave the 1 Recce base in Durban in the early morning hours and head up the coast. Take a seat against the aft gun turret around midmorning and look out over the ocean to the growl of the engines.

Every now and again you will see the fish jump out of the water and glide across the surface from one swell into the next. Take bets with the other crew members on how far they'll go.

If there are two barracuda crash boats on deck, the back of the strike craft will be quite low in the water. When a fish flies into the side of the gun housing, grab it before it slides off the deck.

Take it to the chef in the galley and ask him to prepare it for you.

In light of how difficult it is to catch a flying fish, and that so few people know how to cook this fish, this dish is sure to impress your guests.

Clean the fish as best you can, keeping in mind that it is quite bony.

After removing the guts, replace with a mixture of chopped parsley, lemon slices and garlic.

Make a batter using the flour, milk and spices. Then dip the fish in the batter and deep fry in oil in a pot.

If you are on a strike craft, then the designated person to serve it to will be the ship's captain. He will accept the meal with dignity.

BARNACLE STEW

A bag of barnacles
Tabasco sauce
Lemon
Salt

This is a tough and uncompromising dish. Barnacles have to be prised off the rocks (or out of the units).

Cook them as you would periwinkles, which means simply boil them in water and remove from the shell. The barnacles will be chewy but nutritious.

If you have British guests, call them 'periwinkles' and hope no one notices the difference.

---

[22] The SAS *Oswald Pirow* was a strike craft named after a former Minister of Justice and Defence.

SPECIALISED COOKING – THE RECCE WAY

> A good decision is based on knowledge and not on numbers.
> — PLATO

SUNNY SKIES AND A SUBMARINE BRAAI

One submarine (the boat, not the sandwich)
Meat
Stuff to braai with
Sunny skies

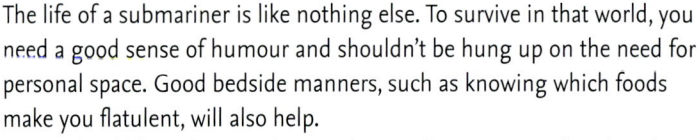

The life of a submariner is like nothing else. To survive in that world, you need a good sense of humour and shouldn't be hung up on the need for personal space. Good bedside manners, such as knowing which foods make you flatulent, will also help.

You should learn how to sleep in the rain forest,[23] to read and to play tap-tap, as the scenery is limited. You'll also come to realise quickly that giving fellow crew members weird and wonderful haircuts is a great form of entertainment. Once this is done, settle into a routine in which all members have to give a three-minute show on the stage, that is the one-metre-square area in front of the torpedo tubes.

After seven days on board a Daphné-class submarine planning the same job over and over again, it's recommended that you start doing an exercise launch every night. For this you'll have to climb out of the conning tower with the Zodiac engine on a hoist rope. Assemble the craft on the deck and launch without capsizing.

Return to the belly of the submarine and debrief. Do the same thing the following night but this time with diving gear. The next evening the exercise should be repeated with Klepper folding canoes.

By this time you will be healthy and hungry.

On a calm day, go to the surface for fresh air. Make sure the captain is onside and drop a hint for a braai. If he agrees, treat the opportunity like a launch and run up the steps at launch speed with the braai and coals. Be very sure it was packed when you left; there are few alternatives at this point.

VARIATION
Let's just accept this is the ultimate braai! The closest you will come to beating a submarine braai is to park an icebreaker in a sea of solid ice in the Arctic. For this you will need a hipflask of sherry or vodka. Volume 2 of this book will expand on this.

No matter the size of the galley, the submariners always made the most amazing food, even for formal dinners.

---

[23] The 'rain forest' was the section in the front of the boat where the torpedo tubes were located. This was allocated to us when we came on board and we slept on top of and inside the tubes. There was a lot of dripping water because of condensation, which made it much like a rain forest. Many of the guys put up their bivvies just like in the bush.

SPECIALISED COOKING – THE RECCE WAY

From the Galley

The whole of the galley – only magicians allowed.

Being on board a naval vessel as part of a Special Forces raiding party brings with it numerous unique experiences. It starts with where you sleep. All the additional soldiers need to be fitted in somewhere. If you are slightly senior, then at least a bunk would've been assigned to you. The rest fill up the vessel from the back, with the juniors having to sleep on the floor in the gun bay. The privilege of sleeping on the floor amid the smell of the grease and diesel fumes from the big engines is only partially offset by the advantage that you will be the first to get out on deck to get some fresh air.

The food you are served is prepared in the galley up front, and a raiding party representative would be sent to collect it. The trip there and back is more hazardous than the actual raid, as the route goes through the engine room (at night) and up and down the gangways, and involves the opening and closing of doors and locks. All the while, you have to balance the containers of food.

In the containers, though, you'll find the most amazing creations, especially on raid or launch night. On those nights the food would be had under red-light conditions. This means that the inward leg to the coast had started and no lights would be visible on the vessel. Only red lights inside the hull were allowed.

During the day, all prep and packing would be completed, and what remained was mentally working through the routines again and again. At about L-minus two hours, it was eating time. Thereafter it was get dressed, kit inspection and blacken up. Let's go.

IF IT SWIMS 65

FOR THE RECORD

4 Reconnaissance Regiment

OCs ROLL
Commandant M Kinghorn	1978–1982
Commandant JJ (Hannes) Venter	1982–1994
Colonel KE (Krubert) Nel	1994–1998

RSMs ROLL
WO1 JWA (Chilli) du Plessis	1972–1980
WO1 EJ (Tilly) Smit	1980–1988
WO1 WJ (Koos) Loots	1989–1995
WO1 GJ (Gerrie) Heydenrych	1995–1997[24]

The 4 Recce unit flag is lowered at Operators Kop, Langebaan.

Operators Douw Steyn (left) and Tuffy Joubert after a parade at 4 Recce in Langebaan.

ABOVE Members carry their 'leader' to the annual Viking Party at Donkergat.

LEFT A 4 Recce operator's diver's log book.

---

[24] WO1: Warrant Officer First Class.

Dishing up food in the aft quarters of a strike craft.

Compass Rose, the 4 Recce yacht, on a visit to the Durban harbour with the Bluff in the background.

Members of 1 Recce play volleyball on the deck of the SAS *Drakensberg* during rehearsals for Operation Kerslig.

You can discover more about a person in an hour of play than a year of conversation.

PLATO

A tug of war at a 1 Recce reunion held in Saldanha.

IF IT SWIMS 67

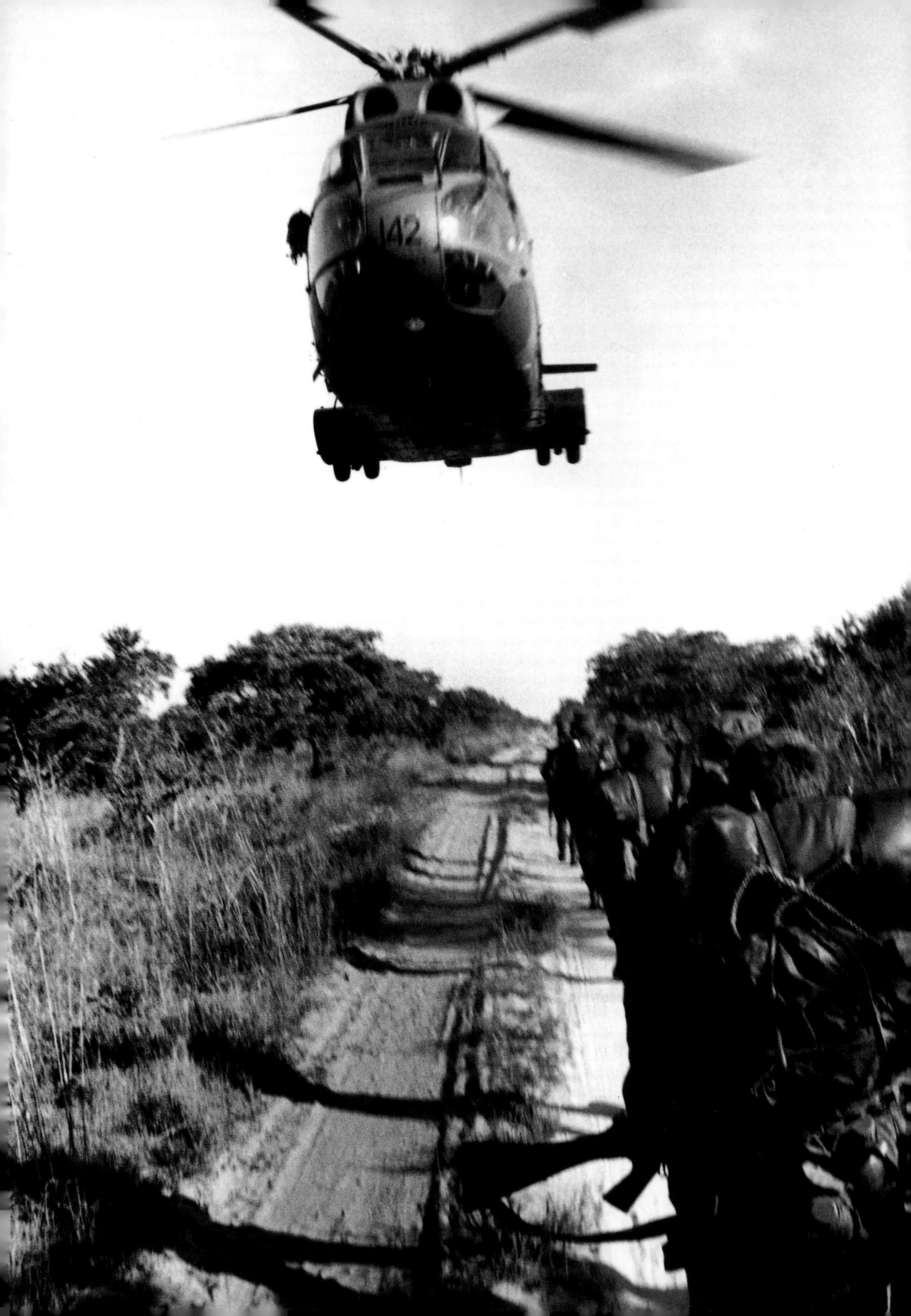
142

IF IT FLIES

You've probably guessed it already but 'If It Flies' refers to food with wings. Of course, having wings doesn't guarantee that something can fly or has qualified for flight. Ostriches and penguins have wings but, quite like the guys from Air Supply, you've never seen one fly.

Then there are those with limited flight ability, such as chickens. You'll find they make a lot of noise in their effort to briefly make it into the air to get into their coops – much like paratroopers making noise to get up into the *aapkas*.[25] They have wings but can't really fly.

Birds such as ducks are truly skilled and could be classified as the gods of the sky. They do intercontinental migrations with ease. Some humans would like to consider themselves as sky gods, even though skydiving is really just a matter of falling through the sky. You will easily recognise a 'sky god'. They walk on drop zones with those funny running pants and elastics tied to their shoes. Perhaps it's caused by the lack of oxygen when they do HALO (High Altitude Low Opening) or HAHO (High Altitude High Opening) jumps.[26]

In this chapter we don't discriminate against birds that can fly and those that can't. We offer recipes across the board on how to eat them.

A Puma helicopter flies low over a foot patrol. Note the sleeping bags tied to the top of the backpacks. This leaves more space for equipment in the pack.

---

[25] An *aapkas* (literally, 'monkey cage') is used as a training aid for student paratroopers. They jump from this elevated structure, about six storeys high, to which a cable is attached. Getting up the stairs is always done with a lot of shouting.

[26] A HAHO jump is done from above 18 000 ft and requires oxygen. These jumps can be from as high as 36 000 ft. Jumping requires you to pre-breathe and also to wear protective goggles and gloves to combat the extreme temperatures at high altitude.

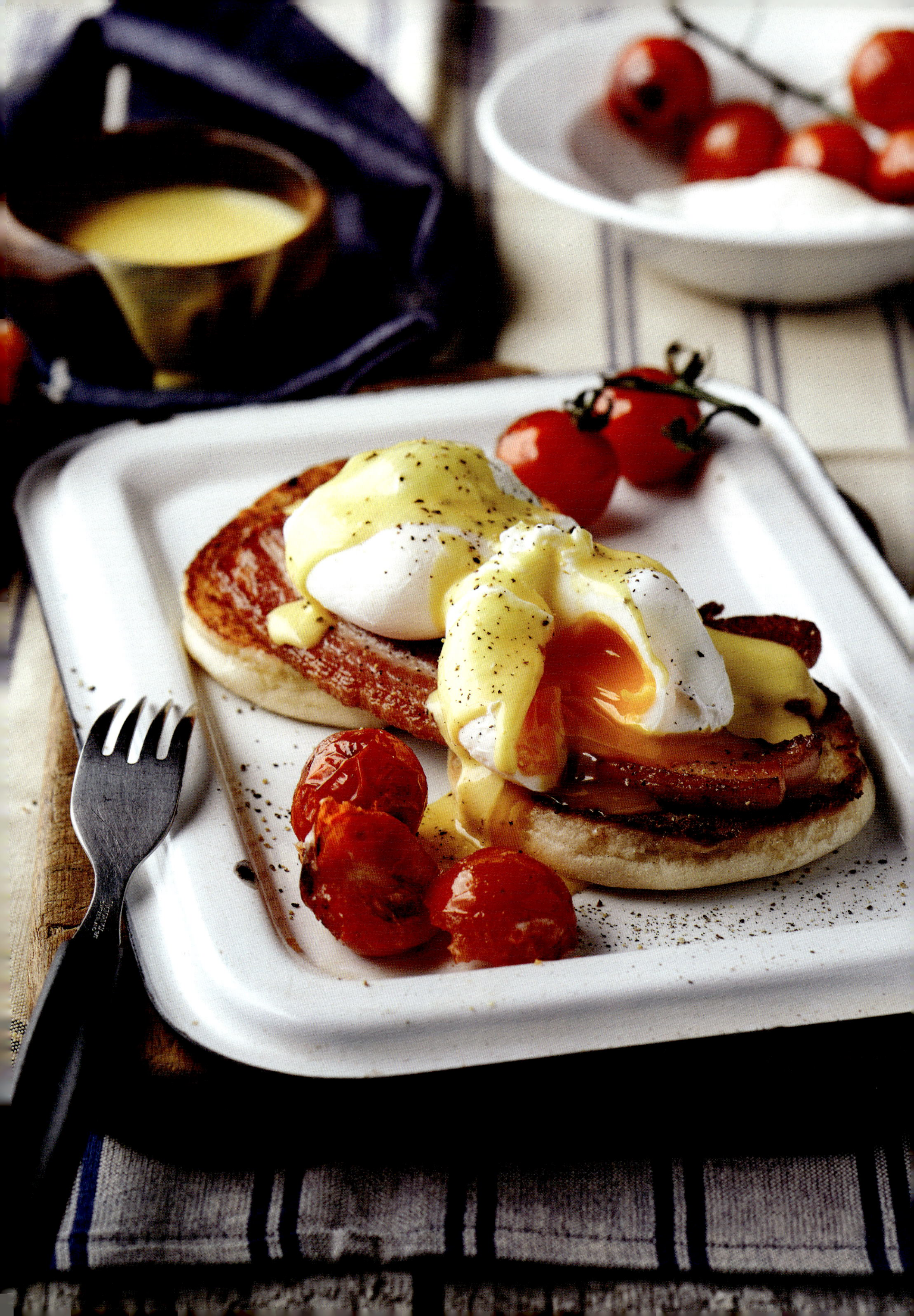

EGGS BENEDICT

This traditional American breakfast is made with poached eggs and bacon, ham or smoked salmon on a muffin or piece of toast and covered with a hollandaise sauce. It is a tried and tested hangover cure, but, most importantly, it is sure to impress even the shyest girl from the Teachers' Training College[27] in Durban. If you serve this the morning after the first sleepover, you are likely to get return visits.

HOLLANDAISE SAUCE

Make the hollandaise sauce first, but be warned: it can be quite tricky to make. If you don't get the hollandaise sauce right, you will need to seriously improvise. See the variation below if this happens.

Beat the egg yolks before adding the lemon juice, salt and cayenne pepper.

Slowly pour melted butter into the egg yolk mixture while whisking.

Heat in microwave for 15 to 20 seconds.

Whisk one last time after taking it out.

POACHED EGGS AND BACON

Briefly cook the bacon in some oil; it should still be soft. Set aside.

Cut the muffin in half and lightly toast in the pan you used for the bacon or make two slices of toast.

Bring the water to simmer – in a pan or pot – then add some vinegar. Break the eggs into a saucer first and then flow each gently into the water. Allow the egg to boil for about three minutes. It is ready when the outside is white and the inside slightly runny. This will allow it to spread over the muffin when cut.

Butter the muffin, and layer the ingredients with the poached egg on top. Add the bacon/ham/salmon and pour the hollandaise sauce over and serve with fresh or fried cherry tomatoes and salt and pepper.

VARIATION

A much simpler version of this breakfast is with fresh rolls from the Spar and without the hollandaise sauce. Slice off the top third of the rolls and hollow out the bottom part slightly. Spread with butter. Place the poached egg in the roll and season with salt and pepper and chopped parsley. Add grated cheese and serve.

FOR THE HOLLANDAISE SAUCE

3 egg yolks
Lemon juice
Salt
Cayenne pepper
Butter

FOR THE EGGS

Bacon, smoked salmon or ham
Oil
Muffin or toast
Water
Vinegar
2 eggs
Cherry tomatoes
Salt and pepper

Brighton Beach in Durban in 1980.

---

27 When 1 Recce was stationed in Durban there was a strong link between the local Teachers' Training College and the unmarried contingent on the Bluff. So much so that regular meetings were held between the Dean and the then OC of 1 Recce.

IF IT FLIES

The Infantry School

(aka Mafafa School)

No book on the Special Forces would be complete without a mention of Oudtshoorn, because it is here – at the Infantry School – where the story of the Recces actually begins. The Infantry School was established long before conscription was implemented and it was the most prestigious unit in the infantry.

The founding members, or the so-called Dirty Dozen, who started 1 Reconnaissance Commando in 1972, including Colonel Jan Breytenbach, were all stationed at Oudtshoorn when the unit was formed, so we can say that the Recces were a product of the School. (1 Recce only moved to Durban in 1975.)

All infantry soldiers passed through the Infantry School at some point if they served long enough, because this was where you attended the mandatory courses to get promoted. The curriculum included the courses for support weapons such as mortars, the 106 mm recoilless gun and the Milan guided missile, as well as the young officer's and non-commissioned officer's (NCO) course for junior leaders and the more senior courses for officers and senior NCOs.

During their career, all Special Forces soldiers would also spend some time in Oudtshoorn. We would always mentally prepare ourselves before meeting the infantry for the first time, since they were a bit different from us. They were career soldiers who really loved the army environment. They thrived on routine and structure and had great respect for rules, procedures and discipline … and extremely short hair! They loved to drill and do parades, cut their hair, write curriculums and do mock exercises.

However, they also had to train all the rest of the G3K3 infantry who had gotten lost in the woodwork and needed to do certain courses to get promoted, so let's not give them too much grief. Even if they are very regimental, they compare with the best in the world.

The nickname 'Dirty Dozen' was given to the founding members who started the original Reconnaissance Commandos in Oudtshoorn, which evolved into the modern Special Forces Regiments. Pictured here are PW van Heerden, Koos Moorcroft, Barry Visser (Sr) and Jimmy Oberholzer.

On Course in Oudtshoorn

The promotion system for Recces was somewhat strange at times. For instance, to qualify for a promotion, you had to attend certain courses, such as one of the support weapons courses, at the Infantry School, even if you were a seasoned soldier.

By that time you would most likely have had six years of operational experience and you would have completed the Recce heavy weapons course[28] early in your career. And you would definitely have deployed operationally with 81 mm mortars and/or 106 mm rifles on modified Unimogs or Sabres.

Also, the course would have been presented by an instructor who was doing his two-year conscription as a national serviceman and had seen no operational action. Weird but true.

Under such conditions, it is time to bring forward one's special qualities to adapt, adjust and stay in the moment. It's impossible to take course life too seriously, especially if you do the 106 mm course with Spik Botha, Dave Tippet and Jimmy Oberholzer. Rather make a plan to enjoy the beautiful surroundings on weekends, but see to it that someone from the Recce team comes top of the class – as Recces should. Spending a weekend at the Holiday Inn was a great stress reliever that offered a break from the intense classes, the marching, the ironing of uniforms and polishing of boots every morning.

The best way to explore the scenery around Oudtshoorn on a limited budget is to negotiate with the chef in charge at the Infantry School. By this time, you should have a few negotiating skills: explain that the four of you who are on course will not be there for the seven meals served on the weekend and can he please pack your rations in bulk? The mince, fish and other intended rations should be substituted with steak, cheese, tomatoes, onions and a few loaves of buttered bread.

With this one move you've secured the Swartberg and Vic Bay for the weekend. Bye, bye barracks – hello mountains!

Spik Botha and another Special Forces operator practise using a Soviet-made B10 recoilless gun. Note the Cuban helmet he is wearing.

---

[28] All operators did the heavy weapons course within two years after qualifying. The course included operational training with LMG, RPD, 60 mm, 81 mm mortar, 106 mm recoilless, B10 recoilless, 14.5 mm, ZU23 mm and the SA-7.

SWARTBERG CARPACCIO

Coarse salt
Ostrich fillet
Balsamic vinegar
Vinaigrette
Rocket (the leaf, not the weapon)
Parmesan cheese
Capers

It's not that easy getting ostrich steak as tender as mature beef or pork fillet. To sidestep this potential pitfall and still enjoy its deep flavours, simply serve it as carpaccio.

To do so, pick an outdoor venue such as a campsite in the Swartberg. Once settled, make a fire; the air will be chilly and you'll also need the warmth. Since the piece of meat should be thick, start off with a full rump.

Rub coarse salt into the ostrich fillet. Take care not to puncture the meat.

Sear the meat over hot coals for about 8 minutes, then wrap in foil and let it stand next to the fire. DO NOT COOK.

Sit back in your camping chair and watch the flames as they slowly dance over the deep-red coals.

When everyone's hungry, cut the ostrich rump into paper-thin pieces, overlay and display.

Pour the balsamic vinegar and vinaigrette over the meat in broad strokes.

Serve it as a fancy starter on a bed of rocket, topped with some Parmesan shavings and capers, as you prepare the *braaibroodjies*.

SCRAMBLED OSTRICH EGG AND BRAISED STEAK

by IJ (Tuffy) Joubert

1 tin of military-style braised steak
1 stolen ostrich egg

Join the 1973 selection course in Oudtshoorn.[29] This will be one of the first Recce selection courses ever to be presented.

You will have limited food and it is expected that you will improvise to get food.

After ten days of extreme exercises, the selection course will enter the all-in phase (this last part of selection is when you have to evade capture). Chris Schutte will lead the chase (by the instructors) to find you as you try to move unseen from national key point to national key point. He will be supported by a company of infantry troops.

Meet with your 'Agent', MJ Potgieter, every second day to get your next instructions and to show that you are still alive.

When you pass through a farming area, make sure you obtain an ostrich egg. Don't worry about the ostrich and its aggressive, protective instincts. When the female sees the desperation and determination in your eyes, she will be the one backing off. However, don't waste any time getting back over the fence again.

Make a hole in one end of the egg and empty it into your dixie. Cook the egg.

Heat the tin of braised steak provided by the Agent in the other part of the dixie.

Mix and eat. Soon you'll start feeling much better.

---

[29] 1 Reconnaissance Commando was based in Oudtshoorn between 1972 and 1975. At the time the selection courses were done in the Swartberg range around Oudtshoorn. They were based on SAS methods, that is, no rules applied. After 1 Recce moved to Durban, the selection courses were presented in various locations, including northern Natal and at Fort Doppies.

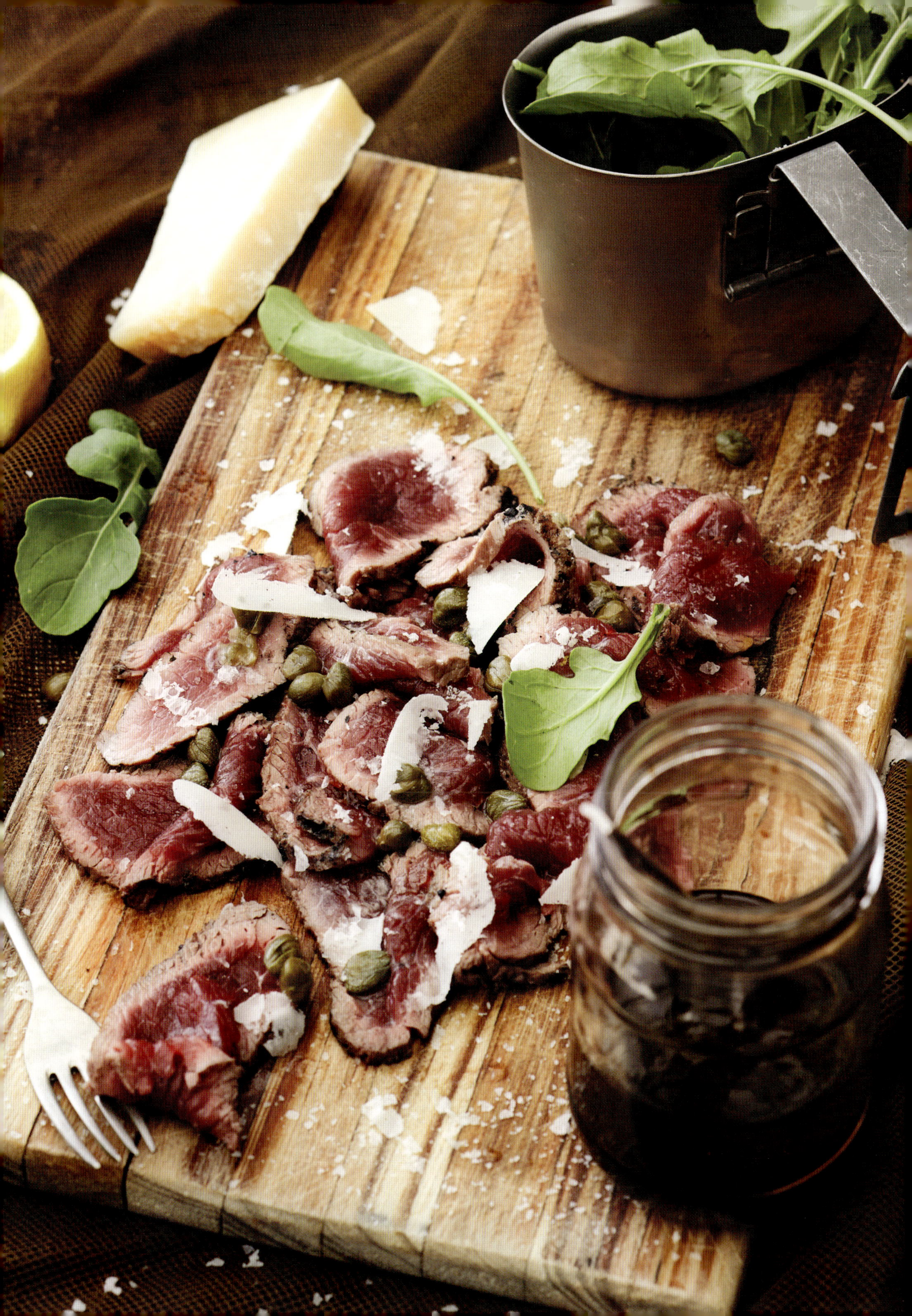

Drop Zone, What Drop Zone?

All Recce students did an air orientation course after completing their parachute jumping course. On this course they were taught how to call in choppers and air strikes, do fast-roping from choppers, prepare landing zones and sharpen their jumping skills in a more operational type of environment.

During the training, they were required to keep their kit packed at all times as this would help them get used to living from a backpack. To check that they were following this instruction, every now and then the instructors would pick up their kit to feel the weight. If an instructor noticed that the packs weighed much less than they should, there was a simple way to teach the students a lesson …

Before every static-line jump, the drift was calculated and the exit point of the jumpers was adjusted accordingly so they would land in the middle of the designated drop zone (DZ), that is, if you actually wanted them to land accurately in the landing zone.

If the students were taking short cuts with their packs – and it happened on every course – the course instructor would move the intended landing zone for the last light jump just enough so they would land in the trees and not next to them. The pilots would then adjust the run into the drop zone by some 300 m off the intended track and also delay the start of the drop by 15 seconds.

Once the red light came on, the dispatchers would quickly check outside to make sure the plane was indeed over the trees. Then they let the students go. Once they were all out, you as dispatcher pulled in all the static line bags that were fluttering outside the door, sat down and smiled. Tonight they would learn a simple lesson.

As with all these jumps, the jumpers still had to do the ground grouping before they could call in for a pick-up – and it had to be before dark. That of course didn't happen this time.

By the next day, the rumours about the pack weights have filtered through. Amazingly, when you test the packs again, they are all the correct weight.

A parachute instructor's handbook.

Amilcar Queiroz (middle) with former colleagues at his restaurant in Angola. From left to right: Manual, Martiens Verster, unknown and Rieme de Jager.

With free falls you didn't need this kind of intervention. The pilots of the old Dakotas created the right mix of chaos all by themselves. On a night exercise in 1984 in Natal (today KwaZulu-Natal), they were supposed to drop the two-man scout teams between Bhangazi and Sibaya lakes over carefully marked open spots in the fever tree forests.

But, before the arrival of GPS (Global Positioning System), the world was a very different place. As usual they were out but this time by a full 45 km. You see, before the arrival of GPS (Global Positioning System), the world was a very different place so the majority of the teams were strung up in the fever trees. But by the time the last team exited they were over Mozambique. Luckily, Amilcar Queiroz[30] – an experienced operator of Angolan descent who speaks Portuguese – was part of this two-man team. At first light as they were walking with their parachutes they got to a big fence. Assuming it was a game fence, they decided to follow it until they reached a gate.

A while later they saw two Frelimo soldiers who were walking towards them on the same side of the fence. They walked past each with their heads turning in unison to keep eye contact. Neither side knew what to do.

As soon as enough distance had been put between them, the two Recces threw over their parachutes and clambered over the border fence and back to South Africa.

---

[30] On his first jump during the free-fall course at Pietermaritzburg airport, this very colourful and competent soldier fell through the roof of a house near the drop zone and landed in the kitchen. This young paracaidista (Portuguese for 'paratrooper'), as he always referred to himself, was discovered by the search party several hours later having soft drinks with the kindly homeowners.

SPECIALISED COOKING – THE RECCE WAY

Not All Men Jump

Being a free-fall instructor with the Recces has its benefits – you get to jump a lot. It's a lot of fun, until you get to jump with people who either don't want to jump or simply can't jump. As Dave Tippet – master instructor – always said of such instances: 'All you have to do is keep a cool head and a tight ass.'

Take the following example. Your student is one Mendez, who is 34 years old and of Angolan descent. By this time, he has been in 5 Recce for seven years and needs an additional qualification to get promoted, such as completing a free-fall course …

It is jump number six of his accelerated free-fall course. Up to this point none of his jumps has been stable. For those unfamiliar with parachuting, in accelerated free-fall, the student and the instructor exit the aircraft together, with the instructor holding the student by his shoulder straps to assist him to fall in a stable manner. The student must arch his body so that his stomach is the centre of gravity, keeping him pointing downwards. All extensions, that is, arms and legs, must be balanced to avoid instability, otherwise you will quite literally spin and tumble through the air as opposed to having a controlled and exhilarating fall at 200 km/h. At this velocity, the wind drowns out your voice and if you let the student go he will be even more unstable.

Back to Mendez. By jump six he should've been stable and been able to respond. The idea is that by now you could leave him as he falls and does his routines. Not Mendez. He hasn't opened his own chute by himself or gone solo, even if the course requires one-on-one jumping. As the instructor, you have to get him stable.

As you exit the door, he flops in underneath you – again. His arms come up to his face and the two of you start to somersault. You push back as far as you can with your arms, only to see him trying to put back his false teeth – blissfully unaware that his supposed arch has turned into a hunch.

This is when you have to rely on what Johan Burr-Dixon, Dave Tippet, Frans van Dyk, Anton Retief and the old free-fall masters taught you in your student days. Extend your arms in full – prepare – then jerk him closer at full speed so you can hit him with your head.

Out pop the teeth and the arch comes back. Finally, a stable free-fall.

PS: Mendez qualified, but he still doesn't have front teeth.

TOP Static-line jumpers prepare to land in the cold waters of Langebaan while boat crews wait to pick them up.

This photo shows Kenaas Conradie (foreground) preparing for a test water jump with Dewald de Beer (rear, left) and John More next to him.

IF IT FLIES   77

CHICKEN SANDWICH
Havana style

Chicken breast
Bacon
Oil
Lime
Sliced white bread
Mayonnaise
Mustard
Lettuce
Gherkin
Tabasco sauce
Salt and pepper

The Cuban intervention in Angola played a pivotal role in ensuring that the Popular Movement for the Liberation of Angola (MPLA) came to power after the Portuguese withdrew from the country in 1975. During the Border War, Cuban support for Fapla, the armed wing of the MPLA, included the supply of weapons, personnel, training and strategic battleground support.

Another big part of Cuba's support was in training Angolan pilots and assisting in the aerial defence and attack strategy. It is estimated that some 9 000 Cubans were deployed in Angola during the war.

Havana, the Cuban capital, is a tropical city where people spend much time outdoors, and you'll often find tables put out on the pavements. The city is also famous for its vintage American cars, which predate the Cuban revolution of 1959.

In Havana, the humble sandwich plays an important role in the daily diet and routine. Much care is taken in preparing it, as it is often the main meal of the day (just as the 10 o'clock tea was for many 'living ins' at Recce bases across the country). The bread used for the sandwich has Spanish/Portuguese origin and is similar to the *pau* you find in Angola and Mozambique. When lightly toasted it's a most amazing base for a sarmie.

Fry a sliced chicken breast and some bacon in a lightly oiled pan.

Squash a bit of lime over just before it's done.

Toast the sliced bread and trim off the crusts.

Spread with mayonnaise and mustard.

Layer with lettuce and thinly sliced gherkin before adding the chicken and bacon.

Add Tabasco and salt and pepper to taste.

The Angolan flag. During the Border War, Cuba supported Angola's MPLA government in the civil war against rebel movement Unita. The Cubans provided high-level planning skills and much-needed equipment that gave the Angolans air superiority.

Taking time out in a café in Havana.

SPECIALISED COOKING – THE RECCE WAY

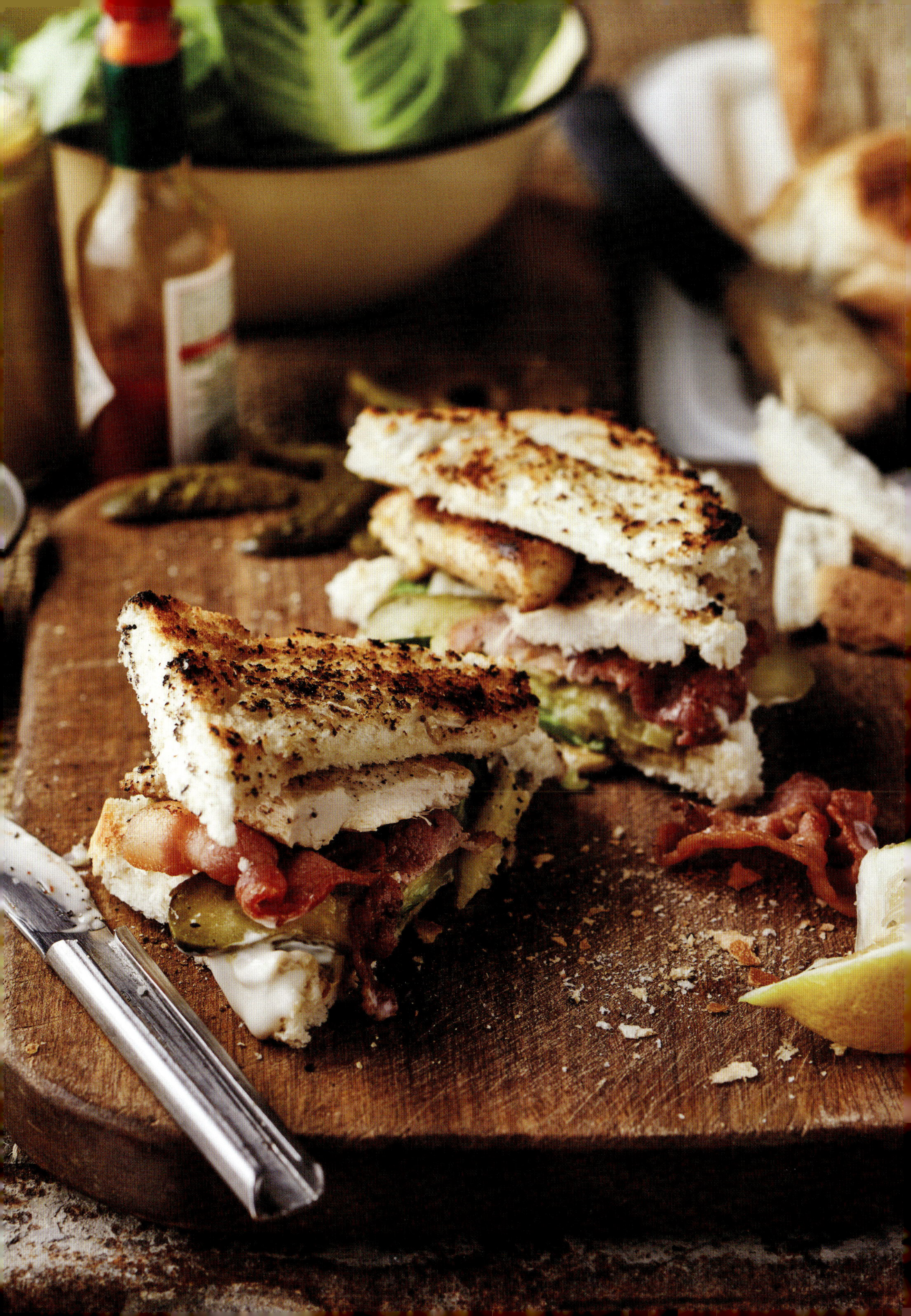

Let's Boogie, Swiss Style

ABOVE The view under canopy when jumping onto the sports fields at Phalaborwa during the 'Swiss boogie'.

LEFT One of the most thrilling and risky skydiving experiences is to fly in a canopy formation. You need to manoeuvre the canopies into position but once coupled, it provides for an intimate experience in the air.

In the 1980s South Africa was subjected to economic sanctions, as well as cultural and sport boycotts, due to the government's apartheid policy. However, the neutral Swiss broke ranks to come and enjoy the African sun during a few Decembers.

They would organise a C-130 transport plane and for two weeks Phalaborwa would become the jump capital of the country. In attendance would be the Swiss military's free-fall team, plus the Springbok team sponsored by Gunston cigarettes – and all wannabe sky gods.

Imagine two weeks of dirt dives, take-offs, skydives with formations, parachute packing, after-jump debriefs and, of course, the evening entertainment. It was here that mere mortals got to know the sky gods and where the real learning took place. As per all skydive boogies, the first beer could only be popped after the last flight had taken off.

Amid all the excitement and frenetic activity, it was important to do a jump or two that would be burned into your mind forever. For this you could organise a two-way Canopy Relative Work (CRW)[31] jump for the late afternoon. Exit over the Kruger National Park at just about 15 000 ft and do a 'hop and pop'. Fly into the CRW and get your fellow jumper – Peter Lamberti – to hook his feet in front of your canopy.

You will now have 15 minutes to glide down and enjoy the view while he steers you in long, slow S-turns all the way down into the DZ (the local sports stadium). So kick back in the seat strap and enjoy the moment. The magnificent flat bush landscape with its dotted hills stretches from one end of the horizon to the other and the quiet flapping of the canopy's stabilisers acts as confirmation that your flight is in good hands.

You can now open the beer you took along for exactly this purpose. As Lamberti feels you flare, he will disengage his feet and you can both land gracefully – knowing the moment is etched into your memory forever.

This is as close to real flying as you can ever come.

---

[31] Canopy Relative Work is a sporting discipline in which two jumpers open their parachutes directly after jumping – called 'hop and pop' – and then continuously manoeuvre the parachutes until the two canopies are vertically aligned. By slowing the top chute the bottom jumper then flies into the lines, or legs, of the jumper above. The jumper at the top grabs hold of the jumper below's lines and then hooks into the lines with his feet. This allows the two to fly together with the top jumper steering for both. Turning away while hooked in this way causes a down-plane that provides for a spectacular adrenaline rush.

Showjump Chicken Wings

As a meal, chicken wings doesn't really stand on its own. It's a snack or finger food that is best served as part of an expanded offering at some or other occasion. No self-respecting specialised chef will waste his time making them.

Rather find an event where chicken wings will be on offer somewhere in a hospitality suite. Places like air shows, big sporting events or military tattoos always have showjump schedules, so get a spot on the team.

For extreme showjumping, you must use a Para-Commander (a round parachute) and jump into the military tattoo in Durban, as there is no margin for error. Once square parachutes arrive (about 1980), it gets a bit easier to make jumps at cricket and rugby stadiums. It is a great feeling to hang under the orange white and blue with 'RECCE' emblazoned all over it. After landing, remember to follow protocol and march off with chute over shoulder, keeping faces hidden by goggles and helmets. A more relaxed jump at the agricultural shows of Eshowe or KwaMbonambi will also do, and even fundraisers for schools or charities probably will have them.

Just get out there and enjoy it; after all, you can jump and eat for free.

Jimmy Oberholzer (left) and Frans van Dyk (right) do a tribute jump at Westonaria, Johannesburg, with the 1 Recce flag in October 1980. Prior to their jump, Major John Murphy (ex-Selous Scouts) was killed when his parachute malfunctioned.

1 aeroplane
Group of jumpers
1 showjump organiser
Ground crew
Department of Civil Aviation approval
2 500 ft cloud base

Assemble a group of jumpers from whoever is not deployed in Angola. Try to match the experience levels with the venue you will jump at. Some places are really tight, and jumping into King's Park Stadium in a 25-knot wind is a bit more difficult than, say, landing on the double rugby grounds of a local school. Do all weather checks and plan the take-off to coincide with the scheduled jump time. Add smoke canisters, flags, etc. for dramatic effect. Whatever you do, if it has been announced that the Recces will jump, you go and jump! – no matter what. It is inconceivable for an announcer to inform an audience that the Recces were too chicken to jump!

TIPS:
- Make the jump, and make the DZ!
- Do not jump into stadiums in a 25-knot wind – unless printed on the programme.
- Do not open below 2 500 ft; appoint someone to look at the altimeter.
- Do not do not break arms or legs; you will miss a deployment.
- Do not land downwind; you will break arms and legs.
- Do not land on the braai fires; you are looking for chicken wings.
- If you're at the Cape Town Air Show, do not jump over low clouds.
- If you do jump over clouds at the Cape show, do not land with your Recce canopy in Gugulethu.
- Do, however, get yourself invited to the sponsor's tent, and go in search of the chicken wings. Once you identify the location of the chicken wings, you will find the rest of the food close by.

IF IT FLIES

ROADRUNNER CURRY
Menongue style

1 roadrunner
Oil
Onion
Garlic
Curry spice mix (Gorima's is best)
Potatoes, cut into small cubes
Water

A SABRE TEAM CONSISTING OF
1 x 106 mm recoilless gun
1 x 81 mm mortar
2 x 14.5 mm anti-aircraft guns
1 x 0.50 Browning machine gun
1 x twin 7.62mm MAG
2 stopper groups
Kwêvoël support truck

A Unimog is prepared for a Sabre-type deployment from Fort Rev in Ondangwa. Note the mounted 7.62 mm light machine gun.

---

[32] Every year Fapla would mount an offensive aimed at Jamba, the Unita 'capital' in southeastern Angola. The staging area was always Menongue, with Cuito Cuanavale the last 'big' town from which operations were conducted.

[33] This is a term for an adapted vehicle – particularly a Land Rover or Unimog. Originally designed as reconnaissance vehicles, they were armed with light machine guns. Later they were fitted with 81 mm mortars, 106 mm recoilless guns and other weapons normally deployed on their own carriers.

To the uninitiated, all chickens might look and taste the same, but that is simply because you haven't tasted roadrunner. The chickens you buy in the shops usually sit on their thighs for 40 days before they find their way onto the shelf.

But 'roadrunners' are a different breed of chicken. They outrun everything that comes their way. They confirm Darwin's theory of evolution, and the ones on the road to Menongue are the pick of the bunch.[32] They had to dodge convoy after convoy. By the early 1980s, no Fapla convoy, whether of tanks, Urals or BRDMs, on their way south to Jamba fazed the birds any more. And no convoy of Elands, Kwêvoëls, Ratels, Casspirs or Buffels going north could outpace them.

In full 'flight', with its wings swept back, the roadrunner looks like a MiG-21 fighter jet. Their extended thighs, which permit those long strides, make ostriches look ungainly. Whenever you did manage to pick up a roadrunner, you assumed it had probably died from exhaustion. That is why you would treat it with the respect it deserved.

Get a Sabre[33] team together and make your way to Longa (a town about 60 km east of Menongue) on your adapted Unimogs. Good guys to have around are Herman van Niekerk, Lafras Luiting, Gif Opperman, Adriaan Steyn, Mac van der Merwe and the ground teams.

Longa is about 450 km into Angola, so you will need to live in the bush and stay hidden for a few weeks. Once there, set up the planned ambush of a Fapla resupply convoy and remain patient; it will take a week or more of waiting in this position.

When the time comes, execute the ambush with focused efficiency. You will have only about 15 minutes. Sweep the ambushed vehicles for important documents. If you happen to find some Grant's whisky and Pushkin vodka, it's yours to keep. Vacate the area rapidly before the Mi-24 helicopter gunships arrive.

During the hasty withdrawal you will be faster than a roadrunner for once. Throw your roadrunner on the back of the Unimog and continue driving for at least eight hours. Set up camp once you're at a site where the trees form a thick canopy.

Once the bird is plucked, marvel at the length of its femur and the small amount of meat.

Cut into pieces; if there are eight of you will need two roadrunners as they can only be cut into four.

Sauté the onions (and garlic if available) in oil until softened and add your curry mix. The oil should be entirely absorbed into the curry mix.

Add roadrunner pieces and fry.

Cut potatoes into very small cubes and add a cup or two of water.

Let the potatoes boil a long time while you sample the Grant's from the ambush. It is, oh, so good …

Don't forget to eat the roadrunner.

SPECIALISED COOKING – THE RECCE WAY

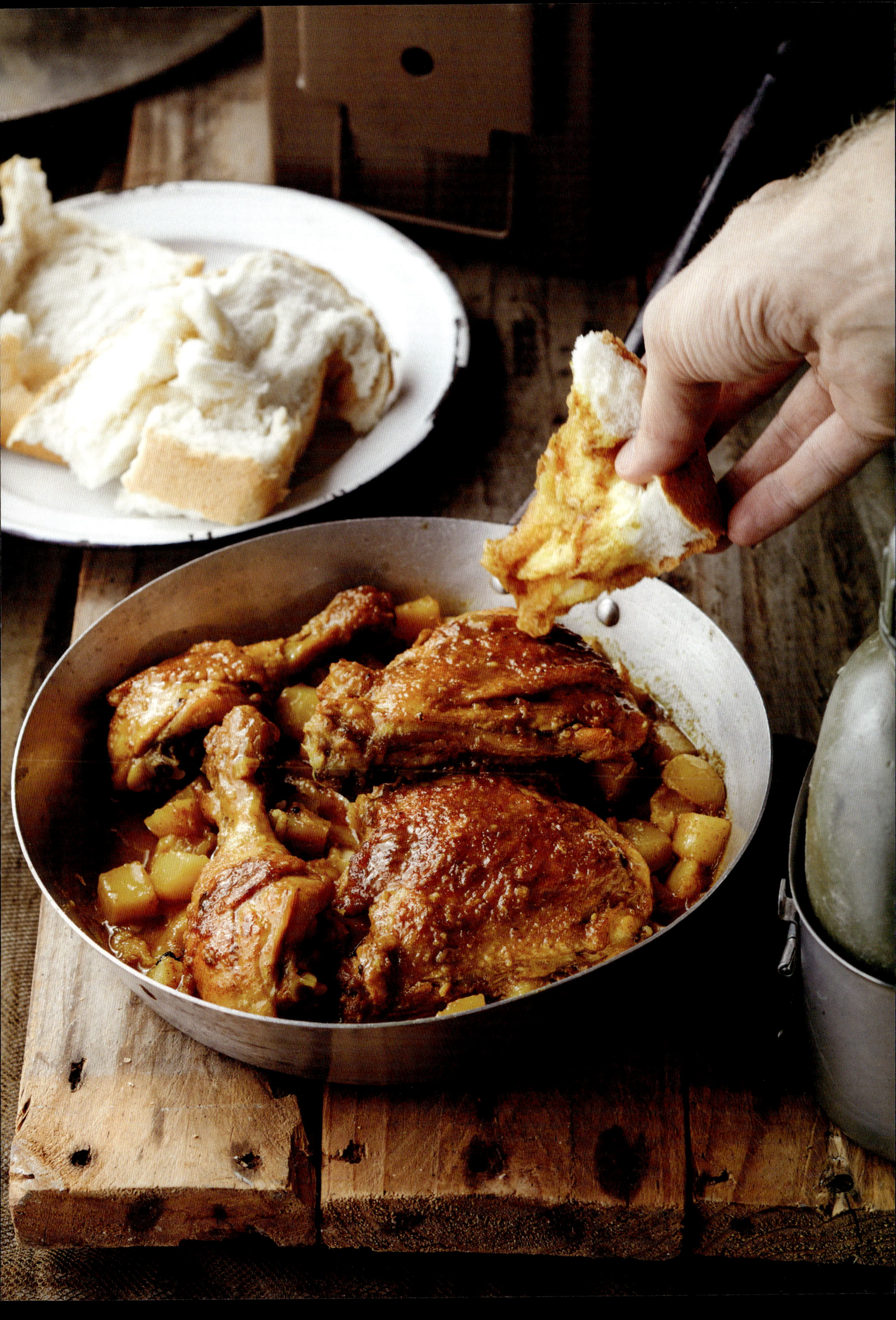

Flying Back For Supper

A 'flock' of Pumas refuel on the runway at Epupa before flying Recce teams into southern Angola.

In the introduction to this book we stressed that there are certain basics needed to create a special moment: good presentation, the ability to adapt and a sense of occasion. If you have been lazy and have only flipped through the book, let's recap by looking at a wonderful example of how a sense of anticipation can be created.

Get yourself on a 14-day deployment into Angola from Rundu in the mid-1980s. Deploy in one of three teams that consist of eight men each. In these teams will be guys like Niek du Toit, André Meiers, Steward Sterzel and José da Costa. Carry all your supplies in your rucksacks, leaving some space for explosives, medical material, radios, RPGs, mortars and ammo belts.

You will walk only at night to get to the intended areas, and will hide during the day. Once you get to your destination – a railway line – place the explosives and withdraw from the area. Make good speed to get to the landing zone (LZ) where the choppers (Puma helicopters) will come to collect you.

This is not a time to be late. Prepare and secure the LZ and keep your ears open for that first faint swoosh-swoosh sound of the rotor blades.

That first time you recognise the sound of the rotors is the moment your sense of anticipation starts to build. In fact, it's pure adrenaline rushing through your veins. Get your red filter strobe ready to guide the chopper in to the site in the last glimmer of daylight. Make the radio call to the pilot and brief him quickly.

The moment the chopper lands, scramble in; you have only 30 seconds before it has to be airborne again.

For the next 90 minutes you'll fly at low level over the African bush. Finally, you can talk out loud again and start wiping the 'black is beautiful' cream from your face. Most importantly, now that you're done with counting the food you packed so carefully, tonight there will be seconds at dinner.

As the Puma passes over the cutline (border) you know there are only seven more minutes left before you will be 'home' for supper. By the time the sound of rotor blades changes pitch and you feel the chopper slowing down, you can almost smell the smoke of the fires. At this moment all your senses are alive.

Unload, drive to the base and stash your kit. In the shower, you will first smell the soap as you wash off two weeks of dirt. Then the smell of the smoke from the fire and the meat on the braai will come wafting through. Stay focused. Put on a clean T-shirt and shorts and head out for your first ice-cold beer; a medium-rare rump steak with pap and sous will be served shortly.

Now that's what we call having a sense of occasion!

What Goes Up Comes Down

Whether it's a parachute or plane, the golden rule applies: what goes up must come down. The only question is when and under what circumstances.

If you have been instructed to jump out of a plane, you have many choices. For a static-line jump it may be a 'pampoen' or a steerable Mk 2. For free-fall you might want a Para-Commander (PC) MT1 or Cruiselite.

If you have been deployed with the aim of getting air superiority for the South African Defence Force (SADF), you will be deployed with an SA-7 and you will need training in how to use it. Gus Davidson is a specialist in this regard and will teach you how to lock on the infrared eye and how the buzzer changes pitch once you are locked on. When you are ready to use it, your number two will move the eye after lock-on to make sure the weapon is ready before you release the missile.

Once you are successful in preventing an enemy fighter plane from bombing your troops, they will know where you are and come after you – and it won't be to congratulate you. Expect a few Mi-24 gunships to be part of the enemy's search party. These choppers have a large arsenal of nasty stuff on board and they will be very eager to offload them on you and your team.

This should not distract you, though. You still have the initiative. Remain packed up for withdrawal and stay properly hidden. You will be able to work out the square search plan they are flying by timing their turnaround times. Light a dummy fire a few kilometres from your site to distract them and send the search in a false direction.

Now you have to run, so do not loiter on the objective. Start the 70 km walk south to the pick-up point, where friendly choppers can come and collect you.

TOP An SA-7 surface-to-air missile is aimed at an aircraft.

BELOW The wreckage of a downed Mi-24 gunship. In any conflict, losing a plane to an SA-7 missile has a very high deterrent effect and leads to changes in strategy and tactics.

CHICKEN SCHNITZEL
à la Sport Parade[34]

Chicken breast (2 per person)
Cooking oil
Lemon
Salt and pepper

FOR THE BATTER
Cake flour
Baking powder
Bottle of beer
Salt
Egg
Onion flakes
Tabasco sauce
Chicken spice

The Amanzimtoti golf course made some of the best chicken schnitzels in town. Luckily for us, they always had a special on for the soldiers who played there on a Wednesday afternoon.

If you play reasonable golf and know how to count all your shots, then you will normally win enough money to pay for a schnitzel at the club so you don't have to make it yourself at home. Just check that you don't play with André Bestbier, because he actually knows how to play golf *and* he can count.

Also, don't play with the guys from the LWT (Light Workshop Section) because they don't know how to play and they also can't count. You will end up making lots of schnitzels.

If you are the one who lost the bet at golf and will be paying, then offer to make the schnitzel yourself – at home.

Tenderise the chicken breast with a blunt object. If you don't have a hammer-type object, then you can do it with the side of a saucer or plate.

Tenderise until the meat fibres are properly broken, just as you would do with perlemoen.

Mix all the batter ingredients together.

Dip the schnitzel in the batter and quickly pat it in flour.

Fry on low heat in shallow oil.

Squeeze lemon on the battered schnitzel.

Serve direct from the pan with salt and pepper.

All the members of 1 Recce do Friday-afternoon PT before knocking off for the RSM's parade.

[34] 'Sport parade' refers to the opportunity afforded to soldiers to practise a sport on Wednesday afternoons, be it athletics, rugby, soccer, golf or fishing. All you needed was a sports club, a constitution and members. If you had any organisational skills, you would join the golf and fishing clubs.

SPECIALISED COOKING – THE RECCE WAY

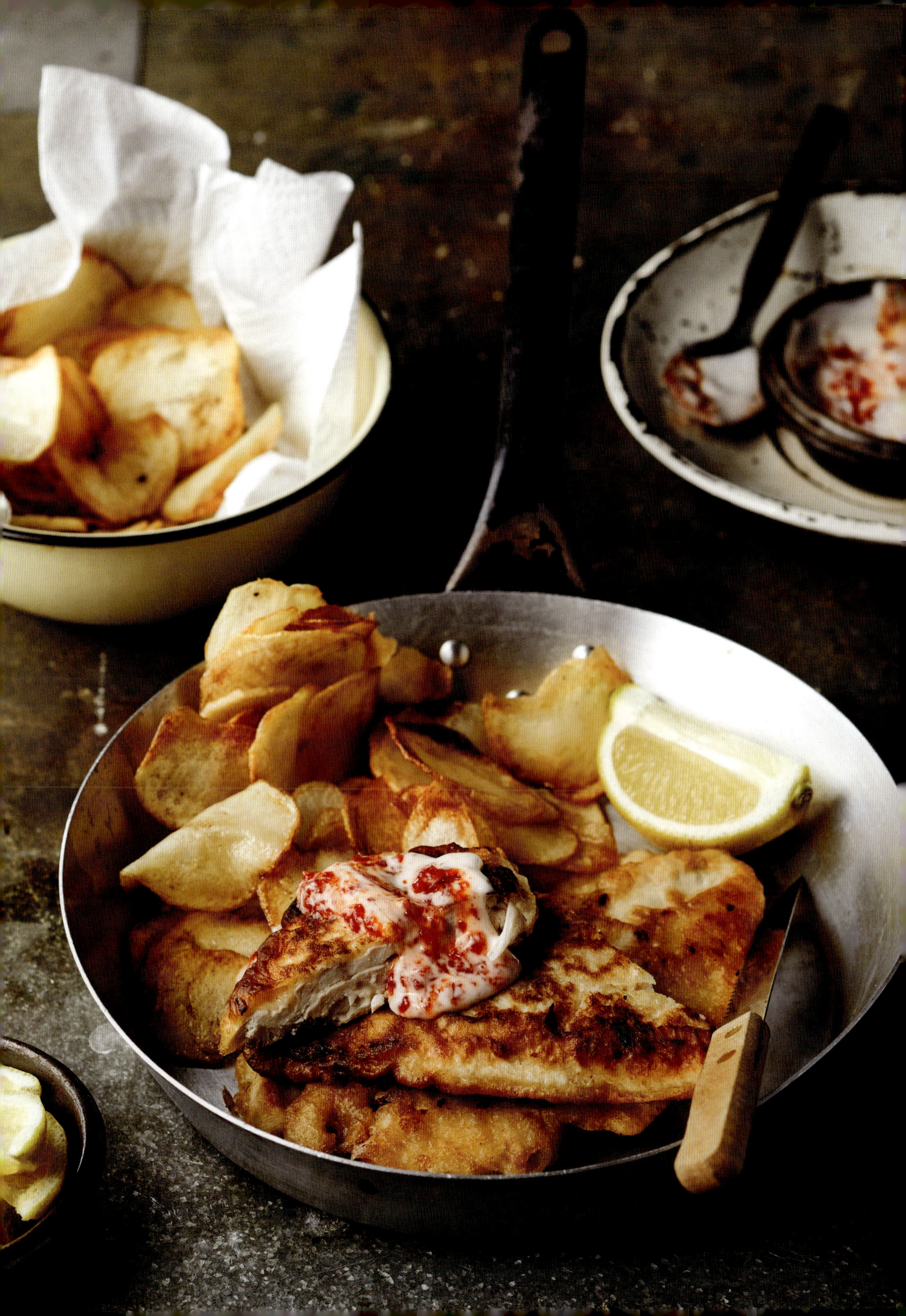

FORTY-MINUTE TURKEY
à la Fort KZN

Sasfa evening

Ex-Recces

1 air rifle

1 drinks trolley

1 x 6.5 kg turkey (marinated in brine overnight)

3–5 litres of cooking oil

Lemon pepper

Garlic

Cajun spices

(Do not substitute any of the ingredients!)

The South African Special Forces Association (Sasfa) operates according to a so-called fort structure, which provides an opportunity for former members of the Special Forces to meet once a month.[35] Fort KZN is a jovial bunch and the monthly meetings are well attended by a regular group. The meetings are organised by their inspired *bendeleier*, Taffy Pelser, who has run Fort KZN since its inception.

When the regulars were told of the call for recipe submissions for this book, they got straight to it. The pictures on this page are of the actual event. The guys have suggested that, if repeated, one should try to make it less black. As a specialised chef you should be able to work out how.

Assemble with other Fort KZN members on the first Monday of the month with a turkey that has been marinated in brine overnight.

Pour enough oil into a large pot so that the turkey will be covered. While you're waiting for the oil to heat up, entertain the wives, friends and colleagues with an air-gun competition. AK-47s are no longer allowed.

When the oil reaches the right temperature, place the turkey in the pot as is – no foil required – with the spices. The skin will seal quickly and allow the meat to cook.

Allow 5 minutes of cooking time per kilogram of turkey. A 6.5-kg turkey will take about 36 minutes, but add a few minutes to be sure.

Take the turkey out after exactly 44 minutes.

This is the moment everyone has been waiting for.

Now is the time for you to display your specialised chef abilities, because the turkey will come out pitch black. You'll note the look of concern on the faces of most of the guests. Explain that the charred skin acts as insulation, and that this is how it should be. Offer a tester to the unbelieving crowd. Once they nod their heads in approval, continue carving up the rest of the turkey.

Add all the side dishes and present with confidence. Remind everyone how it took only 44 minutes to prepare.

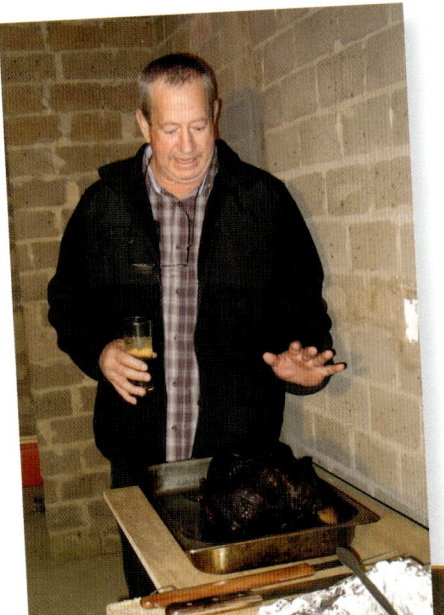

The specialised chef will not display any signs of surprise when he takes this turkey out of the pot – it's supposed to be this charred.

[35] The forts offer an easy and natural way for former members of the Special Forces to stay in contact and also to assist them or their families in time of need.

SPECIALISED COOKING – THE RECCE WAY

CHICKEN LIVERS

à la Nando's

This meal requires no recipe – just a telephone number. It doesn't get better than Nando's medium chicken livers. Simply go out and buy them! If, however, you insist on doing a lot of work for lesser effect, then follow these steps.

Brown the livers with onions as per the rules of cooking.

Add pepper and meat seasoning.

Add a tin of tomato and onion (and a bit of sugar) and some soy sauce and simmer for about 45 minutes.

Add Nando's mild sauce.

Serve with *roosterkoek* or fresh rolls.

PÂTÉ

This goes with anything on biscuits, as part of a starter or as an in-between if you don't want to cook. When you order your Nando's, be sure to get an extra portion. Put it through the blender until it is puréed. If you don't have chicken livers, then any livers and breast meat combination can be turned into pâté; just add a bit of fat/butter and spices to the meat pieces before you blend them.

1 portion chicken livers
1 onion
Pepper
Meat seasoning
1 tin of tomato and onion mix
Sugar
Soy sauce
Nando's mild sauce
Roosterkoek or rolls

IF IT FLIES

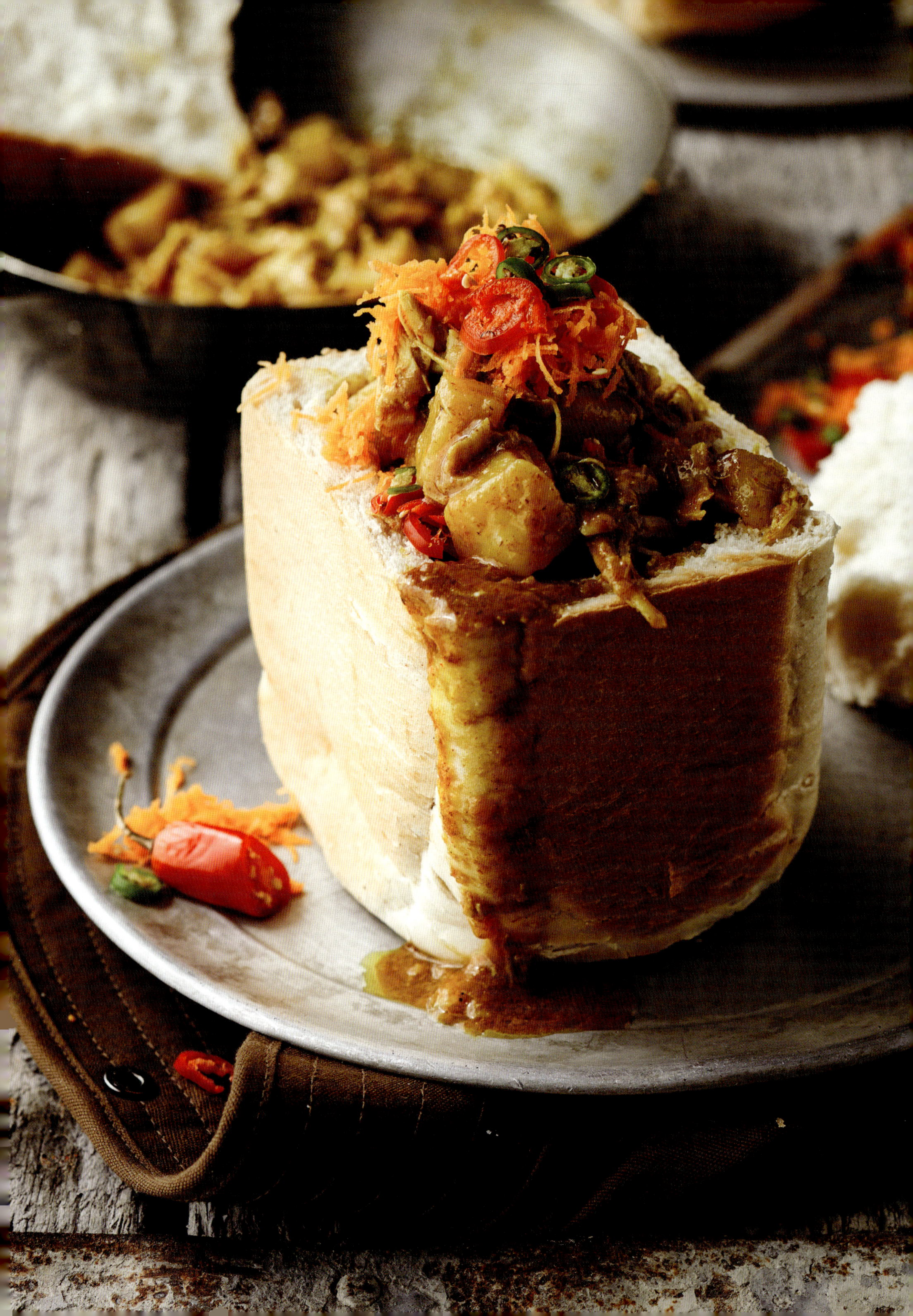

BUNNY CHOW

This humble yet tasty and filling meal originates in Durban's Indian community but is now a firm favourite with all South Africans. It's great value for money, simple to enjoy and a lifesaver for many a hungry soldier when the month-end pay seems far away.

Loaf of white bread, unsliced
Chicken curry
Grated carrots

Cut the bread in three, leaving two parts with the end crust still intact.
Use a knife to carefully remove the inside and pull out the 'bunny' as a single piece.
Fill the hollow bread with chicken curry and place the 'bunny' on top.
Serve with the sweet grated carrot.
Use the extra piece of bread to wipe the curry pot clean.

The infamous Smugglers Inn in Point Road, Durban. This club was a must see, especially if you came from Langebaan or Dukuduku.

BLITZ CHICKEN
à la Hannes Britz

Fry chopped onion and chicken pieces in a deep frying pan with a lid.
Add atjar.
Close the lid and cook for about half an hour.
Done!

1 onion, chopped
Chicken in portions
Cooking oil
Mango atjar

BLITZ CHICKEN
à la Tannie Phil

Fry the chopped onion and the chicken pieces in a deep frying pan with a lid.
Add the apricot juice and the diced potatoes.
Close the lid and open some white wine.
When the bottle is empty, the chicken will be ready.

1 onion, chopped
Chicken pieces
Cooking oil
1 litre apricot Liqui-Fruit
2–3 medium potatoes, diced
White wine

IF IT FLIES

Menno's Chickenpot

The 5 Recce Potjiekos Floating Trophy is awarded, with Menno's infamous little pot mounted on it.

by T Timmerman

This moment occurred in 1987 at 5 Reconnaissance Regiment in Phalaborwa. It happened at the unit's potjiekos competition, which was ops normal on closed weekends and also after church parade[36] at Savong.[37]

Families, including the 'living in' family, assembled at the swimming pool area of the base. People had organised themselves into teams for this auspicious event. On this particular day, the 'living ins' under team captain Sakkie Seegers were ready, thirsty and starving.

Our usual team comprised myself, Chris Scales, Ertjies Bezuidenhout, Beyers Burger, Paul Dietriech and John Brokaar (when he was not away). We set up our position at the braai closest to the bar, because all of our methods and ingredients were timed per beer. In that way, we were *gaar* before the pot was.

While we were well into our fourth beer (browning the meat), Menno Uys sauntered over and joined us. We found it strange that he had not joined Dave Scales and the other manne from 54 Commando and thought he was spying on us. Despite Sakkie's use of bizarre evasive tactics, Menno still stuck around and assured us that he had entered his own pot and all was under control.

As the afternoon progressed, Menno stood his ground and engaged all of us drink for drink. By now the judging team were also concerned that Menno would not have enough time to prepare a potjie, let alone cook the food too. Once again, he calmly assured everyone that everything was under control.

At precisely 15h45, a mere 15 minutes before the bell would ring to signal the cut-off time, Menno disappeared into the mess and returned with a small parcel. He scratched together a few coals and proceeded to place the smallest potjie I have ever seen. He jealously guarded the potjie and would not allow anyone near it. He stood there with his broad smile camouflaged by his walrus moustache.

If memory serves me right, the judging team comprised Colonel James Hills, RSM Koos Moorcroft, WO1 Bokkie Kitching and WO2 Gordon Powell (Mess Boss). Everyone had gone the extra mile to ensure that they would win. The tiffies' team had even organised bales of straw as part of their decor.

When the judges got to our potjie, Sakkie proudly offered them a taste of an amazing potjie, accompanied by a glass of chilled wine.

They then walked over to Menno, where the judges were treated to a detailed explanation of the fine detail under which a chicken potjie should be prepared. When he delicately lifted the lid, the judges were greeted with a single egg boiling in the potjie.

By the time the laughter had died down, many drinks had either been consumed or knocked over. I am not sure who won the competition that day, but I will always remember Menno's comment to an astounded Colonel Hills: 'But Colonel, what came first, the chicken or the egg?'

That small potjie became very famous and RSM Moorcroft arranged for it to be mounted on an ornate piece of wood. It became the official 5 Recce Potjiekos Floating Trophy.

---

[36] Church parade was a compulsory event that took place once a quarter. The dress attire was step-outs with full medals and badges. It was always a stressful event for 'living ins' as it seemed nearly impossible for them to get the full dress code correct.

[37] Savong was the recreational facility of choice for the men from 5 Recce.

Dropping by, Halo Style

If you like surprise 'parties' then doing a HALO/HAHO infiltration is just the thing, because nobody will see you coming.

Fly to the destination on a normal transport route at airline altitudes (over 28 000 ft). When the aircraft is over the targeted landing area, exit from the rear. Let them open the ramp of the plane and out you go. It will be −50°C at that altitude, so be sure to prepare for the few minutes of extreme cold, freezing fingers and iced-up goggles.

Carry on down while the plane continues to its commercial destination many hours from here. In addition to a parachute, you will need the following:

- A C-130/C-160 or similar aircraft that can fly at 28 000 ft; the rear-opening door helps
- Oxygen units in the plane and bail-out bottles to jump with
- Helmets to hold goggles and oxygen tubes
- Gloves and KAP3 parachute-opening devices
- A reception party and a good extraction plan.

When you land, be sure to stay hidden, otherwise it will spoil the surprise. Eat your supper in private with your buddy on the mission.

Do whatever you went there to do and meet up with your extraction party. Nobody will ever know you were there.

Many Recce soldiers loved parachuting and did it as a sport. With the Air Force providing the aircraft, who could say no? The team assembled here in front of the Dakota in their slick jumpsuits were practising their skills before the Defence Force championships, in 1985 or 1986.

FOR THE RECORD

A 1 Recce rugby team in 1984 in their black unit jerseys.

1 Reconnaissance Regiment

OCs ROLL
Commandant JD (Jan) Breytenbach	1972–1974
Commandant JC (Jakes) Swart	1975–1980
Colonel E (Ewald) Olckers	1981–1983
Colonel A (André) Bestbier	1983–1988
Colonel G (Gert) Keulder	1989–1993
Commandant AD (Diedies) Diedericks	1994–1994
Lieutenant Colonel FE (Frans) Fourie	1995–1996
Lieutenant Colonel CF (Fred) Wilke	1996–1997

RSMs ROLL
WO1 TI (Trevor) Floyd	1972–1980
WO1 PP (Pep) van Zyl	1981–1988
WO1 JMJ (Boats) Botes	1988–1992
WO1 BMM (Bruce) Laing	1992–1995
WO1 GD (Maddies) Adam	1995–1997

A logbook to keep track of parachute jumps.

A showjump team lands on Durban's main beach in front of the Malibu Hotel. From there, everyone would be off to Father's Moustache pub at the Malibu.

94 SPECIALISED COOKING – THE RECCE WAY

Corporals with 1 L rum, 2 L Coke and 3 L Cortinas at Cuban Hat on Durban's main beach after a long night at Smugglers Inn.

All the top dogs at the mess for non-commissioned officers at 1 Recce in Durban. From left to right: Jack Greeff, Tim Timmerman, Jimmy Oberholzer, unknown, André Bestbier, Bruce McIvor, Pep van Zyl and Dewald de Beer.

A proudly Special Forces showjump in the 1980s.

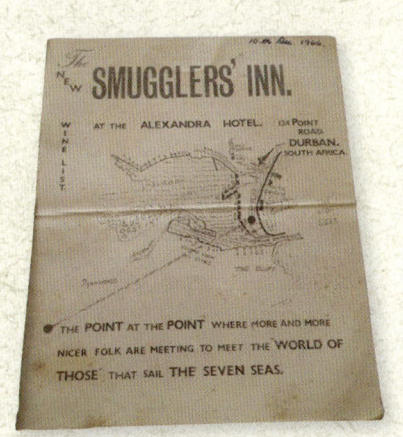

A flyer for the infamous Smugglers Inn in Durban.

Soldiers discuss matters of importance in the 1.1 Commando room at 1 Recce on the Bluff in Durban some time in 1986.

IF IT FLIES   95

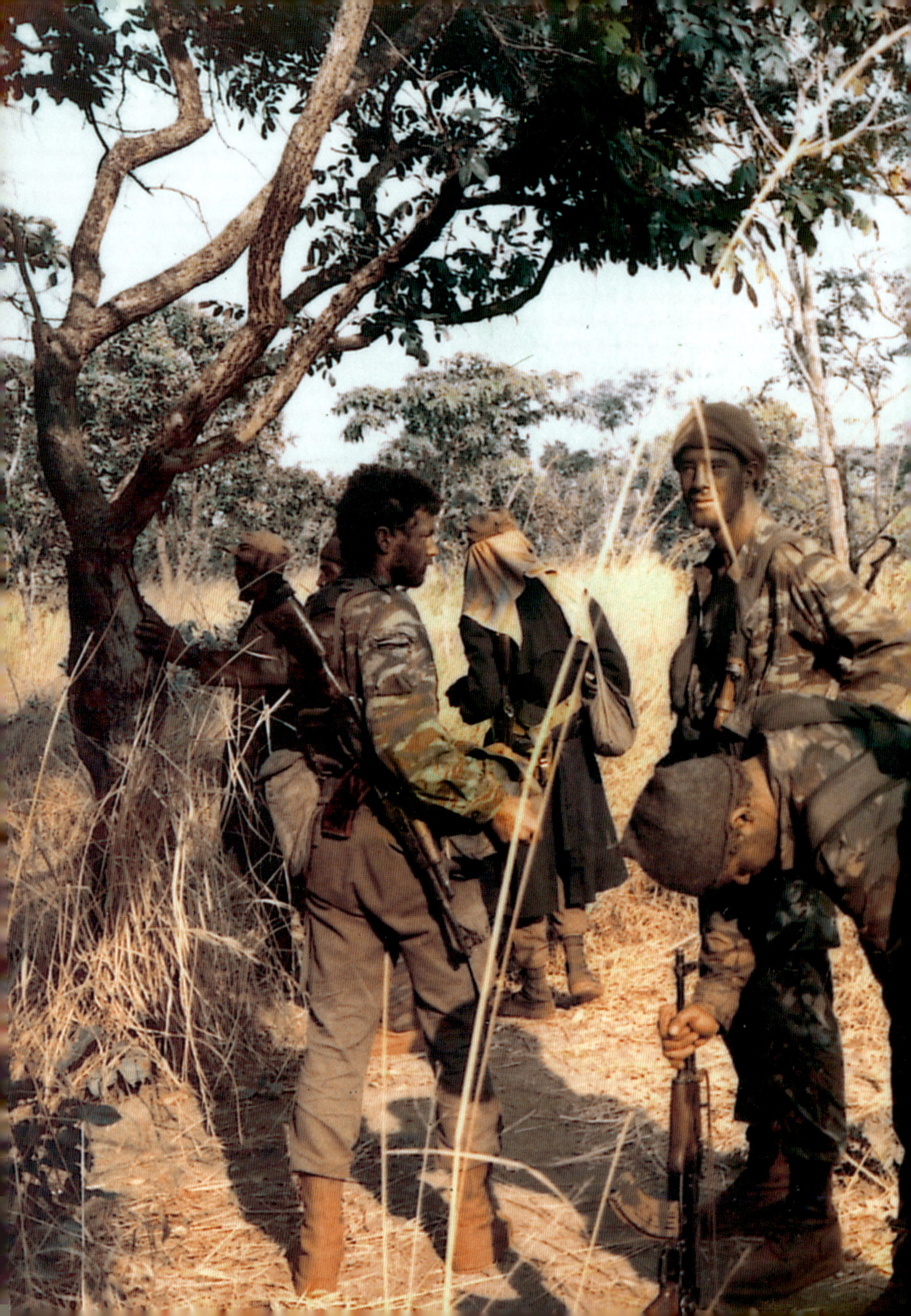

4

IF IT WALKS

Soldiering and terrain are synonymous. To control a conflict needs good understanding and use of the terrain and for that you need feet on the ground.

This chapter covers things that don't have wings and don't swim, but that walk. This includes cattle, warthogs, mopane worms … and of course Recce soldiers.

All Recces are good walkers. If you want to operate in the vast open spaces of Africa, you need to be a good walker, even if most of the distance to get to a target is often covered by helicopter, plane or vehicle. During your career as a Special Forces soldier, you will have walked thousands of kilometres with a rucksack on your back, and on some missions you could do 500 km or more by foot.

During the Border War, the Recces also used a wide variety of wheeled transport. These included Casspirs, Unimogs, Sabres (modified vehicles), motorbikes and even bicycles. For this reason, this chapter will include a few 'meals on wheels', as technically it is still all about being at ground level.

Let's not delay it any longer. Let's do a Johnnie Walker and keep walking.

A group of soldiers in enemy camouflage in 1985 after a long stretch. Being deployed deep into Angola meant walking long distances on foot and spending long periods in the bush.

Making a Fire

When you're living from your rucksack it usually means you're on a stealth operation in enemy territory. You are supposed to operate unseen and undetected, which means no fires and no gourmet food – just ratpacks and freeze-dried food on a gas or an Esbit stove.

Still, there will be ample opportunity to cook on a fire or have a braai. Every self-respecting South African – never mind Special Forces operator – knows how to braai. But not everyone knows how to make a fire. The easiest way is to use Blitz firelighters and windproof matches. But that is for Sunday afternoons. Let's review how to make a real fire under specialised conditions.

Option 1: Old school
Find a hard stick and a softish chunk of very dry wood. Rub the hard stick on the base so it makes an ember. At this point cover with the driest and finest of tinder. The ember should gently ignite the tinder. To prove that you can do this, attend the Special Forces survival course. On the course you'll be deployed at sunset some 15 km from base with only the clothes on your back and one uncooked egg. To pass the test you have to arrive back at base before sunrise with the egg cooked …

Option 2: Tracer bullet
During exercises, fire tracer bullets into dry grass. It will set the grass on fire. It will also get a few other things burning, so it's not as efficient if you only need a small braai fire. It will, however, get you back to base very quickly to haul the firefighting equipment.

Option 3: Illuminating flare or 60 mm illuminating mortar
Before using this method to light your fire, check your timings and height. If you get it wrong, the bomb will reach the ground while it is still burning. If done in the forests of Dukuduku you will get a fire that lasts three days. No need to bring your own wood since there is about 2 000 ha of forest … Expect a tremendous choice of coals. Sadly, you won't get to choose where and when you braai as you will be fighting the fire all the time.

Option 4: SA-7 into an Mi-24 helicopter
This is the fastest way to make a huge fire – and it's instantaneous. Just keep in mind that there is usually very little time left to use the fire for anything as the explosion caused by the SA-7 hitting the Mi-24 attracts unwanted attention. In unique circumstances you can create a second fire in a similar manner when the search party arrives, but this is extremely high-risk fire-making. Only use this method with the help of experts who have done it once before.

It's not the easiest way to make a fire, but you have to be able to do it to pass the survival course.

Option 5: Limpet mines and oil tanks
This method requires a raiding party, boats, limpet mines and weeks of planning and preparation. Sneak into an oil refinery in a foreign city and place the devices on the oil storage tanks. Get off the premises before they go off, otherwise your friends will have to rescue you from the burning refinery.[38] Next time exfiltrate to the barracuda boats on which you arrived, and use a remote control to detonate the charges on the storage tanks first. It will light up in the most spectacular fireball you have ever seen and add a glow to the Beira skyline that is any photographer's dream.

[38] This happened during Operation Kerslig, in 1981. During the operation, against the oil refinery at Luanda, Captain K de Kock was killed and other operators were seriously wounded.

ABOVE Tracer bullets draw lines of light during a night shooting exercise.

BELOW A white phosphorous grenade explodes and burns.

Selection courses are finely designed to place Special Forces recruits under extreme mental and physical strain and then test whether they can operate successfully under these conditions.

1-minute Steak, Selection Style

à la Dave Jenkins

When you are on the Special Forces selection course, you measure time in how long it takes to the next smoke break.[39] Around you there are constant mumblings about withdrawing, and speculation about when the course will finish. To survive, you have to block it out and simply carry on walking.

By day 18 you have seven days of Omuramba *opfoks* behind you, as well as six days of dark phase, with its Swapo songs and rotten baboon stew. You are also burping diesel from the doctored dog biscuits. It seems to be one long, slow torturing walk from the Botswana cutline to 'first elbow' (the first bend in an otherwise dead-straight road) and then on to the Kwando River, before going back again.

Sometimes you walk through the bush, at other times along the road. On the dead-straight roads and cutline stretches, you'll see the dancing mirages in the midday heat of those way in front of you, so you try to keep up. Every now and then just check that you are not last.

Once, maybe twice a day, you'll see the instructors. In the afternoon, they'll greet you from the back of the Landy (Land Rover), where they sit on folding chairs drinking ice-cold brandy and Coke from flasks. They will mockingly invite you to have a cold beer with them rather than spending another night with the mosquitoes in the bush. You will also be told that you are useless and that they won't stop until everyone has given up. So you might just as well give up then and there, they say.

On this day, 18 August 1980, the group of instructors consisted of Carel (Fabes) Faber, Marius (Bone) Boonzaaier and course leader Major Peter Schofield. It was late afternoon when they drove up to us. They duly extended an invitation to us to withdraw and also advised us that we must fill our water bottles from the canisters on the side of the vehicle. Their flasks must have been low, too, as could be expected on a Saturday afternoon.

Our morale was as low as our water bottles; we were tired, raw, sore and desperate. That didn't mean that we couldn't talk back with great bravado. So we hinted for a beer and asked them where they kept the rest of their stash. And how many did they have left over?

Foot care on the go during a selection course.

This lasted for about a minute or so before Faber, in his gruff voice, reminded us in unpublishable language that it had bugger all to do with us and that we should mind our own business. 'You lot look pathetic and you will never make it. Just give up now,' he said before driving off, laughing.

The sounds of the vehicle had just started to fade away when Justin (Totti) Vermaak called to us from within the treeline, 'Hey guys, come here. Quickly!'

I am not sure who of us looked worst at this point. Obie Oberholzer had raw shoulders from carrying the old army webbing filled with mortar canisters for days. Frans Marais looked like death warmed up, BC Greyling had blisters on his feet the size of oysters, and I was also in a bad way. Still, the urgency in Totti's voice spurred us into action and we disappeared into the treeline.

From under his shirt he pulled out a fistful of big T-bone steaks. While the instructors had been taunting us, Totti had sneaked his hand into the back of the vehicle and stolen as much steak out of their braaibox as he could grab with his one hand. He clearly understood Lesson 4.

It wasn't a minute before we had a few small sticks burning – and I mean small, they were the tiniest bloody twigs. The moment we had flames, we scorched the meat. It was like braaing on a candle. We were in a race against time, because we had no idea if or when the instructors would notice our fire and come to beat us up.

The meat couldn't have been on the fire for more than two or three minutes before we took it off and gulped it down. The evidence was gone! For tonight at least we had the upper hand.

The selection finished two days later with all of us still together.

---

[39] In the 25 years covered by this book, the selection courses varied quite a bit. The course referred to here was called the 'long selection' and relied purely on time to break down the candidate's resistance.

UNDERDONE STEAK, E BLOCK STYLE

by Johan Raath

1 group of corporals
1 piece of steak
lots of rum

For many years, E Block on the Bluff in Durban housed the 'living ins', or unmarried soldiers, of 1 Reconnaissance Regiment. With sea views rivalling those of any hotel and rules appropriate to a Permanent Force unit, E Block spawned a variety of mentionable and unmentionable activities.

Rumour has it that there were illegal bars and ladies who slept over, or even moved in semi-permanently. Add to that a kitchen that served food three times a day (for free) and Shorty the Cleaner, who ensured the block was always spick and span, and this was a 'residence' of note.

The stories that emanate from E Block warrant their own book, but for now the following recipe best captures the spirit of the corporals who lived there – whether they owned Cortinas or not.[40]

> If the enemy is in range, so are you (unless you have a G5).

It was a Saturday afternoon like any other in the late 1980s when a group of us 1 Recce corporals walked past the late Neil (Bez) Bezuidenhout's room in E Block. He was sitting flat on the floor next to his bed, with a pair of braai tongs, a small gas stove and a large steak that just fitted into the pan on the stove.

This member was even more clattered than we were. We had spent the whole morning on the stoep of the Malibu Hotel (a Southern Sun hotel) and were getting ready for an evening outing to the Father's Moustache, the hotel's pub.

Bez duly invited us to come in and share his meal. On closer inspection we noted that the gas was not turned on, but he continued frying the meat. Every time he turned the meat, you even heard a tsssssssssszz ... It was the most ridiculous and hilarious moment.

To fully appreciate it, we asked him for some Red Heart rum ('RHR' for short) and Coke, which he kindly offered to us. After a few rounds we were all equally raw – on par with the meat.

So, we cut it up and ate it as good corporals should. I can't recall exactly who shared in the meal, but I wouldn't be surprised if it included myself, Barry Visser, JJ (John) Raath, K Croucamp and two other corporals.

I can't really say what it tasted like, but I realised that day that it is possible to cook and eat meat without a flame or coals. The only conditions are that the diners must have had enough RHR and like their steak very underdone. There is nothing a corporal can't do. Just don't ask him to do anything!

Men of E Block at 1 Recce in Durban discuss the contents of their potjie during a potjie competition. From left to right: Johnny de Gouveia, PJ Johns, C Castelyn, Bez Bezuidenhout – the specialised chef in the above recipe alongside – and JJ Raath.

---

[40] All Recce soldiers had to complete at least three years' military service before they could join the Special Forces. After 18 months you would normally be promoted to corporal. Unmarried personnel lived in the base, so E Block, with its 54 rooms, had at least 20 unmarried corporals.

ON THE SPIT
à la Feeskomitee

Feeding a crowd requires a little more additional planning. A spit braai is a great way not only to get your better half to attend a unit function but also to feed a big group of people. Just remember that moms with children are a different breed. There is a fine line between making someone just hungry enough and making someone angry, so stick to the timing or have a separate kids' menu.

Appoint a committee who will be responsible for recreation. Let them choose their own theme for the function. After you have allowed Wayne Ross-Smith, Spik Botha and the rest of E Block at 1 Recce to choose a hobo party as the theme, and they don't wash for a week, you can rein in the committee's freedom.

Rather pick a more family-friendly theme – like 'summer spit braai' at the unit swimming pool. Pitch a few tents, lay out straw bales, bring in a nursery full of plants and, voila, instant atmosphere.

Let your men start the braai in the early afternoon. Issue them with lots of coals and only a few beers. Warn the wives not to try to break off the crackling loin meat from the sheep as the braaiers will defend it aggressively, to the point of chopping at them with the braai knives.

Get five big potjies going with pap, sauce, potatoes, rice and chicken à la king.

After a few hours, when you've reached the moment where people are about to start losing control due to hunger, cut the meat and serve with all the side dishes. Then stand aside and shake your head at the amount of beer and rum that can be consumed at such an event.

Make sure Kriek Kruger doesn't have his gun with him, otherwise he will have another hole in his artificial limb.[41] Either way, before midnight he will probably set himself alight leaning back into one of the paraffin torches and then he will have to hop on his one leg into the pool.

On Sunday, after church, go and check that everything is restored to normal. The place will be spotless – *dankie, oubaas se DPs* (thank you, national servicemen).

2 sheep
Half a pig
Pap and sous
Potatoes
Rice
Chicken à la king – a lot
Salads

---

[41] Major Kriek Kruger lost his lower left leg in an operation and thereafter used an artificial limb. However, unless he took off his socks it was impossible to know he had a prosthesis. Once, while attending a course in Pretoria, he took a bet with someone that he could shoot himself in the foot and not even blink, which he proceeded to do, much to the surprise of the gaping onlookers. Now this is how rumours about tough Recces are started …

LAMB CHOPS WITH TZATZIKI

1 cucumber
Salt
1 cup plain yoghurt
Garlic, crushed
Olive oil
Mint, chopped
Lamb loin chops

TIP
Tzatziki is all about the garlic, so there is no limit on the allowed quantity – heap it on!

The Greeks have been making this dish for 2 000 years, and for good reason: the tzatziki really enhances the taste of the lamb. In the 1980s, the Greek restaurant chain Mykonos had an 'eat as much as you can' special. It was quite handy if you were living off army pay and only had money to eat out once a month. Their restaurant in Durban was very popular among the Special Forces operators, especially after a few hours at the Smugglers Inn.

Peel the cucumber and grate it.

Press out all the liquid from the grated cucumber and place in a bowl.

Add one teaspoon of salt and rub it in. Then let it stand for an hour.

Add the yoghurt, garlic, olive oil and mint to the cucumber and mix. Place in the fridge to serve chilled.

Braai the chops.

LAMB KNUCKLE POT
à la Omuthiya

by Roland de Vries[42]

1 onion, chopped
Cooking oil
Lamb knuckle
1 packet of bacon
Salt and pepper
Garlic powder
Mixed herbs
Parsley, chopped
Water
Potatoes
Carrots
Patty pans
Baby marrows
Green peas
Soy beans
Mushroom soup
Cream

[42] Major General (retired) Roland de Vries is widely regarded as the father of mechanised warfare in the South African Army. During his time as commanding officer of 61 Mech, he played a leading role in operations such as Protea, Meebos and Moduler/Hooper.

In the weeks between the operations 61 Mechanised Battalion (61 Mech) was deployed on there was always time to experiment with different potjies at Omuthiya, the battalion's home in the north of then South West Africa. My favourite potjie is made with lamb knuckle and is preferably served at last light.

Heat the potjie and fry the onion in cooking oil.

Brown the lamb knuckle and fry the bacon.

Season with salt and pepper, garlic powder, mixed herbs and parsley.

Add a cup of water and let the brew simmer for at least an hour. Probe for readiness with a bayonet or trip-flare peg.

Add potatoes and layer all the other vegetables from hard to soft (as one would an army on the march).

Stir in the mushroom soup.

Cook slowly for at least three hours.

Supervise the progress of the potjie with beer in hand and taste every now and then.

Add the cream moments before you declare the meal mission completed.

EDITORS' NOTE: It is most interesting that soldiers who have the luxury of wheels have lists of ingredients that read like an encyclopaedia. Not so their walking counterparts in the Recces.

SPECIALISED COOKING – THE RECCE WAY

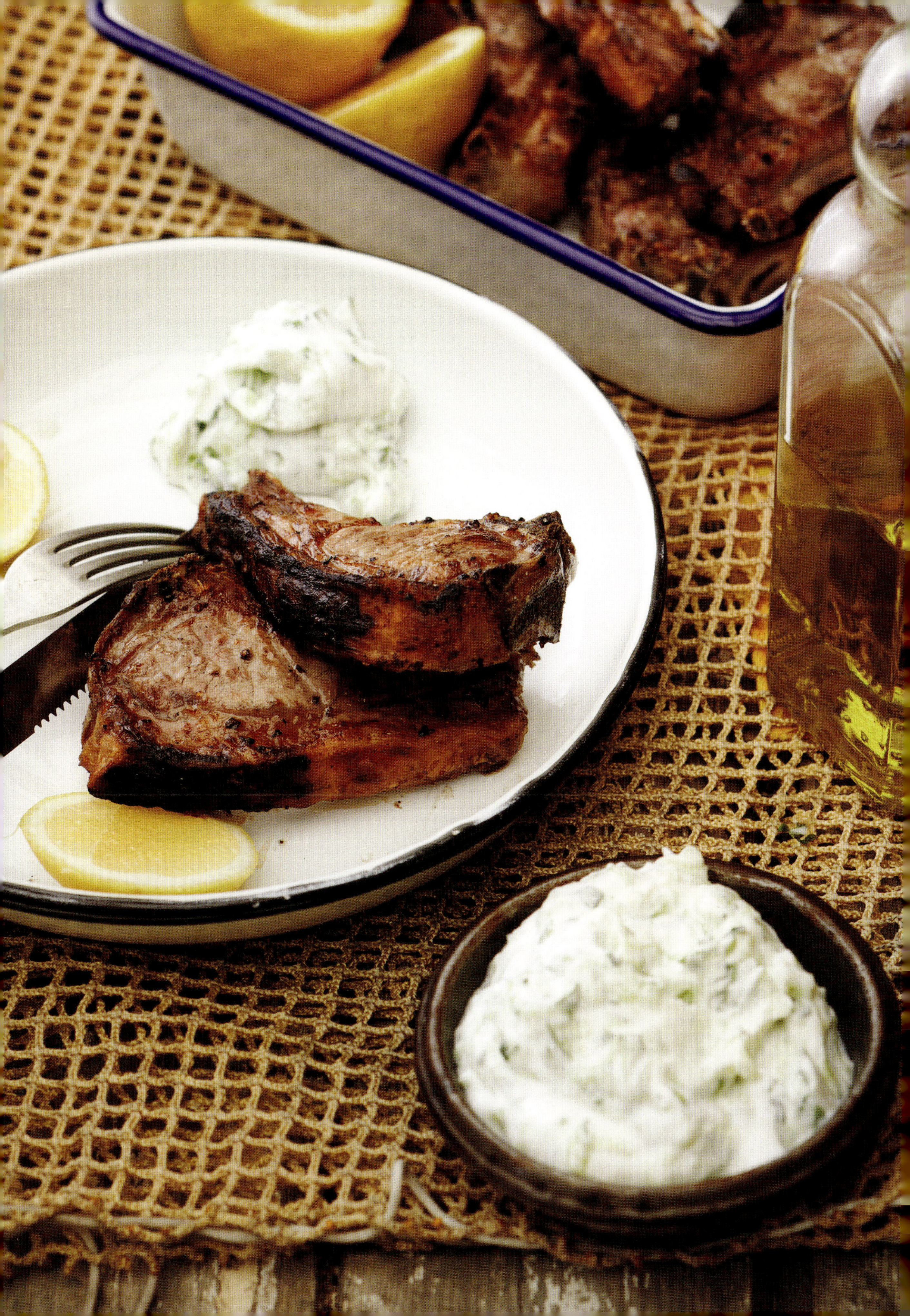

A Place Called Dukuduku

The Dukuduku forest on Lake St Lucia has seen it all.[43] What started as a temporary base for 5 Recce soon became an integral part of the Special Forces story. It was here at Dukuduku that 5 Recce forged their culture. They did everything with limited resources and in quiet isolation – out of sight and out of the way – whether it was in training the Angolans or Mozambicans who joined the Special Forces or in preparing for operations.

If you were part of the lucky few, you did your basic parachute course in Dukuduku with instructors including Dave Tippet, Ouboet Kruger and Anton Retief, using the same equipment that was used to train the Renamo troops. At Dukuduku there were no hangers, *aapkas* or smart fans – only blue gum trees, stiff cables and steps made from planks that went up the trees. This is true to the spirit of 5 Recce – focused, uncomplicated and efficient.

After 5 Recce moved to Phalaborwa, the site was used for initial training, retraining and operational rehearsals. The bush paths will tell many a story of the characters who walked on them, the sweat spilled on selection courses and personal successes and failures.

The bush church under the trees at the Dukuduku training base.

If you listen carefully, the trees will also whisper about the Small Teams and snipers who went there to hone their skills. You might even hear a murmur about a commando rally or two with Dawie Fourie.

---

[43] The base consisted of prefabricated houses, bungalows and other rudimentary structures. To reach Dukuduku in those years you had to take the turnoff to St Lucia at Mtubatuba, cross the railway line and continue. At the railway crossing it's important to look out carefully for trains. Buks (Fala Merde) van der Berg has the full story but, believe me, it's rather embarrassing to hit a stationary train.

Puff Adder On Rice

Apart from the central Copperbelt in Zambia, you'll find some of the biggest snakes on the continent on the northern coast of KwaZulu-Natal. Snake catching became quite a regular sport among the men of 1 Recce in the early 1980s.

The Fitzsimons Snake Park in Durban was always keen to buy live snakes, especially if they were big. If you found a really big snake, you could sell it to the park when you finally went back to the main base in Durban.

The going price was R25/m of snake. If you take into account that a double rum and Coke cost R2 in those days, one snake would've covered the bill for an entire evening. Guys like Wentzel Marx and Etienne (Snakes) Snyman quickly learned how to get by on their *slangvanggeld* (money earned from catching snakes).

As can be expected, snake also ended up on the menu from time to time. Some time in the mid-1980s, while doing duty on the training cycle at Dukuduku, Schalk (Swapo) Prinsloo caught a big puff adder out in the field. He 'donated' the snake to chef Pat Sinclair, who was in charge of the kitchen on that cycle. Major Kobus (Kragvarkie) Human was the officer in charge of training.

The snake was prepared and served with the rest of the food, without any fanfare. The truth only came out after the meal. Then old Pat had to run for his life because Major Human did not take kindly to the idea of puff adder on rice. That's probably because he came from the engineers.

Wentzel Marx, in black 1 Recce T-shirt, holds a serious-sized rock python captured in the Dukuduku forest.

EISBEIN

à la Daan van Zyl

Eisbeins (back hock)
1 stock cube
Water
Thyme
Garlic
Bay leaves
Onions, quartered
Potatoes, cubed
Dijon mustard
Sweet and sour pickles
Sauerkraut

Eisbein is not an entrée. It is a dish reserved for those who have already demonstrated their healthy appetite.

When the dish is served, it is vital that you observe the face of your guest. At first he will sit back in his chair and assess how he is going to tackle the Eisbein. Then a smile will spread across his face as he contemplates achieving the end result. After that he will shuffle slightly in his seat to get the bum settled solidly on the chair before bending forward as he gets ready to attack.

Serve with a large glass of cold beer – beer fest style – and mustard.

Preheat the oven to 220°C.

Rub the hocks (Eisbeins) with the stock cube.

After rubbing, dissolve the rest of the stock cube in boiling water and add the thyme, garlic and bay leaves to the stock.

Place the Eisbeins in a roasting pan and add the stock. Add water until the Eisbeins are half-covered.

Add onion quarters and cubed potatoes and cook for 20 minutes.

Turn and top up the liquid in the pan.

After 20 minutes drain the sauce and grill the Eisbeins until the skin is crispy.

Serve with Dijon mustard, sweet and sour pickles and sauerkraut. Ensure that there is ample space at the table so your guests will have enough elbow room.

BUSH PIG IN SWEET AND SOUR SAUCE

Leg of a bush pig
Pork fat, cut into cubes
Bay leaves
Onion
Orange juice
Sugar
Salt and pepper

SWEET AND SOUR SAUCE

1 stock cube
12 prunes
Peppercorns
Chilli peppers
24 cherries, pickled in vinegar
1 bottle of red wine

When you live in a forest and have good connections at the provincial parks board who will allow you to enter all their otherwise restricted areas, it is inevitable that you will end up with some bush pig on your table.

Boar is obviously the more well-known variant and is served in Western Europe in a sweet and sour sauce. Apparently this dish originates from Gaul. But, true or not, this recipe works really well for bush pig too.

Marinate the leg for 24 hours.

Heat the oven to 180°C.

Make small incisions in the meat and insert pork fat cubes. Add bay leaves.

Season with salt and pepper. Place in the oven with the onion and a bit of orange juice and braise for 40 minutes per 500 g.

Once cooked, drain and place in a long dish. Strain the braising liquid and pour a few tablespoons over the leg. Sprinkle with sugar and glaze in the oven.

SAUCE

Reduce the remaining braising liquid.

Add the stock cube, prunes, peppercorns, chilli peppers and pickled cherries to the sauce.

Serve with red wine.

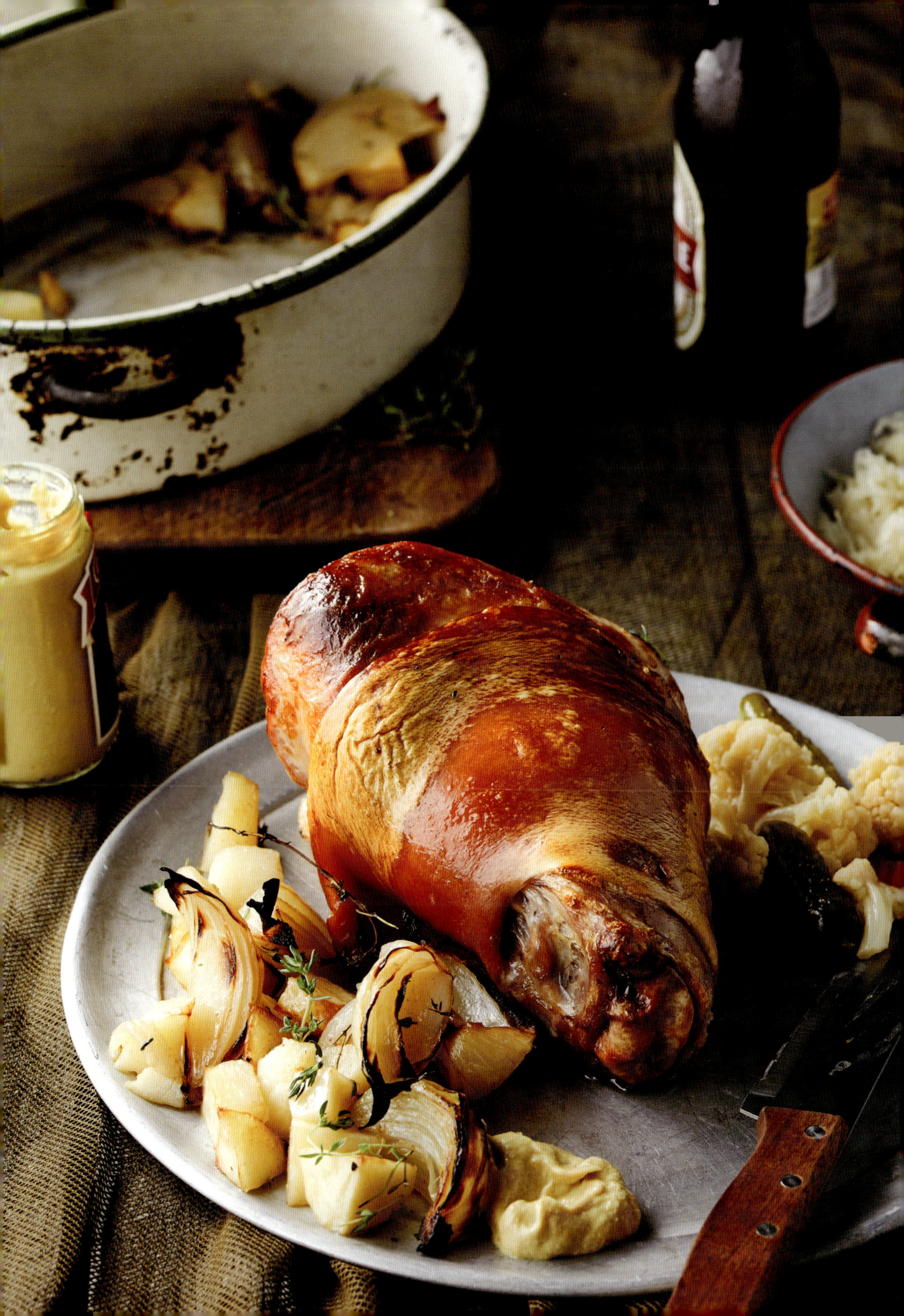

GIANT FRIKKADELLE

Bread
Onion, diced
Salt and pepper
Meat spices
500 g mince

Knowing your way around mince is a crucial life skill, if only because it can be used in such a wide variety of dishes. So, even if you are Spik Botha and can't even heat a hamburger patty in a microwave, it will be worth your while at least to learn these basic meals that can be made with mince.

Break bread into very, very small pieces or use a grater (the pieces should be of the same size as you would put on a hook to catch carp on Hartbeespoort Dam).

Dice the onion finely.

Add the salt and pepper and spices of your choice to the bread.

Mix with the mince and knead thoroughly. Roll into fist-sized balls. Don't use Basil Liebenberg's hand as a guide because his fists are so big you'll end up with 500 g *frikkadelle*.

Bake in the oven at 180°C, fry in a pan or wrap in tin foil and cook on the fire.

MICI[44]

Romanian style

Bicarbonate of soda
Lemon juice
Mutton mince
Fatty pork mince
Beef mince
Savory (or basil and thyme)
Coriander
Salt and pepper
Cooking oil
Mustard
Pickles

This dish is made with similar ingredients to wors, meaning minced meat, except that it consists of a combination of equal parts beef, mutton and pork and requires no casing. This makes it a very useful recipe if you want to braai anywhere in Africa but don't have any skin to make wors.

Any true traveller will want to visit the country where *mici* is the national dish and is sold in every stall at every shopping centre and cooked by everyone – Romania. If you do travel there, you will also learn how to slaughter the pig yourself and how to make and drink țuică,[45] the national drink.

Dissolve the bicarbonate of soda into lemon juice. Use one full teaspoon of bicarb per 500 g of meat and just enough lemon juice required to dissolve it.

Mix the three types of minced meat and add the lemon juice, savory, coriander and salt and pepper. (If you can't find savory, which is a member of the mint family, you can substitute it with basil and thyme – but try to get the savory.)

Roll the minced meat out into cylinder-shaped sausages of about 100 g each.

Place them on an oven tray and coat with cooking oil. Let the sausages stand for a few hours.

Pack them on the braai grid; they should be touching each other. Roll them forward and backward 90 degrees at a time so they will brown all around.

The dripping oil and fat will cause a lot of smoke, giving the *mici* a very specific flavour.

Serve with mustard and pickles. And cold beer.

---

44 *Mici*, n [small] pronounced 'mietsch' in Romanian.

45 *Țuică* (pronounced 'twee-cha') is a witblits made by every household in Romania and consumed by all ages and sexes. You start drinking it around age ten and carry on until you are 100.

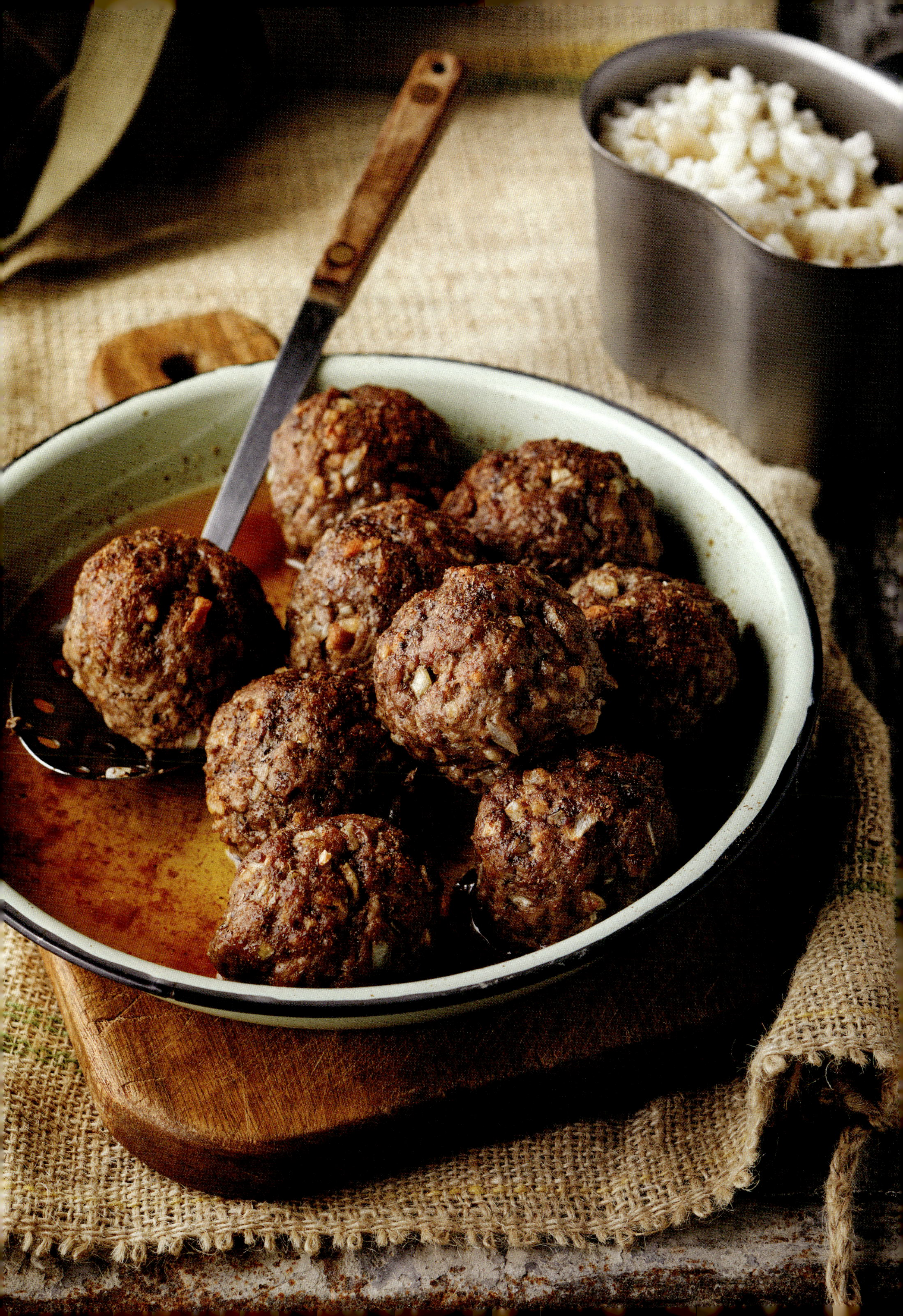

Food on Wheels

A regular SADF force, using Casspirs as troop carriers, assembles for an attack.

by Roland de Vries

Deploying with a conventional fighting force offers a change in routine for the Special Forces soldier. Normal deployments were done in small groups and clandestinely – meaning unseen and unheard. However, when you deployed with a convoy of Ratels and other vehicles from 61 Mechanised Battalion you couldn't really go unnoticed. The upside was that you also had more options in terms of the food you could prepare.

What such a deployment would show you is that it's not only Special Forces soldiers who adapt and stay in the moment – every soldier had to learn these principles. It is a hallmark of our forces. The extract below, from Roland de Vries's book *Eye of The Firestorm*, about an incident during Operation Meebos in 1982, offers the perfect example of the South African soldier's ability to adapt.

61 Mech followed the Mui River via Mongua back to Ongiva – it was like a dusty highway. One more spectacle would befall my eyes on the way to Mongua while travelling down the Mui. It would make me adore and appreciate the troops of 61 Mech so much more.

One early morning a Ratel-mounted infantry section of Captain Jan Malan's forever spirited Alpha Company was passing by, dust trailing. Tethered to the spare wheel on the roof of said combat-ready Ratel was a goat (for messing purposes only it was later to be confirmed by me). I said to myself, De Vries let it be, a mobile mechanised goat, what the hell next?

However, the next day the same Ratel passed me by. This time there were a few mechanised chickens neatly tethered to the camouflage net, cackling happily on the move!

I was curious and stopped the Ratel for a moment with a hand signal. I asked the troops what the hell was going on, were they farming or what and what had happened to the goat of yesterday? They said to me in a serious tone: 'No, Commandant, we had swapped our goat for a few chickens yesterday, it is a bargain, the goat had died – we gave them ratpacks (24-hour ration packs) as well.'

I told them sally forth and enjoy their dinner that evening in the dust, wherever.

Good-bye Ratel, good-bye chickens …

SPECIALISED COOKING – THE RECCE WAY

RESUPPLY POT ROAST
à la Bone

Some people simply love cooking, and regardless of what they are preparing, you know it will be good. Usually their attention to detail and the intention to please is very apparent.

Top of the class in this regard is Marius (Bone) Boonzaaier, an operator who qualified during the early days of the Special Forces but was wounded in action. This left his right hand and arm with limited functionality, so he transferred to the support unit. Once you heard Bone would be manning the base, you deployed with ease, because as a former operator he knew what getting a hot resupply meant for morale.

Draw the weekly rations at HQ in Rundu.

Once you get the departure times of the choppers doing the resupply, you can start planning your cooking.

Cook the roasts with garlic and lemon in the oven – maximum 60 minutes – but leave slightly undercooked.

Wrap in foil and leave in the oven at 60°C.

Remove from the oven 30 minutes before take-off and place in hot boxes with other food.

Personally deliver to the choppers. Hand over the hot boxes to the flight technician, pointing out the names you have written on masking tape on the boxes.

Relax in the knowledge that your food will reach your men some 300 km away and it will be warm. This is teamwork at its best.

- 4 beef roasts
- Garlic
- Lemon
- Aluminium foil
- 3 hot boxes
- 4 six-man Special Forces teams out in the field

ABOVE A hot box.

LEFT A team displays their raisin beer 'prizes' after resupply from their cache during Operation Sea Warrior. Deployed for a full 99 days near Luena, in central Angola, they had to live off what they could take with them. From left: Gary Yaffe, Pierre Schweyer, SW Fourie and Hans Delport.

IF IT WALKS

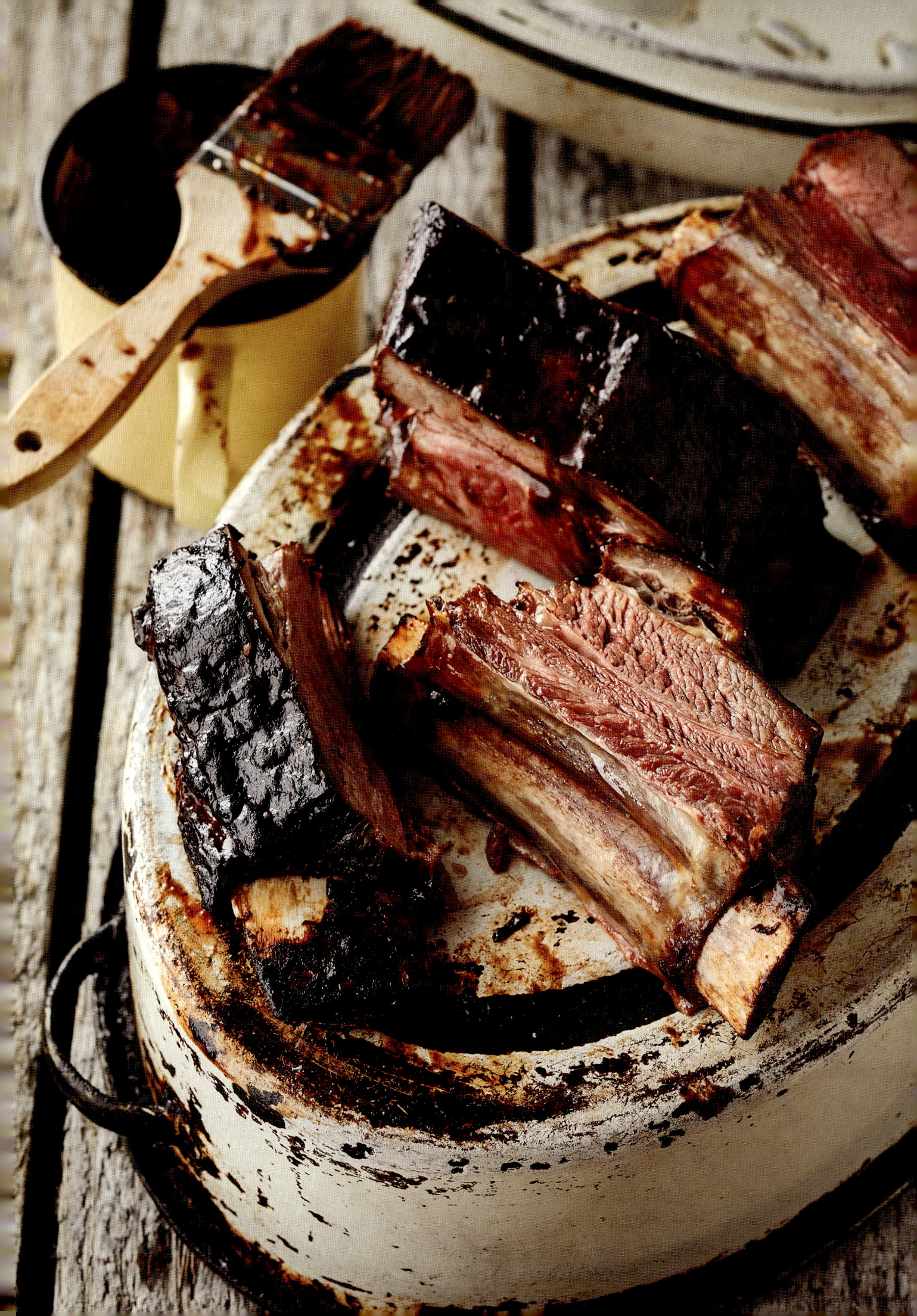

BEEF RIBS IN THE OVEN
à la Oshakati guesthouse

One cannot have a book about the Recces without some reference to Oshakati and Ondangwa. Oshakati is not high up on the list of popular tourist destinations. History tells us that it was once the hub of Sector 10's war effort. Many senior army personnel lived at Oshakati permanently.

Oshakati had proper houses, some schools, a few general dealers, a real school and even a proper guesthouse. After a few weeks at Fort Foot – the Recce base at Ondangwa – or in the bush, this was the closest to civvie street one could get.

Oshakati offered you a chance to meet people who weren't employed by the army or the police. You might even meet someone from the opposite sex. Needless to say, for all this the base dwellers of Ondangwa, some 25 km down the road, saw Oshakati as a serious weekend-out destination.

The best dish at the Oshakati guesthouse was the oven-baked beef ribs. You could order this every time. It took a long time to prepare but you were not in a rush and the company was always good. Just beware of the older women sitting alone in the pub; there are good reasons why they don't have company.

Freshly grated ginger
Salt and pepper
Worcestershire sauce
Tomato paste
500 g beef ribs

Heat the oven to 200°C.
Mix the spices and the Worcestershire sauce with the tomato paste. Baste the ribs.
Bake the ribs on the bone for 30 minutes.
Turn the oven down to 160°C and turn the ribs. Bake for another 20 minutes.
It is good to baste the ribs every 10 minutes to keep them moist.
Turn down the oven and keep warm until ready to serve.

Warrant Officer Peet (Oom Pote) Coetzee relaxes under a tree outside Fort Rev.

Fort Rev at Ondangwa

The Sector 10 headquarters were at Oshakati, and the airfield for this region was at Ondangwa, some 25 km to the east. The Special Forces units always established their bases close to airfields so as to have direct access to the helicopters and other aircraft that would take them into enemy territory.

Fort Rev[46] at Ondangwa was consequently built right next to the airfield. In addition to this being a staging station for all the Recce units, the base also functioned as a permanent home for a section of 5 Recce operators, many of them former Angolan soldiers.

One would get there by C-130 or C-160 transport planes, which was quite a long trip from Pretoria, Durban, Ysterplaat or Phalaborwa. (A good way to pass the time during the flight was by playing bridge.) In later years, the arrival would be marked by a rapid spiral descent to limit the threat of an SA-7 attack.

As far as garrison bases go, Fort Rev was as bleak as it gets. The permanent staff stayed in mobile homes. The wooden bungalows provided bulk accommodation, but it was in fact better to be deployed than to be base-bound. This was not a place to laze around; it would only lead to late-night sessions, kitchen raids and dirties around the airstrip.

---

[46] The name refers to being 'revved', meaning 'being in a contact'. With so many operations done from here ending in a firefight, the fort was aptly named Fort Rev.

PORK ROLL

1 kg pork belly
Salt and pepper
Sage, chopped
Garlic flakes
1 cup of water
1 cup of orange juice
Tin foil

TIP: Leftovers should be left in the juice for 'sarmies' the next day.

In the Lowveld heat of Phalaborwa, you don't want to spend too much time in the kitchen. Let the oven do the work while you enjoy a crisp dry white wine in the shade or by the pool.

Preheat the oven to 220°C.

Score the meat but don't cut through it.

Rub salt, pepper, sage and garlic flakes into the pork belly.

Place on roasting rack and pour 1 cup of water and 1 cup of orange juice into the pan below the roasting rack.

Go and play bridge on the veranda. G&Ts with lots of ice will keep you hydrated.

After an hour, turn the temperature down to 180°C and cover the pork with foil.

Place dry white wine in the deepfreeze 30 minutes before serving the meal.

After cutting the pork into slices, drizzle with juices from the roasting pan.

STROGANOFF IN BLAAUW CHEESE[47]

Water
Pasta
Sirloin, fillet or rump (well rested and almost as blue as the cheese)
Salt and pepper
Onion, diced
Mushrooms
Cooking oil
Mustard
Sour cream
Gorgonzola or any other strong-flavoured blue cheese.

With a bit of planning, you can work even the stinkiest cheese or other strange item in your fridge into a dish. So, if you end up with a strong blue cheese after a formal supper or a cheese and wine event, it is a sign to try your hand at something unconventional. Instead of the usual braai, switch to specialised cooking mode.

Bring water to the boil and cook the pasta.

Cut the meat into small, finger-sized strips. Season to taste with salt and pepper.

Sauté onions and mushrooms in oil.

In a different pan, fry the meat strips on a high heat for no longer than 3 minutes – the meat should be seared but still moist.

Add the onions to the meat, as well as the mustard. Cover with the sour cream and crumble over blue cheese.

Bring to the boil and stir for 5 minutes. Serve on pasta.

Three members of 51 Commando enjoy a cold Lion Lager after work on a Friday afternoon in Phalaborwa.

---

[47] Hennie Blaauw is a long-serving officer of 5 Recce. He has a treasure chest of stories as tall as he is himself.

SPECIALISED COOKING – THE RECCE WAY

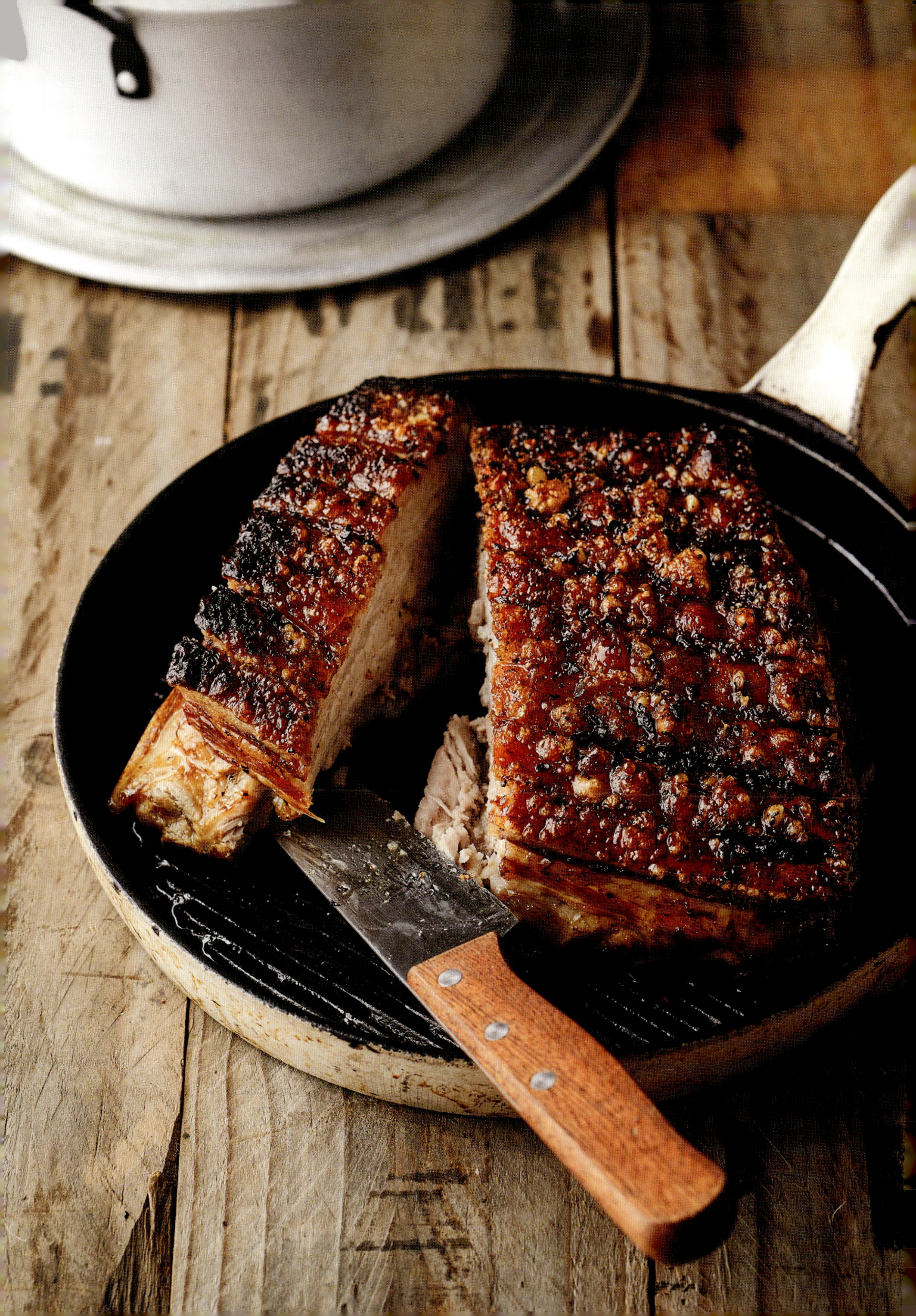

OXTAIL

by Johnny Maass

1 bottle red wine
2 kg oxtail
Flour
Onions
Garlic
Rosemary
Cloves
Mixed herbs
Bay leaves
Beef stock cube
Carrots
Baby potatoes
Celery sticks
Salt and pepper

This is a dish for connoisseurs. It takes a long time to cook, so the sense of expectation will rise among the guests as the rich aromas start escaping from the pot.

Oxtail is excellent for winter time, so you and your guests can share a great bottle of wine in the warmth of the kitchen. Preparing an oxtail will give you more than enough time to catch up. I normally make it as part of a routine in which I serve brunch and then this for an early supper. This allows adequate time to relax, chat and do things slowly.

My cooking is much like my skydiving. No two jumps were ever the same, just as none of my dishes are exactly the same. I am unsure if I ever cooked the recipe below, but it is sure to be a good one.

Pour a glass of red wine for yourself – the rest is for the oxtail.

Coat meat pieces with flour and brown on high heat in the pot.

Sauté the onions and garlic until golden brown.

Add all the other spices and the bay leaves.

Pour half a bottle of wine into the pot and let it simmer ever so gently for 90 minutes. Once the gelatine/fat has formed a layer on top, scoop out most of it into a jar.

Dissolve the stock cube in a little water and add to the pot.

Add the rest of veggies and celery sticks and season with salt and pepper.

Cook on a gentle heat until the meat falls off the bone. The estimated cooking time is about another two hours, or, for me, a half bottle of Captain Morgan and water.

Serve with mieliepap or rice.

ABOVE LEFT **Johnny Maass**

LEFT A selection course ends with a small celebration in the middle of the bush. At this point, recruits have only earned the right to learn – nothing more.

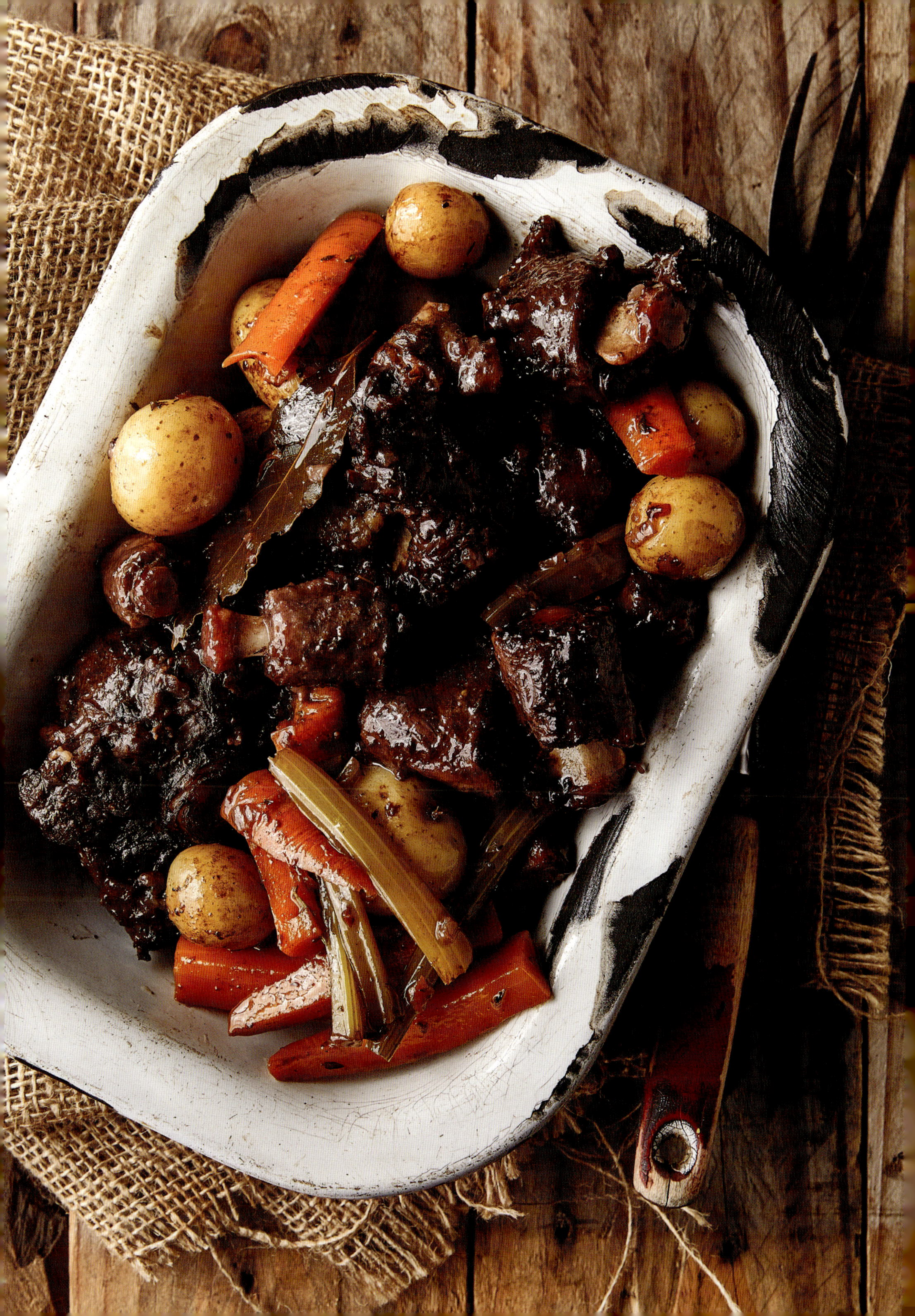

FOR THE RECORD

5 Reconnaissance Regiment

OCs ROLL (5)

Major PJ (Joe) Verster	1976–1980
Commandant HM (Hennie) Blaauw	1981–1981
Colonel HW (Willie) Snyders	1981–1982
Colonel AG (Burt) Sachse	1982–1984
Colonel JR (James) Hills	1984–1988
Colonel C (Corrie) Meerholz	1988–1989
Colonel AG (Burt) Sachse	1990–1993
Colonel Julius W Engelbrecht	1993–1998

RSMs ROLL

WO1 JL (Kenaas) Conradie	1976–1978
WO1 JJ (Koos) Moorcroft	1978–1991
WO1 GJ (Kitcha) Kitching	1992–1993
WO1 JJ (James) Teitge	1993–1996
WO1 GD (Maddies) Adam	1997–2000

ABOVE James Teitge seems ready for action at Fort Rev in Ondangwa.

LEFT 51 Commando get ready for Friday afternoon festivities with Warrant Officer S Seegers leading the group into action.

Dave Tippet, one of the founding members of the Special Forces.

The gates to 5 Reconnaissance Regiment in Phalaborwa.

120 SPECIALISED COOKING – THE RECCE WAY

ABOVE Two operators prepare for a free-fall.

RIGHT Mother Earth, here we come!

ABOVE The Camel's Inn, a building occupied at Xangongo, in southern Angola.

RIGHT RSMs parade on a Friday afternoon in the pub at 5 Recce, outside Phalaborwa.

A group of 5 Recce seniors in a relaxed mode.

A medal parade at 5 Recce with Major General Eddie Webb (left) and Colonel Burt Sachse (third from left).

IF IT WALKS 121

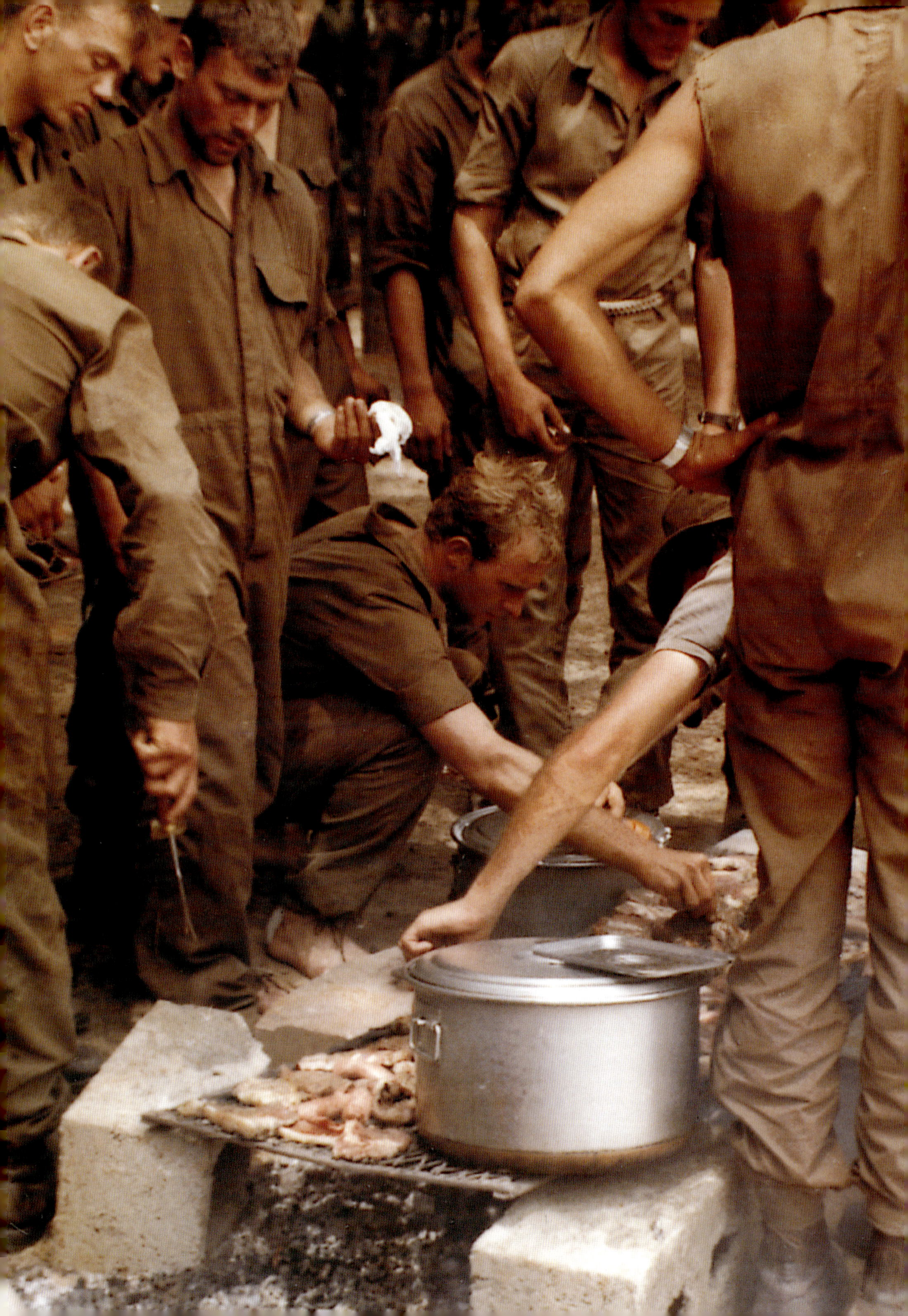

5

IF IT GROWS

This chapter covers everything that comes from the ground, mainly vegetables and fruits. It also deals with the baking side – flour is just wheat, after all. It is said that vegetables are smart food, and that smart people eat lots of them.

The spectrum of food within this category is very wide and diverse and allows for truly spectacular cooking. In previous chapters we focused on the units themselves, so this one will focus a bit more on the Special Forces Headquarters elements. The more cynical will note the irony that Headquarters should end up in the vegetable section. With an iconic senior who goes by the nickname 'Oom Kool', one may be forgiven a sardonic smile.

> It is impossible to make anything foolproof because fools are so ingenious.

We survived it … Recce recruits are treated to an end-of-course braai with *pap* and *sous*.

Starch

CHEESY JACKET POTATO

Potato
Cheddar cheese
Potato spice mix
Salt
Sour cream or mayonnaise

This method reduces cooking time and adds flavour all the way through. For best results, cut the potato in half slices, meaning don't cut right through.

Sprinkle with grated cheese, potato spices and salt.

Fold in foil and cook on coals. If you have an oven, cook in the oven for the same time. Don't forget to preheat. Allow at least 40 minutes at 200°C.

Serve with sour cream or mayo.

POTATO BAKE

Cooking oil
Potatoes, sliced
Onion, sliced in rings
Cottage cheese
Salt and pepper
Mustard
Parsley, chopped
Cheddar cheese, grated

Oil the bottom of a baking pan, leaving it just covered.

Cut and layer the slices of potato and onion rings in the pan.

Mix cottage cheese, salt, pepper and a bit of mustard together. Pour over the layered potato and onion and add chopped parsley on top.

Bake for one hour in an oven preheated to 160°C.

Sprinkle over grated cheddar cheese and put back in the oven for 15 minutes.

Smile – you have a winner!

POTATO ROSTI

Potato
Salt
Spice mix (optional)
Cooking oil
Cheddar cheese, grated

Peel the potato and grate like carrots. Squeeze out as much moisture as you can.

Add salt and spice mix as you wish. Mix well together.

Make little balls, squeezing as hard as you can.

Fry the potato balls in oil in a pan.

Garnish with grated cheese and serve.

If there is no pan, you can wrap in foil and cook in the coals. Open up the foil before serving and sprinkle cheese on top.

> There has never been a protracted war from which a country has benefited.
>
> SUN TZU

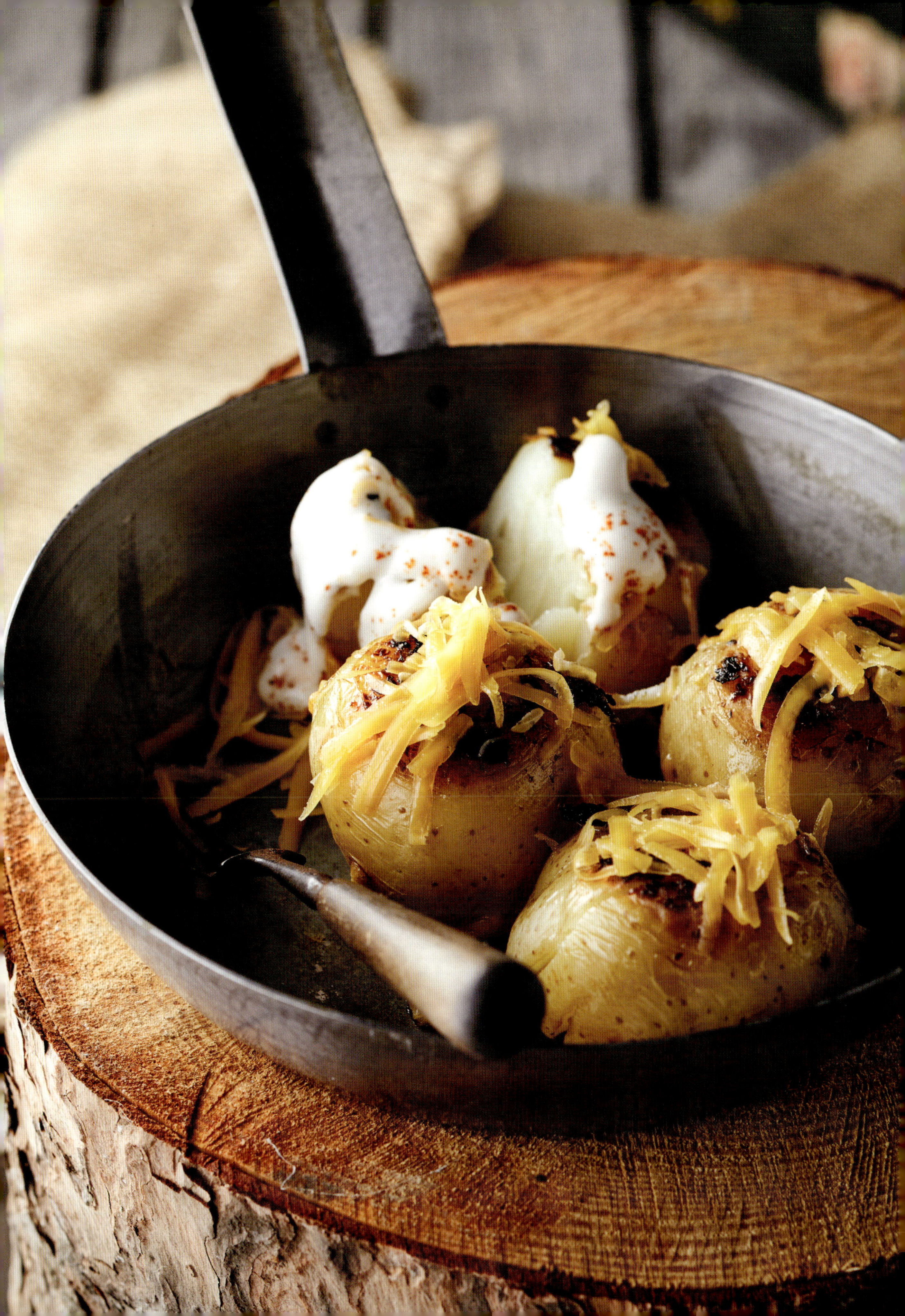

PEP'S HOT POTATOES

by Magda van Zyl

2 cloves of garlic, grated
Fresh ginger (2 cm long), grated
1 cup of fresh green chilli
2 onions
Cooking oil
Vinegar or balsamic vinegar
4 potatoes, cooked and cut into small cubes
Salt and pepper
Brown sugar
Spices

After we sent out a call for recipes, there came back a number of requests for Pep's Hot Potatoes. We asked Joe Hunter and a few other people who were close to Pep van Zyl, the regimental sergeant major of 1 Recce,[48] for the recipe. They came back with different variations.

The truth of this recipe lies in the following letter from *Tannie* Magda, Pep's wife. She called him Peet, instead of Pep.

There has never been a recipe for this popular potato atjar that Peppa loved to make. During the Border War we lived in Rundu. Well, at least I lived there, since the men were mostly at Buffalo [32 Battalion's base].

We were transferred to Rundu, if I remember correctly, because Peet hit the neighbour over the fence and his punishment was to spend time in the bush. All I did was to be married to him at the time.

Either way, this was the start of one of the most marvellous experiences of my life. In Rundu I met Warrant Officer Charl Roza, a man for which I had utmost respect and fear, and his wife, Helen. I had the privilege of eating these potatoes at their house for the first time.

Peet struggled to get the recipe from them for a long time. Then one day he went over and made it with Helen. He 'stole' the recipe with his eyes and in turn I did the same as I watched him prepare the dish over the years.

Peet always sat in the corner of the kitchen at Kromdraai and cut up the ingredients with painful precision. The garlic and ginger were grated. I use a ratio of one cup of chillies for two onions alongside two cloves of garlic and a two-centimetre-long piece of ginger. (The blender will also make everything really fine.)

For every cup of oil for the sauce, I added a quarter cup of vinegar or balsamic vinegar, which adds even more flavour.

Cook about four potatoes, then cut into little cubes.

Mix all the other ingredients with the sauce and pour over the potato.

If you are brave enough, test the sauce before you add salt and pepper, a little brown sugar and spices. When Peet felt that it wasn't hot enough, he would add red chilli or from the bottle of red chilli sauce.

The warm dish must be stored in the fridge as the starch ferments easily. A good idea is to label it so that small children won't be tempted to try it and burn their mouths.

Chilli stays on your hands a long time and I use lemon to stop it from burning the eyes. I get tears in my eyes just thinking about it and also about how much fun and how many fights Pep and I had over the years when we made this meal – and tried to get just the right amount of burn into the potato atjar …

Warrant Officer Pep van Zyl had a moustache as big as his character. Next to him at a formal supper in Durban is his wife, Magda.

EDITORS' NOTE: While we often say a meal is 'to die for', this one is 'to die from'. You have been warned.

---

[48] Warrant Officer Peet van Zyl was also the first WO Special Forces.

CASSAVA

Whenever you're travelling in Africa and you see banana trees, you will find cassava close by. In countries with a warm climate, such as Angola, almost every rural family has a few of these plants.

For Special Forces operators, cassava is prime opportunity food that will augment the rations as you venture further and further north. If you are on the move, just dig out the tuberous root and peel as you would a sweet potato. Then cut it into slices and eat raw. While cassava is rather starchy, it has a pleasant taste. It's simple and nutritious.

For more sophisticated versions of cassava dishes, you will need to go fairly deep into Angola. Joining an operation with Unita presents a good opportunity.

You will stay deployed – on foot – around Luena for over 12 weeks. This means you will learn to eat and drink only what is locally available, and this means cassava, cassava and some more cassava. In fact, you will eat so much of it you will be overjoyed when you get to your cache[49] and see a ratpack again.

Fortunately, you will have company on the trip in the form of stellar individuals such as Frans van Dyk, SW Fourie, JJH (Johnny) de Gouveia, Gary Yaffe and others.

Cut cassava into slices.

Dry slices in the sun.

Put the cassava into big hessian bags.

Get lots of very thin Unita guys to carry the bags wherever you go.

When ready, grind the cassava slices into a flour.

Boil with salt and water.

Eat.

VARIATIONS FOR SPECIALISED CHEFS

This is a great opportunity to adapt, adjust and stay in the moment. Even if you are not that good at adapting, you will get the hang of it after six weeks and start to experiment. Dig out one forgotten ratpack milkshake packet from your rucksack. Mix the contents with a little water and pour over the cassava porridge. When you find some tinned food, look for corned beef and layer it on top. Make a very dry cassava porridge and roll it into balls, then flatten them and roast on the flames. After a few more weeks, you will work out more variations.

Fernando dos Santos and Celeste at one of the unit bases. Note the basic structures in the background and different enemy camouflage uniforms they are wearing.

> I am not afraid of an army of lions led by a sheep; I am afraid of an army of sheep led by a lion.
>
> ALEXANDER THE GREAT

---

[49] When we deployed deep into foreign countries such as Angola, resupply was impossible. We had to take everything along with us, which required meticulous planning and preparation. Since we didn't want to carry all our rations with us due to the weight, we would store some in a cache. Finding the right cache wasn't easy, since it must be properly camouflaged so as not to be discovered, but you have to be able to find it again. If a cache was discovered, you would be compromised, which led to mission failure and extraction.

Maize

PAP THREE WAYS

by IG (Taffy) Pelser

Water
Salt
Maize meal
Butter (if available)

VARIATIONS
Medium water with meal = *putu pap*
More water = *slappap* (porridge)
Less water = *krummelpap*

This method of preparing pap was developed when I was doing Special Forces training in Oudtshoorn in 1973.[50] In those days the students/troops also had to do some of the cooking. If you got the pap or the sauce right, you were given a 'learner's licence'. After three successful attempts at making pap you got a full licence, and after a sustained performance you were elevated to 'tester' level.

Make a fire under a large black pot and pour in one fire-bucket full of water. Once the water boils, add salt.

Add one fire-bucket full of maize meal until it forms a mini-volcano in the water.

Add butter to the heap of maize meal. Close the lid and let it cook for 15 minutes.

Stir the maize meal and then arrange the coals so that the pot is on a low heat. Allow an hour for the maize meal to cook completely. Stir regularly.

POLENTA
South African style

Water
Milk
Salt
Coarse yellow maize meal (polenta)
Feta cheese
Sour cream
Eggs, beaten
Spices to taste

Most South Africans consider pap a staple food. Many would be surprised to hear that some countries outside the African continent eat even more pap, and in a much more sophisticated manner, than we do. Polenta is an Italian word that refers to a style of cooking rather than just the ingredient (polenta can also be made from semolina). But since most South Africans prefer pap, this recipe is made with maize meal.

Boil water and milk in a 50:50 mix. Add salt.

Add the maize meal – a good ratio is 3:1 liquid to solid – stirring vigorously with a whisk to get a smooth texture as if making porridge.

Let it cook through for 10 minutes. Remove from the stove and let it cool.

Tip the solid polenta onto a cutting board and cut the polenta into three layers.

Place the layers in a dish and insert crumbled feta cheese between the layers as if you were making a sandwich or a cake.

Cover the layered polenta and feta with sour cream and beaten eggs. Place in a preheated oven. Bake at 180°C.

Serve with cubes of smoked pork fat and țuică or witblits.

---

[50] In the early years, there were fewer than 30 members of the Special Forces, who were then based at Oudtshoorn. We had to act as instructors while still learning ourselves. Members did everything in those days. This principle played a defining role in establishing the unit's working methods and also established a relationship of equality between soldiers regardless of rank.

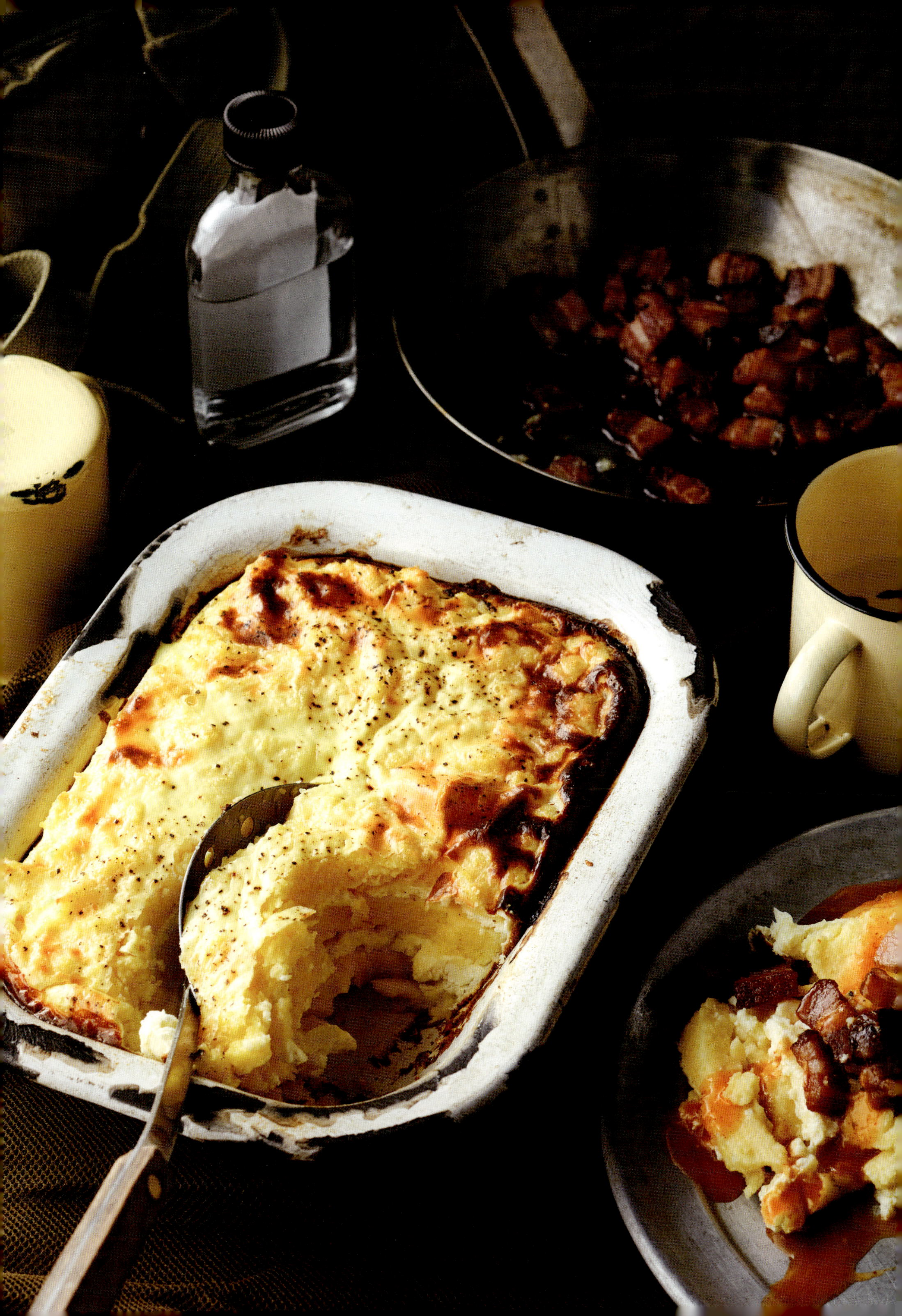

Breads and Basic Bakes

There are few things more heavenly than the smell of freshly baked bread. To eat it hot off a fire with a dollop of butter is the best.

Most basic bakes – from vetkoek to pot bread and pancakes – use the same ingredients, only in different quantities. If you memorise the following table, you will be able to bake it all, provided that you packed the baking powder and instant yeast.

Remember: When preparing dough, always sift dry ingredients first, or mix thoroughly if no sieve is available. Butter should be crumbled and rubbed into the dry mix.

STICK BREAD

Mix the dry ingredients as for *roosterkoek* (see next page).
Instead of making balls for 'cakes', roll these into Vienna-style lengths.
Wrap each piece around a thin green branch and braai it slowly over the coals.
Eat the stick bread bit by bit as it is ready – the warm dough will lift the spirits!

The thick walls of a hollowed-out termite mound store so much heat that it is a match for any convection oven.

Table of ingredients for basic bakes

	Pancake	Vetkoek	Flapjack	Muffins	Roosterkoek/ stick bread	Pot bread	Crust mix
Flour	200 g	240 g	210 g	225 g	300 g	480 g	120 g
Milk/water/ beer	300 ml	250 ml	335 ml	225 ml	200 ml	250 ml	125 ml
Butter				60 g			60 g
Eggs	2	2					1
Oil		500 ml	30 ml		30 ml	30 ml	
Baking powder		10 g	20 g	15 g			15 g
Instant yeast					7 g	20 g	
Salt	3 g	7 g	3 g	3 g	6 g	17 g	3 g
Sugar			13 g		13 g	4 g	
Extra ingredient			Vinegar 10 ml	Castor sugar			

130　SPECIALISED COOKING – THE RECCE WAY

VETKOEK

Mix the dry ingredients with the water or milk. The dough should be slightly more moist than for pot bread.

Ladle into a pot or pan that has lots of oil and cook.

Turn once the dough has turned a deep golden brown.

Serve hot and crispy with filling of choice – cheese, mince, jam, anything will do. This is a real morale and energy booster if you need it.

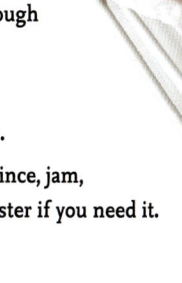

ROOSTERKOEK

Mix the dry ingredients together in a pot or bowl.

Add the oil to the lukewarm water. Slowly add the water/oil mix to the flour and keep mixing and kneading with your hands.

Once the dough is no longer sticky on your hands, stop adding liquid.

Let the dough double in size next to the heat.

Knock back the dough and make flat cakes the size of half a slice of bread. Let these rise again, then cook over soft heat.

BEER / POT BREAD

Mix the dry ingredients together in a pot or bowl.

Slowly add a warm beer to the flour and keep mixing and kneading.

Once the dough is no longer sticky on your hands, stop adding liquid.

Let the dough double in size next to the heat.

Knock back the dough, then let it rise next to the heat.

Place in a pot, making sure the inside is well-oiled. Push down the dough in the middle as far as possible to stop it rising and lifting the lid.

Use heat only from sides and top – no coals below. The bread will be ready after four more beers.

For pot bread, add yeast and water.

> Have a plan. Have a back-up plan, because the first one won't work.

IF IT GROWS

BRAAIBROODJIES

The unsung hero of the braai

Cheese, grated
Sliced white bread (or brown if you really want to be healthy)
Onions, sliced thinly
Sugar
Salt
Tomato
Butter

For each *broodjie*, grate the cheese and sprinkle on both slices of bread.

Slice onions really thinly and rub with sugar and salt.

Layer the onion and tomato on one slice and close with the other. If necessary, wrap with string.

Butter the outside, and the crust in particular, so it doesn't dry out.

Smother the bread when finished – close for a few minutes in a container with a lid – to give a soft feel to the crust.

Tea-time Sandwiches

No military cookbook will be complete without mentioning tea time. For many soldiers this is the most important meal of the day, especially if you start PT at 07h00 (it doesn't make sense to have breakfast before you go on a 10 km run). Most 'living ins' who wanted to sleep late would often use breakfast as an excuse not to go on the run, but let's not get stuck in this debate.

The big issue is that certain individuals arrive for tea time at 09h50, which means that when the rest of the team rock up at 10h10, tea time will be just that. All the food will have been gobbled down – 'toebie time' over.

It gets even worse at the monthly 'big tea' when the chefs truly show off their skills and the offering is an extravaganza of sandwiches, sausage rolls and *frikkadelle* – all made in miniature sizes, as morning tea decorum dictates.

For maximum enjoyment, ensure that you are in position early around the tables. Practise restraint. The signal to

Bush coffee in a fire bucket on an Esbit stove.

attack the food is when the OC ends his address to those assembled and reaches out to put something in his saucer. Try to look relaxed while being vigilant at the same time; if not, the food will disappear in seconds.

SPECIALISED COOKING – THE RECCE WAY

FRENCH TOAST

Whenever you work in West Africa or the Democratic Republic of the Congo (formerly Zaire), you will meet French people. You'll definitely find a few at the parachute club in Kinshasa/Zaire if deployed to train the Zaire Special Presidential Guard (see Chapter 6, Regional Flavours). If you get your story right, you might even get in a skydive with the guys from the French Foreign Legion. If not, just enjoy the beer and the sight of the aeroplanes, as the rest of Kinshasa doesn't offer much. Order a toasted sandwich and, voila, you have completed step 1 of making French toast.

Beat an egg or two before adding some milk, as well as salt and pepper to taste.
Pour the mixture into a soup plate and soak two slices of bread in it.
Fry the bread in a buttered pan. Serve with honey, fried banana or bacon.
This is a wonderful way to use up three-day-old bread.

2 eggs
Milk
Salt and pepper
2 slices of bread
Butter (or oil)

Use cover or concealment as much as possible.

PIZZA BREAD

Bugger the Italians; who needs pizza dough when bread works equally well?

Preheat your oven to 180°C.
Take a hamburger or other round bun and cut into three slices. Spread thickly with butter and tomato sauce, and top with grated cheddar, grated mozzarella, salami and de-stoned olives.
Bake for 15 minutes in the oven.

Hamburger bun
Butter
Tomoto sauce
Cheddar cheese, grated
Mozzarella cheese, grated
Salami
Olives

When hollowed out, anthills make natural ovens. The walls are strong and hard and absorb heat, creating a heat reservoir. Once the hole is covered, you keep it warm by placing a few coals on and around the anthill.

Rice

YELLOW SAVOURY RICE

Salt
Turmeric
Raisins
Water
Long-grain rice (such as basmati)
Onions
Cumin
Ginger, chopped
Salt and pepper

This fragrant rice dish is the perfect accompaniment to bobotie or any meal with savoury rice.

For plain yellow rice, just add salt, turmeric (1½ teaspoons) and raisins to the rice.

Add water and boil until fluffy.

When used as a stand-alone dish, fry onion and add other spices such as cumin and chopped ginger after the rice is cooked.

Season with salt and pepper.

PUMPKIN AND HAM 'RISOTTO'

500 g pumpkin
Water
3 teaspoons of sugar
1 teaspoon of cinnamon
Cooking oil
Onion
Canned ham (or bacon), cubed
Stock cube
Spice mix for rice
Salt and pepper
Broken rice
Parmesan cheese, grated

What to do with broken rice? The answer is to make a risotto. This is a dish that has its origins in Italy. In Italy they use a short-grain rice variety that is thick and chewy. You can get the same effect with broken rice if you just undercook it ever so slightly. You will find broken rice all over Africa, and it offers an excellent way to make a big meal with little meat.

Cut up pumpkin into squares and cook in water with sugar and cinnamon.

Fry the onion and the ham/bacon cubes in a pan.

Dissolve one stock cube and spice for rice in a cup of boiling water. Add to the water in which you will be cooking the rice.

Bring the rice to the boil and then reduce the heat. Once the water has cooked off, add the cooked pumpkin and ham/bacon and stir in. Sprinkle over grated Parmesan and let it steam for a few minutes until the cheese melts.

Season with salt and pepper. Serve piping hot.

VARIATIONS

You can add any ingredients to the rice as long as you stick to the sequence in which this dish should be prepared. Consider the following variations:

1. Stock, garlic, mushrooms, bacon, peas, onion, white wine, butter, pepper
2. Stock, garlic, chicken cubes, baby marrows, onion, white wine, butter, pepper
3. Stock, garlic, salami, plantains, onion, white wine, butter, pepper

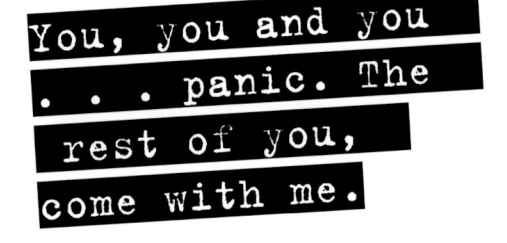

> You, you and you . . . panic. The rest of you, come with me.

SPECIALISED COOKING – THE RECCE WAY

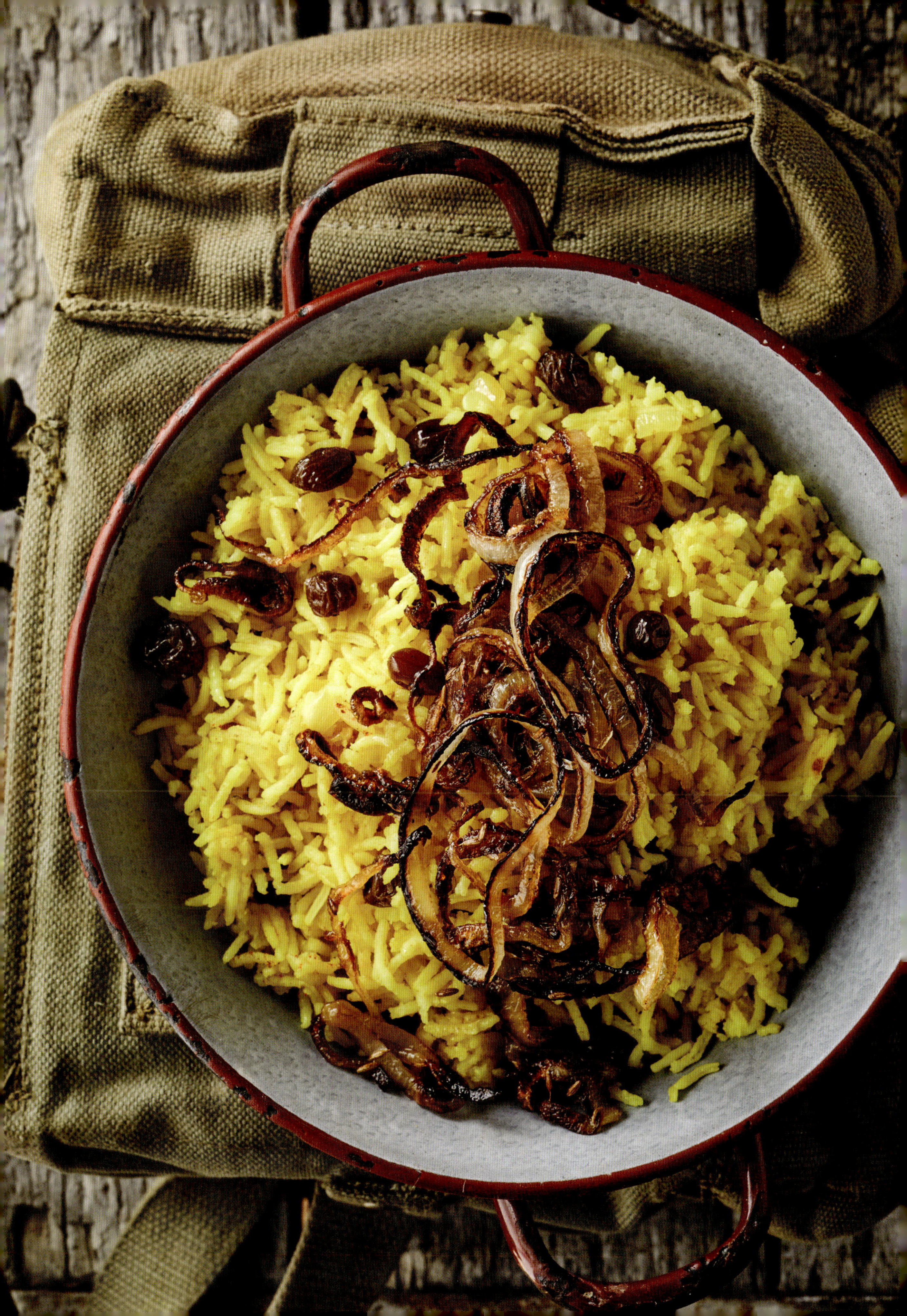

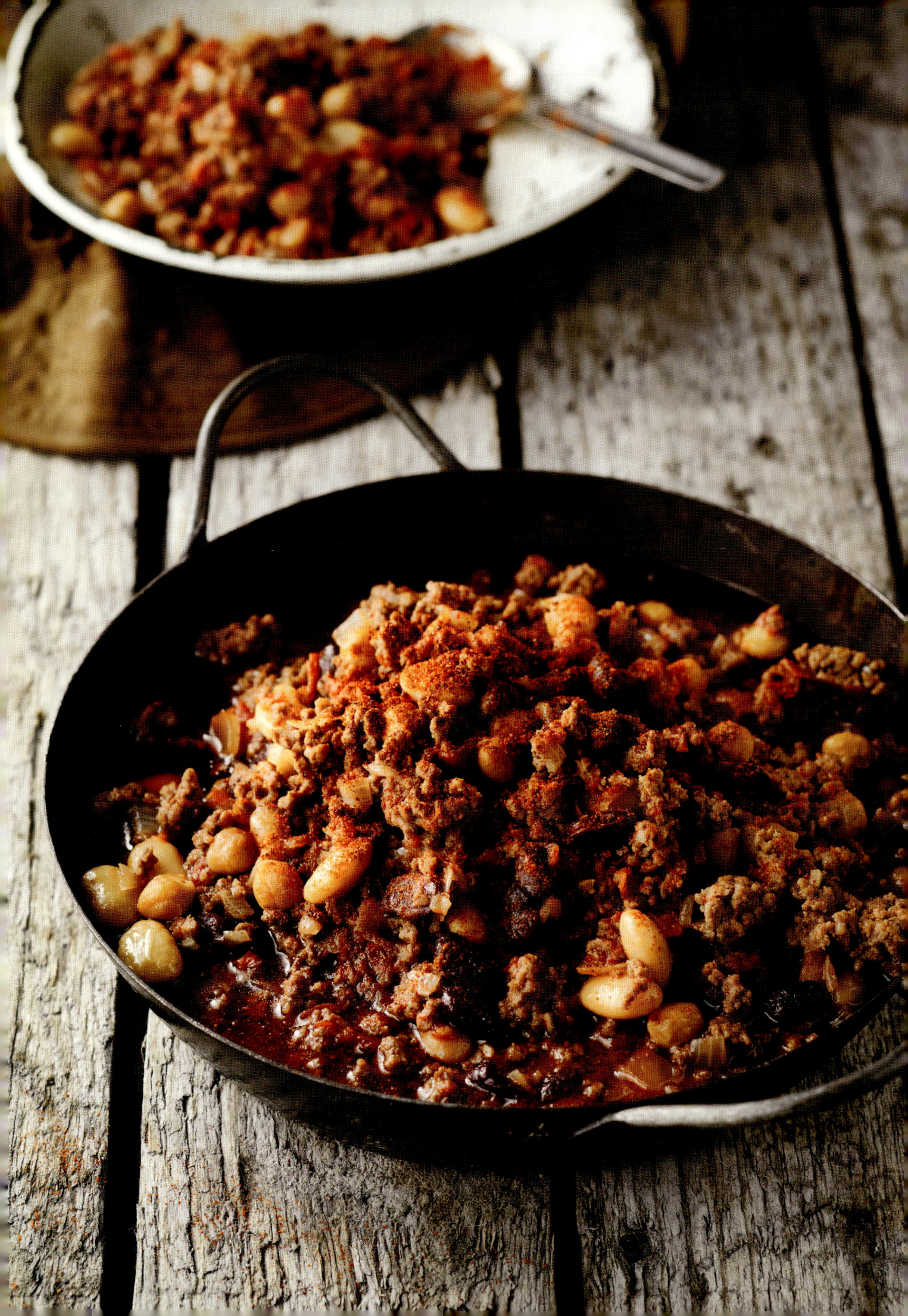

CHILLI CON CARNE
Camping style

This is one of the easiest dishes to make and it can be prepared nearly anywhere and at any time as the main ingredients are mostly canned foods.

But before you get started, you first need to answer one question: how much chilli should be used? There will be varying opinions on this. The macho men will eat the powder by the spoonful, the gourmet crowd will get it right, and the faint of heart will try to shy away from it altogether.

A good test is to feed some to any monkeys that might be in the vicinity and watch their reaction.

Sauté the onions in a pot and add the mince. Add salt; if you don't do this before adding the chilli mix, the salt will taste out of balance.

Add all canned ingredients to the mix, then spoon in half of the intended chilli, the garlic and pepper.

Let it cook through for 10 minutes, then taste. Make whatever adjustments you need to the taste. Serve on rice/*roosterkoek*/samp/pap/potato – whatever you have.

If you didn't spoon out the contents of the chilli packet, but accidentally emptied the whole packet into the pot, you will need to start preparing your defence for when the paw-paw hits the fan among your team members. While you are still busy cooking the meal, tell them exactly how much you like chilli and how you could eat it every day.

After you've dished up, the comments will start coming. When even the most ardent chilli fan scrapes the food off his bread and eats only the bread, it's time to admit your mistake.

If you cooked this dish on a covert trip to Namibia,[51] you will wake up to the sounds of the birds and the nuisance of monkeys in your campsite. Allow the monkeys to come and raid the pot. Their reaction will have you laughing for days. The first one will make a few nervous jumps before sitting himself down at the pot, constantly scanning the campsite. A few seconds later he will grab a fistful and stuff his face, swallowing as fast as he can for about five seconds. Then suddenly he will jump up and scratch vigorously at his mouth while doing the 'wildebeest foxtrot', jumping all over the place as he tries to cough up the food.

When even the monkeys won't eat your food, there's no more denying the truth: it's too hot!

Cooking oil
Onions
Mince
Salt
1 can kidney beans
1 can butterbeans
1 can chickpeas
1 can tomato relish
Chilli powder
Garlic
Pepper
Any starch such as pap, rice, etc.

Monkeys can easily become tame and quickly turn resident. The Doppies training base in the Caprivi Strip was named after a monkey that used to play with all the empty cartridges, or doppies, at the base.

---

[51] A covert operation can be defined as 'an operation that is so planned and executed as to conceal the identity of or permit plausible denial by the sponsor'. That said, a good way of doing reconnaissance in Africa is by way of 'tourist travel'. This entails travelling in a 4x4 with trailer and false passport but staying out of the way in campsites. A clandestine operation can be defined as 'an intelligence or military operation carried out in such a way that the operation goes unnoticed by the general population or specific "enemy" forces.' Before the handover of SWA/Namibia almost the entire 1 Recce went on 'holiday' in Namibia to gather data on the country's national key points.

Pasta

Of all meals, pasta is possibly the easiest one to prepare. So, don't overcomplicate things. Pasta and cream go together like brandy and Coke. When you think of the one, immediately think of the other. Lastly, no pasta can be served without Parmesan cheese.

Also remember that pasta is always better *al dente* (still slightly firm), so follow the instructions on the packet and check a few minutes before it's supposed to be cooked.

SPAGHETTI CARBONARA

Water
Spaghetti
Bacon
Sun-dried tomatoes
250 ml cream
2 eggs, beaten
Mustard
Salt and pepper
Parmesan cheese, grated

Cook the pasta but be careful not to overcook.

Fry the bacon in a pan/dixie and chop the sun-dried tomatoes really finely.

Mix the chopped tomatoes, cream, eggs, mustard and salt and pepper together well and pour over the bacon.

Add the pasta and stir for 4 minutes.

Top with grated Parmesan cheese.

NOTE:
Feel free to use tinned cream. If you don't have fresh bacon, frankfurters from a tin will also do. Both these items can be easily packed in a cache or be taken along when deploying with vehicles.

SPICY CHICKEN NOODLES

Water
Noodles
Canned chicken mix
Tabasco sauce
Garlic
Provita crackers
Salt and pepper
Parmesan cheese, grated

If you are in a buddy pair with the signals guy, you will cook more often than not. For most of the time, he will be preoccupied with laying out the aerials and then tapping out the Morse code at the scheduled comms time.[52] If you are the signaller sitting at Tac HQ during the night shift on 24-hour listening watch, this also makes a good midnight snack.

Boil water in a container.

Break the noodles finely while still dry and put them into the boiling water.

Heat the canned chicken mix in another container.

Add the Tabasco and garlic and stir.

Combine the noodles and chicken mix.

Spoon out the mixture onto neatly arranged Provitas. Offer some to your buddy while he is waiting for the response from the Tac HQ. Dit – Dak – Dit.

---

[52] After deployment the teams had only two scheduled comms times with the HQ per day. The Tac HQ, however, maintained a 24-hour listening watch for use in a serious emergency. The signallers of all units were of exceptional quality and held in high esteem by the teams. Over the 25 years covered in this book, communications changed drastically. It started off with B52s, Morse code, OTLP and throw-away battery packs. Then came the Syncal 30s and soon after rechargeable batteries. Next followed the DET and the sat phone.

SPECIALISED COOKING – THE RECCE WAY

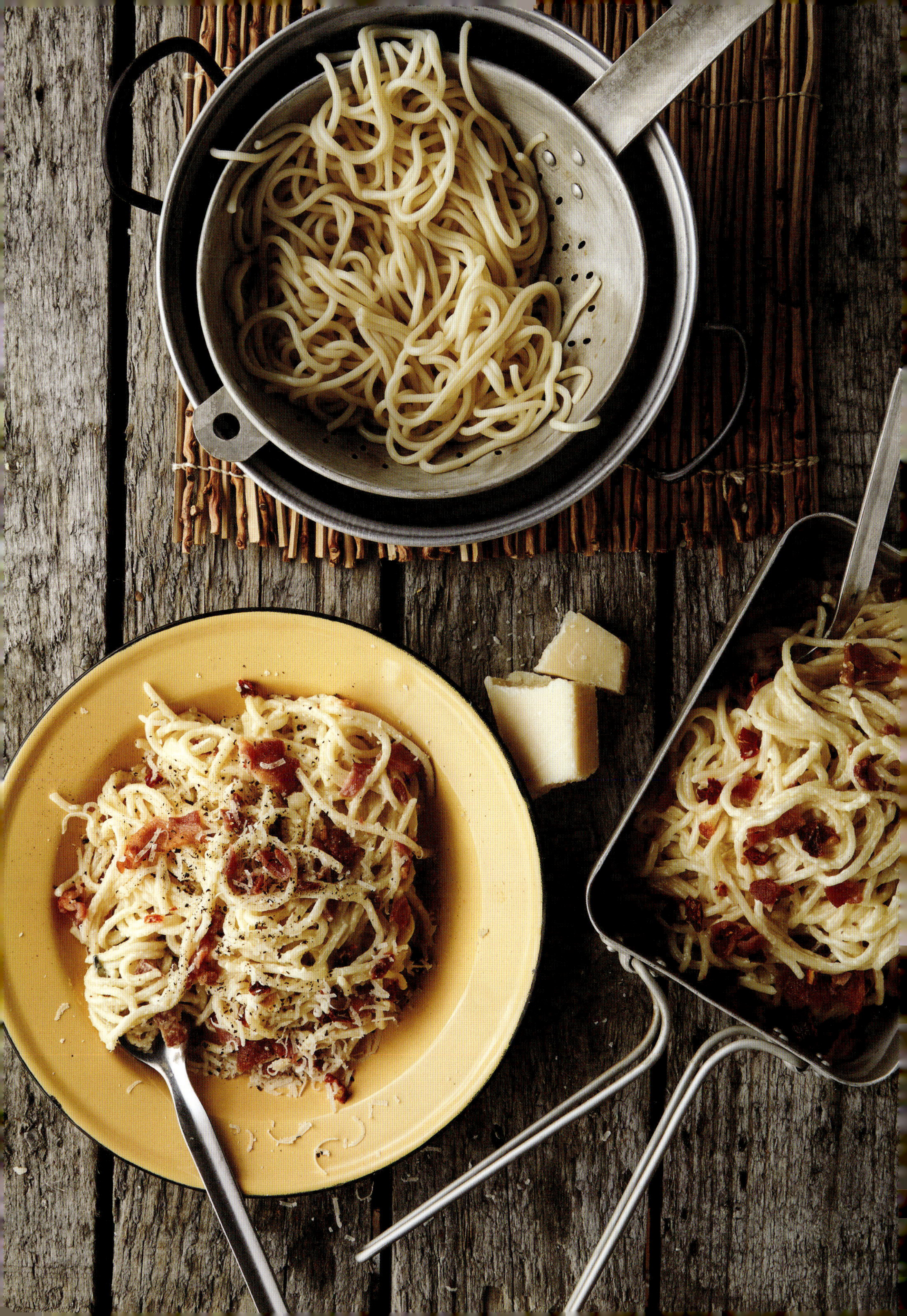

Veggies

SPINACH AND POTATO

Spinach (or other greens)
Water
Salt
Stock cube (optional)
Potatoes, peeled
Salt and pepper
Lemon juice

Chard, wild spinach-like koko (*Gnetum africanum*), marog and many other green leaves make an excellent accompaniment to cooked potato. Use any of these in the following recipe.

Wash spinach leaves thoroughly.

Break leaves into boiling water.

Add salt and, if needed, stock.

Boil potatoes in a separate pot. The potatoes are done when they are almost breaking apart.

Add the cooked potato to the spinach and stir well. The potato should crumble by itself.

Add salt and pepper to taste and a sprinkle of lemon juice.

VARIATION
Replace the potato with sweet potato, or even cassava.

STEAM-FRIED STIR-FRY

Carrot
Cabbage
Onion
Leek
Butternut
Baby marrows
Baby peas
Peppers
Broccoli
Cauliflower
Cooking oil
Water
Salt and pepper
Garlic
Lemon juice

One of the tastiest ways to get some healthy food into your diet is to make a stir-fry. It is also a great way to get people involved in the cooking process. Place the finely sliced and diced array of vegetables in separate bowls and ask your guests to pick their own combinations.

Each serving should not be more than 80 g. Three servings per person is normal. Each guest should try at least five different vegetables with some sauce variations. Offer at least the following sauces: sweet and sour sauce, soy sauce, oyster sauce, red pasta sauce and chutney.

All ingredients need to be sliced/grated really thin so they will cook in under 4 minutes. The name of this recipe comes from the fact that it cooks in the steam of the veggies while you toss and stir it continuously.

Use the cap of the oil bottle to add three capfuls of water and half a cap of oil into the wok. Heat the wok.

Stir vigorously after adding the veggies to allow the steam to do its work. The oil will keep the food from burning. Be sure to add a little lemon juice.

If you ever get a chance to eat this in a street restaurant in Asia, you would think it was a food-tossing competition. That's why we call it 'Steam-Fried Stir-Fry'.

OVEN-ROASTED VEGETABLES

The same principle applies when cooking all chunky, fleshy vegetables. First, you peel and cube the vegetables. Second, you coat them with oil; this will allow the vegetables to roast instead of bake. Remember to preheat your oven or electric frying pan. As an onion lover, you can add onion to any vegetable roast.

Place in the preheated oven and turn every 15 minutes to ensure that all sides stay oiled.

Add cauliflower and broccoli for colour to a mixed roast vegetable dish.

> The more you sweat in peace, the less you bleed in war.

BRINJALS ON THE FIRE

Just the act of making a fire is a good start to any meal. Cooking on it is even better. Whether you do corn on the cob, green peppers or other vegetables, roasting over the fire is sure to improve the taste. The best of all is the brinjal (aubergine).

- Brinjals
- Onions
- Salt
- Garlic
- Rye bread
- Cottage cheese (optional)

Roast the brinjals in the flames, turning regularly.

The skin will go black. The brinjals are fully cooked when the fruit goes softish and you can see bubbles forming under the skin. At this point the skin will start to break.

Allow the brinjals to cool down and then peel off the skin. If the flesh sticks to the skin, just scrape it off with a spoon.

Place all the flesh on a board and chop finely.

Chop onions equally finely. One onion to four brinjals will do.

Add salt and garlic and mix together.

Serve with toasted rye bread as a stand-alone offering.

You can add cottage cheese to the brinjal mix to make an unusual dip.

Table of vegetables and flavouring/roasting time

	Butternut	Pumpkin	Potato	Baby marrow	Cassava	Mixed vegetables
Oil + salt + pepper	Yes	Yes	Yes	Yes	Yes	Yes
Garlic	No	No	Yes	Yes x 2	Yes	Yes
Lemon	No	No	Yes	Yes x 2	Yes	Yes
Secret ingredient	Cinnamon	Sugar		Cheese	Cheese	Cheese
Onion rings	Yes	No	Yes	Yes x 2	Yes	Yes
Roasting time (minutes)	45	30	60	30	60	60

CREAMY RED ONION

Red onions
Blue cheese
Garlic
Lemon juice
Cream or sour cream

For many people the onion serves merely as a taste enhancer, but these recipes make it the star of the show. In many parts of the world, onions are part of the daily rations and are served raw as a stand-alone dish at almost every meal. Don't hesitate to dress and spice it up, but whatever you do, include it and enjoy!

Preheat the oven to 160°C.

Trim roots but leave the outside of the onion intact. Take out the core and fill with blue cheese.

Sprinkle with garlic and lemon juice.

Fill the baking tray with onions so that they don't fall over, and add cream or sour cream.

Bake for 30 minutes.

Take care when presenting on the plate so as to preserve the shape. Serve with finely roasted meats or duck.

> If you find yourself in a fair fight, you didn't plan your mission properly.

SIMPLY ONION

Large onions
Butter
Mustard
Garlic
Salt and pepper

Cover large onions in foil with some butter, mustard, garlic, salt and pepper. One onion per person is enough but have at least one spare for the true onion lovers and vegetarians – they munch these like army worms.

Place in the coals of your braai; if the coals are hot then 20 minutes with frequent turning is adequate, but if the onions are on the side they can take as long as 45 minutes. Once opened, the onion will complete any braaied offering.

Serve with salt and pepper.

RED ONION AND MEATBALLS

Red onions
Sugar
Salt
Sweet and sour pickles
Meatballs

Red onions have a taste that flows around the mouth. Slice one large onion per person into rings.

Sprinkle with sugar and a pinch of salt. Rub into the onion, as this will take out the burn.

Serve with sweet and sour pickles and meatballs.

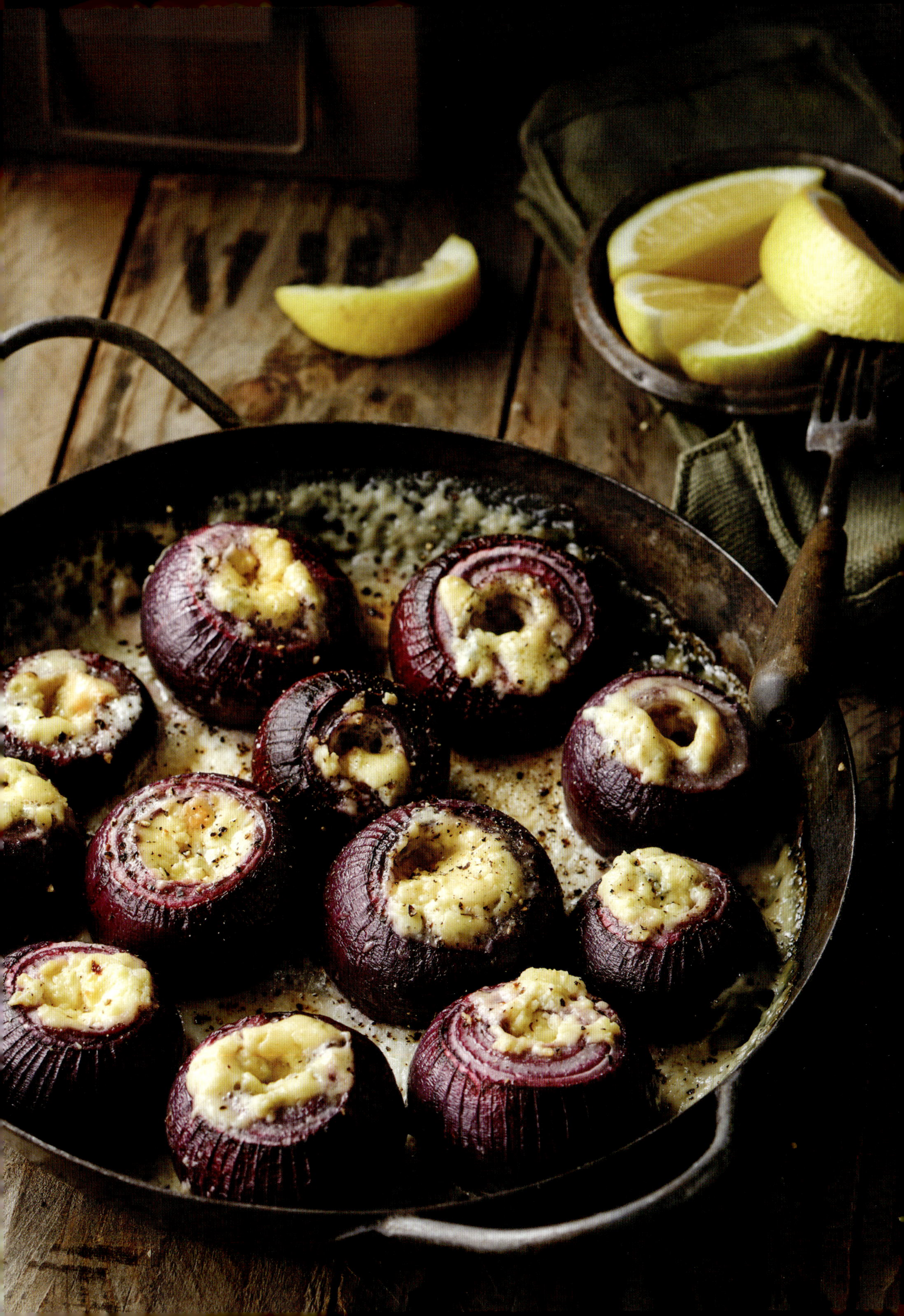

Fruit

There is no substitute for fresh fruit. Whenever you can lay your hands on it out in the bush, eat it. (Cooking with fruit is discussed in Chapter 7.) It also make a great condiment.

All fruits with a firm fresh also fry well. Use a pan with a little bit of oil on low heat. If the fruit is soft already, then it is better to purée it or grate it. Mix with some flour and make patties. You can add nutmeg or cinnamon to the mix and even apples, pears and raisins.

RAISINS

Raisins
Breakfast cereal
Sherry or vodka

Raisins are part of base stock, they are an essential and you should always pack them. Seedless raisins are better but don't be picky.

Raisins go in everything – breakfast cereal, muffins, rice for bobotie, sweet bread, Christmas cake. If soaked in sherry or vodka, raisins can replace cherries in many recipes.

They even make a great beer, with some sugar. That's probably why they are included in ratpacks.

MANGO ATJAR

Mango pieces
Vinegar
Sugar
Onion
Ginger
Red chilli
Salt
Oil

Mangoes are found everywhere. These are easily collected and range from overripe to just starting to get green. When ripe, mangoes make a great base for mango beer, an addition to stews or even just to eat. Mango presents well when it is cut off the stone and quartered into diamonds. When just a bit green and almost starting to get sweet, it makes a great pickle and a great atjar.

Simmer all ingredients together in a pot for about 30 minutes. Spoon into containers and seal.

Pulling a Lemon

Special Forces members on deployment with Unita take some time off to wash in the clear water of an Angolan stream.

Despite careful preparation, we all know that things don't always go according to plan. When an operation goes wrong, we talk about having 'pulled a lemon'. This term is usually used to refer to a self-inflicted negative result caused by poor planning, poor preparation and poor execution, but mostly because of bad information received. Here are a few examples of lemons …

You prepare for a job in Zambia for five weeks. There are rehearsals with the Air Force, repeated ground rehearsals and with agents on the ground. Then you sit and wait for the moment you'll be told to go. You wait a day, then a week. To keep busy, you unpack and re-pack your rucksack. Then word comes and it's a scramble late at night to the departure base. You throw the kit in a truck, speed off to the airfield and get kitted up, only to wait and wait some more. Then you hear that the operation has been called off. This is repeated at least three times over the course of three months before the operation is finally abandoned. Now that's a lemon.

Or, you rehearse for a job for six weeks, then infiltrate to a site in a city. You do the perfect urban raid on the facility – except it is empty. There was a security leak and the place was vacated a day before the raid. Full marks to the enemy.

During Operation Kropduif,[53] the SAAF drops you at the wrong spot and you have to walk some 14 km to reach the target (an enemy base). You report your situation and suggest calling off the operation, but you are ordered to attack regardless. Without the element of surprise and the cover of darkness, you are in a bad position. The enemy is ready when you arrive in mid-afternoon. In the opening exchange you lose seven men, and from there the battle is about limiting your losses and doing whatever is needed to stay alive.

As always, there is a positive side to everything. Each lemon teaches you a lesson. For one, if nobody knows what you are doing, nobody can find out about it, so don't tell anybody anything about the operation before or after it takes place.

---

[53] Operation Kropduif, aka Eheke, in 1977 involved the worst loss of life in a single contact, with seven people being killed in the opening exchange of fire.

Salad

> Left to themselves, things tend to go from bad to worse.

If you consider that tomatoes and carrots have only 20 kJ/100 g compared to meat at 800 kJ/100 g, then it is clear that you will never pack a rucksack with tomatoes and carrots and deploy for a week. As we noted in the introduction, fresh rations are opportunity food, so learn how to exploit it when you get it. Wash carefully!

Salad is the ultimate artistic meal. Anything goes. Therefore salads are best approached as you would an empty canvas: start with a basic foundation and then add the layers to complete the picture.

Start with a base of green and add reds, yellows and whites. Colourful inclusions of purple and orange also present well. Finish with a focal point. Remember, each artist has his/her own style, so don't feel bound by specific styles. Go and play.

SALAD COMBINATIONS

Carrot and pineapple	Grated carrot and pineapple or pine nuts. Sprinkle with sugar and Oros
Broccoli salad	Lightly steamed pieces with salt, pepper and a mix of mayo and yoghurt
Cauliflower base	Lightly steamed pieces with salt, pepper and a mix of mayo and yoghurt or cottage cheese
Greek salad	Tomato and onion sliced or cut in half on a bed of lettuce, with olive oil, vinaigrette, garlic, olives, salt and pepper
Coleslaw	Grated cabbage and carrot, with mayo and raisins
Beetroot	Grated apple, beetroot and onion with yoghurt and mayo
Potato salad	Potato, eggs, peas and pickle with mustard and mayo
Brinjal salad	Fire-roasted brinjal with garlic and salt

Pickles

Anything can be pickled. It is a good way to keep veggies fresh for longer and the taste is perfect for some dishes. Pickles are handy to make and store and use bit by bit. If it is just about preserving the pickle, use as little salt and vinegar as needed, as it only has to last a few weeks. If you want it to stand for months, then a bit more vinegar may be needed.

1 litre water
300 ml vinegar
1 teaspoon salt
1 teaspoon sugar

Selected vegetables – carrots, onions, patty pans, cucumbers, green tomatoes, cauliflower

Mix water, vinegar, salt and sugar together and bring to a boil. Allow to cool down completely.

Wash and rinse the containers – even if you are using 20-litre drums.

Fill with veggies of same consistency. For example:

Mix 1: Carrots, onions, patty pans, cucumbers

Mix 2: Cucumbers and onions

Mix 3: Green tomatoes

Mix 4: Cauliflower and carrots

Then add any of the following to the mix as flavourings: celery, garlic, thyme.

Add cooled pickling liquid and close the containers.

If you are using soft veggies, then 4 days is adequate pickling time. If the veggies are hard, such as carrots, leave them for a few days longer.

Sweet and sour is good as a snack, so add more sugar if you like.

> Someday someone may kill you with your own gun, but they should have to beat you to death with it because it is empty.

Recruits and their instructors on an advanced reconnaissance course at Hell's Gate in Northern Natal with members of the French Special Operations Command (SOC). At the back, from left to right: SOC member, CC Victorino, José da Costa, Koos Stadler, Neves Matias and Japie Kloppers. In front: Faustino da Silva, SOC member, Arno van der Merwe, Steve Seloane, John Dednam and Ric Nicol.

IF IT GROWS

FOR THE RECORD

Special Forces

GOCs ROLL

Major General FW (Fritz) Loots	1974–1982
Major General AJ (Kat) Liebenberg	1982–1985
Major General AJM (Joep) Joubert	1985–1988
Major General E (Eddie) Webb	1989–1991
Colonel M Kinghorn	1991–1992 (acting)
Brigadier JC (Jakes) Swart	1992–1993
Colonel JJ (Hannes) Venter	1994–1994 (acting)
Brigadier CJ (Borries) Borman	1995–1998

WOs ROLL

WO1 PP (Pep) van Zyl	1988–1992
WO1 WJ (Koos) Loots	1996–2008

Founding members

By October 1971, this group consisted of:
Commandant JD (Jan) Breytenbach
Major DP (Dan) Lamprecht
Captain JR (John) More
Captain PJ (Fires) van Vuuren
WO2 TI (Trevor) Floyd
WO2 MJ (Yogi) Potgieter
WO2 FC (Frans) van Zyl
Staff sergeant JJ (Koos) Moorcroft
Staff sergeant JL (Kenaas) Conradie
Staff sergeant DL (Dewald) de Beer
Sergeant JJP (Hopkop/Hoppie) Fourie
Lance Corporal J (Jimmy) Oberholzer
Lance Corporal FG (Wannies) Wannenburg
Lance Corporal DG (Dave) Tippet

It was 'tradition' at formal events for the seniors to do a mock parachute jump off the tables with Jakes Swart (second from left) checking the 'jumpers' before Koos Moorcroft (far right) would despatch them.

True Recces, like Brigadier Jakes Swart, swallow crayfish whole...

Colonel Ewald Olckers at a formal dinner.

The EMLC buildings where all specialised equipment were manufactured.

ABOVE At a memorial at Speskop, headquarters of the Special Forces in Pretoria.

RIGHT A gathering of unit commanders and RSMs in about 1989, with then Minister of Defence Magnus Malan in the centre. From left to right: Pep van Zyl, Fritz Loots, Struis Strydom, Sybrand van der Spuy, Koos Loots, Boats Botes, Hannes Venter, Magnus Malan, Gert Keulder, Jerry Booysen, Burt Sachse, Joep Joubert, unknown and JC Swart.

ABOVE Colonel James Hills of 5 Recce.

LEFT A payslip from back in the day.

IF IT GROWS 149

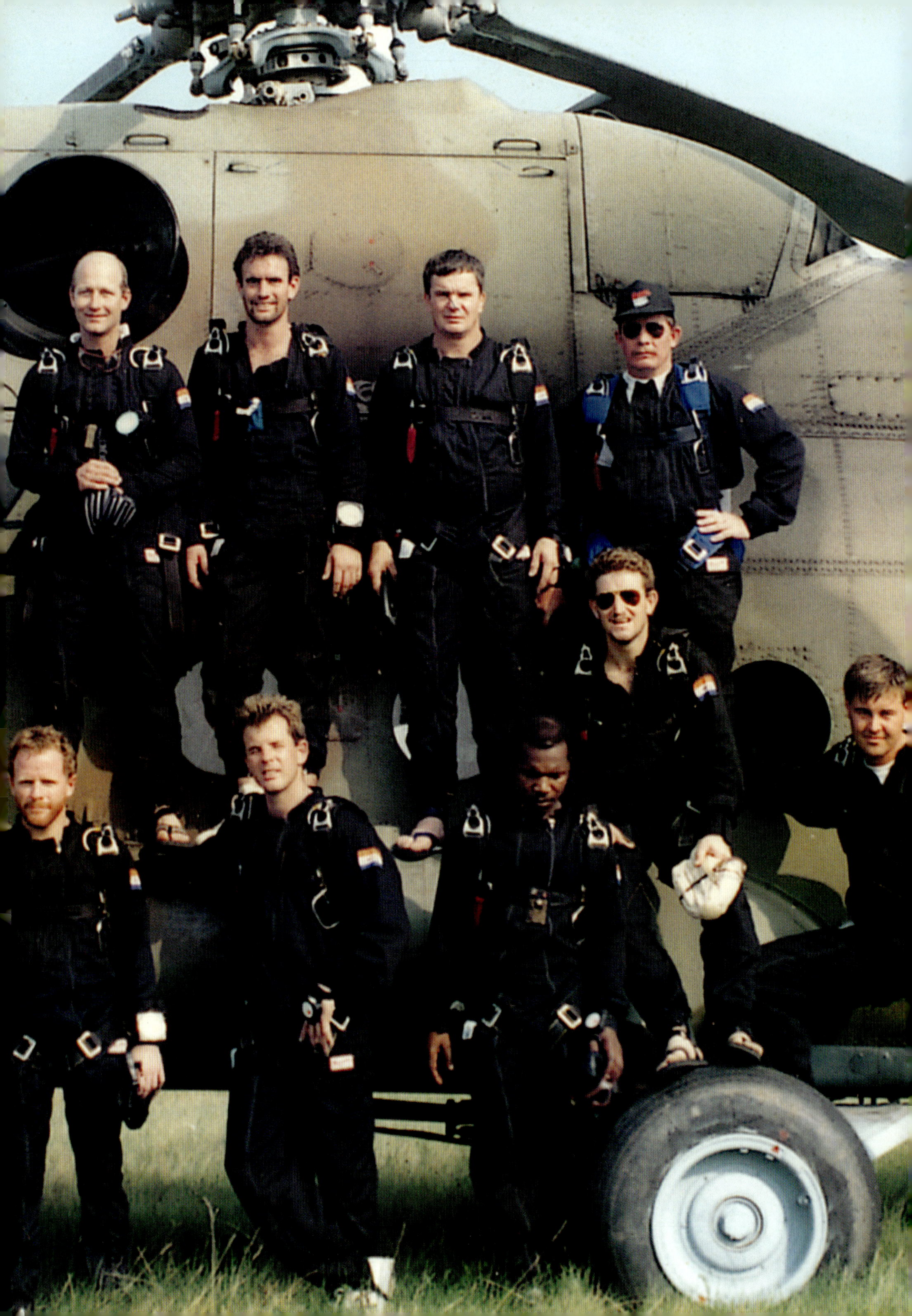

6

REGIONAL FLAVOURS

The Special Forces use the black-and-white compass rose as their base emblem. This symbolises the manner in which they operate – by day and night, by land air and sea, and in any direction. The previous chapters featured recipes from the sea, the air and the land. This chapter goes in new directions, both on the African continent and abroad.

As the age-old saying goes – the enemy of my enemy is my friend, and the friend of my enemy is my enemy. This holds true to this day. The apartheid government saw communism as the major threat, both at home and on the African continent, and was therefore very concerned when a number of communist parties were elected, or came to power, in countries bordering South Africa. The Special Forces participated in many pre-emptive and clandestine operations to assist the forces opposing these parties.

So, in this chapter you can expect to find recipes from countries with which the South African government had an alliance of sorts, from Zaire (DRC) and Israel in the past to the Central African Republic in recent times. In the following pages we travel back to these areas to revive some of the most interesting dishes we encountered.

The first 'relationship building' delegation to visit Russia in 1993, after the fall of communism, consisted of members of the Special Forces and the Police Task Force. The visit was built around parachuting exercises, using different techniques and sharing parachuting styles.

Kaokoland

Kaokoland stretches broadly from the Hoanib River up the west coast of Namibia to the Cunene River in the north, which is also the border with Angola. Apart from the spectacular Cunene River, with its impressive waterfalls, the area is arid. However, what makes this semi-desert landscape so dramatic are its rugged mountains.

On the Angolan side of the river you'll find the impressive Calueque hydroelectric scheme, where the first and last incident of the Border War took place. Operating in the dry, hilly terrain is challenging for soldiers and local hunter-gatherers alike, and dictates a particular type of warfare.

When deploying in Kaokoland, you have to take everything you need with you, especially water. The opportunities for finding food are limited and your survival will depend on your ability to find water in the riverbeds and mountain crevices.

The area is largely unpopulated, but on deployment you could expect to meet members of the semi-nomadic Himba people. They live off seasonal food that is augmented by limited subsistence farming and meat from their goats and cattle. Most Himba lived in then South West Africa (Namibia), although a minority were based in Angola. During the Border War, this was a low-intensity warfare arena, so the Himba were for a time mostly unaffected by the fighting.

Once a patrol walked past a Himba village some 90 km into Angola. A Himba woman, her face smeared red with ochre and glistening in the sun, looked with interest at the blackened faces of the 1 Recce patrol. She had never seen people with white skin before. Such reactions changed during the latter part of the conflict as the Himba were increasingly displaced by drought and forced enlistment into Plan/Swapo.[54]

PORRIDGE AND SOUR MILK

Maize meal
Salt
Water
Cooking oil

The staple food in Kaokoland is pap (porridge). It is mostly made from maize but also from mahangu (pearl millet). The maize kernels are pounded in hollow vessels with logs or any other stamper. Then the coarse flour is boiled in water with some salt in a pot on an open flame. Sometimes cooking oil is added.

The porridge is eaten in the morning but also for dinner, when it is served with seasonal field vegetables. Milk is provided by goats and cattle but turns sour very quickly due to the heat.

---

[54] The People's Liberation Army of Namibia (Plan) was the armed wing of the South West Africa People's Organization (Swapo), the Namibian liberation movement.

Fort Nomad at Ruacana

Deployment from Kaokoland into Angola was intermittent, and this is how Fort Nomad got its name. The deployments from here were mainly directed against Swapo targets. Deployment from Fort Nomad first entailed a 190-km drive from Ondangwa, passing through the towns of Oshikuku and Outapi. The base would be set up close to the airfield runway at Ruacana so the Recces could walk to the helicopters for deployment.

In this sparsely vegetated area, with no trees and little grass, there was little scope to choose a suitable base site. Thus the base would be set up, in true military style, with army tents on the bright white sand. Standard army cooking was done out of 50-man mobile kitchen units, and the food was served in the mess tent. For deployments with vehicles, a mobile workshop would also be deployed.

Deployments from Fort Nomad were generally part of a three-stage process involving first reconnaissance, then search and then attack. This usually meant that the base-bound troops had much spare time. This rarely led to anything good. If you stayed there long enough, you would end up learning how to drive an Eland 90 armoured car (known as the 'Noddy car'), fire the 20 mm Oerlikons from the anti-aircraft pavilions and even do a few exercises with the air supply units at Epupa Falls before you deployed.

Alternatively, you would spend a lot of time with Oom Pote studying black-and-white aerial photos taken by a drone (yes, we had drones in 1982, only they were very big and the resolution was not that great).

MOPANE WORMS

In Kaokoland, mopane worms are standard on the menu. The worms come out with the first rains and proliferate like manna from heaven. There are three ways to prepare this seasonal delicacy.

BRAAI
Gather enough mopanes until you have filled a bowl or satchel. As you collect them, remove the head and gently squeeze from the back to remove the innards. If you have water, you can rinse the worms, but this is not essential. String them on a wet piece of wood as you would for kebabs. There are small hairs on the worms, but the fire will burn these off. Baste with salt, lemon juice and garlic in oil as you braai them over slow coals. It's not quite fillet steak, but they are very nutritious and surprisingly tasty when served with some salt and Tabasco sauce.

FRY
This method requires a fair bit of oil, so is not the best if you are on the march. However, if you are accompanied by vehicles, there should be enough oil. Clean the mopane worms as per above and rinse with water. Cut into three and fry in ample oil. You'll notice that the texture of the worms becomes more crunchy as they fry. Drizzle with your Tabasco and lemon juice before serving.

DRY
In these parts, mopane worms are most commonly eaten dried, since this is the best way to preserve them. The dried worms can be packed and eaten just like biltong. However, dried mopanes are pretty tasteless and eating them feels a bit like eating cardboard, but a true specialised chef will turn even this into something special. Grind the dry mopane worms into a powder and use it in a red sauce (see page 18). Soy sauce or Worcestershire sauce goes exceptionally well with this.

Mopane worms
Salt
Fresh lemon juice
Garlic
Cooking oil
Tabasco sauce
Soy sauce

ABOVE Warning signs at Fort Nomad.
BELOW The colourful mopane worm will look good on any table.
NEXT PAGE Kaokoland in northern Namibia.

REGIONAL FLAVOURS

> Though we have heard of stupid haste in war, cleverness has never been seen associated with long delays.
>
> SUN TZU, THE ART OF WAR

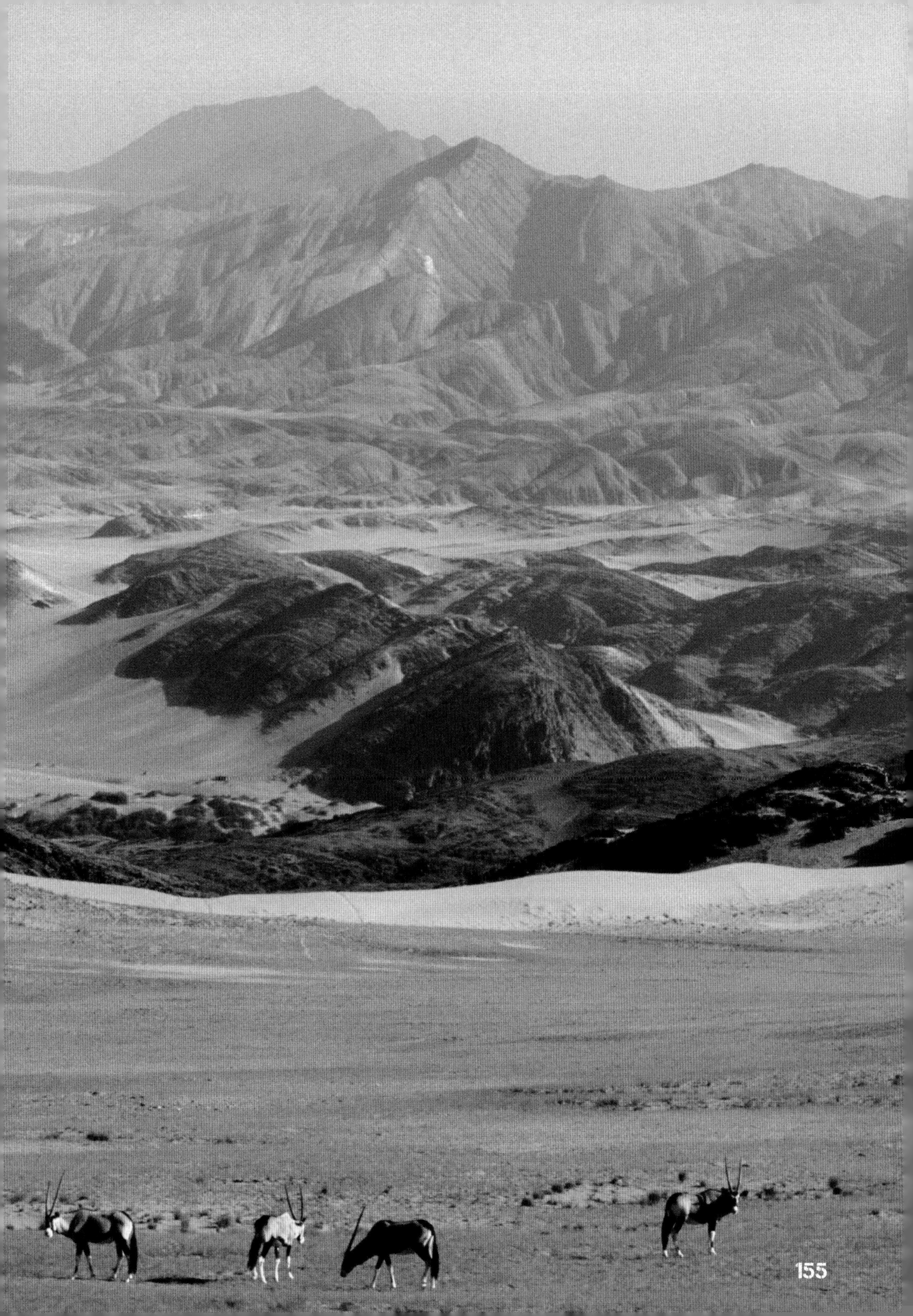

Ovamboland

Ovamboland is mainly an arid alluvial floodplain on top of pot clay with *shona*s (watercourses) or *omiramba* (dry river bed) running alongside the Kuvelai River. In the rainy season, almost 50 per cent of the area is under water as the shallow *shona*s quickly fill up. The *shona*s are dotted with open, unlined wells that provide water to homesteads or kraals.

The Ovambo people plant mahangu and also slaughter animals from time to time. The landscape dominates the cuisine, so expect seasonal fare with mopane worms in spring and small fish during the rainy season. In the dry season, from the end of March to November, sour milk and hand-ground mahangu from the granaries provide the bulk of meals. This is probably not everyone's idea of culinary Eden and only for lovers of the unusual.

For some variety after weeks of army food, you could always check yourself into an Oshakati guesthouse …

LBJ STEW[55] RECIPE

Four LBJs
Hand-ground mahangu flour
Water
Salt

At one time, Recce teams regularly carried out pseudo-operations in Ovamboland. During deployment, the teams – no more than three operators – would disguise themselves as Swapo fighters. The drill was to deploy with whatever the enemy would have available, which meant that you tried as best you could to live as they did. So, you carried only a satchel with the basics and took no (or limited) food along.

Given that there were no white Swapo soldiers, white operators would remain hidden by day. While your black buddy would eat when he visited the local kraals, you could only watch through the night sights. You therefore lived entirely off whatever your black buddy brought back from his visits without looking suspicious. Forget about Banting and Atkins; this is a serious weight-loss plan.

A pseudo-operation team wearing all the right attire.

VARIATIONS

Add two scoops of sand. This will help you to master the technique of not biting down on food but simply rolling it around in your mouth before swallowing. This technique will become very helpful in old age. Whatever you do, don't chew!

Deploy in a buddy pair with a black buddy for three weeks. Just don't pick an operator like Nailokki, because then you will get food only every third day. Pack only one tin of food (per week) for when things get really desperate.

At dinnertime, study the movements around the kraal with your night sights as your buddy enters the kraal as a Swapo operative. When you spot someone sneaking away, try not to get too excited. Send the location of the kraal to your base by DET.[56]

You'll get even more excited when your buddy returns with some food, even if it is cooked LBJs with some salt and mahangu pap in a broken plastic bag. Be grateful it wasn't made from sparrows or rats. Don't look too closely at the stew; you might discover it was mixed with crickets and other things.

If served with potatoes or onions, consider it a special event.

---

[55] LBJ stands for 'little brown jobs', and refers to small black or brown birds, including quelea, sparrows, finches, etc.

[56] DET stands for 'data entry terminal'. These devices were introduced in the mid-1980s and allowed operators to type messages into the terminal and send by radio. Over time, it replaced Morse code as the main medium to transmit messages.

SPECIALISED COOKING – THE RECCE WAY

LATE-NIGHT GOAT IN STRIPS

After three weeks on a pseudo-operation, it will be very easy for you to follow this recipe. All it requires is that you should be part of a group of very hungry and dirty operators whose last meal was LBJ Stew.

You'll find that you'll start thinking differently about the bleating goats you have been listening to for days on end.

Advise and convince the six other team leaders deployed in your area to rendezvous (RV) for an impromptu goat braai. Walk some 25 km to the agreed point. The point has to be carefully chosen to accommodate a large group that can completely hide itself. (Buks Buys, as the senior at the time and overall in charge, will work it out for you.) Allow five hours to get to the meeting point, which means you'll turn up around midnight.

Assign a goat-stealing party – four individuals should suffice. Martin Smith and Schalk Prinsloo are excellent candidates. Sneak into the kraal. The clear instruction will be to swiftly and quietly break the neck of the goat and leave no blood. After trying to twist the goat's head a few times you'll finally realise this method is not working. Strangle the goat.

Do your best anti-tracking on the way out. Walk some 5 km with the goat to the designated braai area and start the skinning and cooking process.

Skin the goat as you would any buck while other team members look for green saplings in the bush. Cut/hack the meat into large pieces. Then take your small knife and cut the chunks into strips.

Start a fire. Create a 'table' from the saplings, which should be built over the fire. Roast the meat by laying it on the sapling table. Whoever has salt should share it. Once the meat is cooked, eat with haste – daylight is coming.

At first sign of light, dig pits to bury any skin and intestines left over. Break up into smaller groups and fan out at least four kilometres to disappear and hide.

1 kraal with goats
18 hungry operators
Salt

VARIATION

Replace the goat with a sheep. However, for that wild and tough taste that lingers, goat is the best.

REGIONAL FLAVOURS

The Kavango

The Kavango region stretched more or less from the town of Oshikoto in the west and ended at the bases Omega and Buffalo, in the east. It was at the western end of the Caprivi Strip (today the Zambezi Region). During the Border War, over half of its population existed in simple, subsistence-type conditions. The local tribes stayed along the river, and so fish made up a large part of their diet. The locals also farmed on the banks of the rivers. The desert-like southern part of the region has been home to the San people for centuries.

The Kavango is flat to the extreme. The town of Eenhana is at an elevation of 1 121 m, with Rundu and Omega at 1 065 m. Over a distance of over 150 km between these towns, the difference in elevation is therefore a mere 56 m.

While the Kavango starts out fairly featureless in the west, there are more trees and fewer people the further east you go. By the time you reach the Okavango River, it has transformed into full miombo woodland, with spectacular river views over grassy plains.

The biggest towns in the Kavango are Rundu, which also had an army base, and Divundu. While Rundu was at the centre of the operations with Unita into Angola, there were a few additional bases with specialised units. Buffalo, on the Okavango River, hosted 32 Battalion. Today, the site of the base is inside a nature reserve.

Omega was the home of 31 Battalion, a Bushman (San) unit. Many a plane filled with hopefuls would arrive at night at Omega on a C-130 for the selection course. From there they would be taken to the Fort Doppies area and go straight into the course.

Fort Foot

Like all other Recce bases, the one at Rundu was built inside the perimeter of the air base. Over an extended period, several regular operations by all the units (1, 4 and 5 Recce) took place from Fort Foot.

This facility was built purely as a staging station and only had room for members on their way into or out of deployments. It was built in a quadrant and had simple rooms with eight bunk beds per room. All the rooms faced inwards and were connected by a veranda. The courtyard was covered in good buffalo grass. In the centre was the heart of the Fort; yes, you guessed right – the pub.

Deployments from here were generally longer-term bush operations that required a fair amount of interaction with Unita. This meant that preparations were done before arrival and the deployment started within a week after your arrival.

The work done from Fort Foot spanned the entire spectrum – from parachute deployment, specialised

Playing bridge at Fort Foot after a long SA-7 deployment with Unita. From left to right: Albie Heigers, Justin Vermaak, Renier van der Merwe, Crokes Croucamp, Anton Benade and Sean Mullen.

vehicle raids, ground assaults, airborne assaults and Unita-supported operations to conventional deployments with battle groups in major operations such as Protea, Meebos, Moduler and Hooper.

BILTONG AND EGG SOUFFLÉ
à la Villa Nova

For the average Special Forces member, it is tremendously exciting to do a specialised vehicle deployment for the first time. The idea that you don't have to carry a 55-kg rucksack over vast distances changes your whole perspective.

There will be adequate water, you will be able to make a fire once in a while, and you can even take fresh eggs along. Wrap the eggs in the cloth used to clean the mortar tube and stow in an empty tube of one of the mortar canisters. Add to this a mounted 81 mm mortar, a 106 mm recoilless gun, a four-barrel 14.5 mm Russian anti-aircraft gun and a towed Zu-23 anti-aircraft gun between the five vehicles and your 15-man team will feel like an entire army and quite invincible.

The 250-km drive in the soft sand through the bush takes about eight days. Being ambushed is a real threat, so it is a stop-start affair, especially if one of the Unita soldiers with you has an AD (accidental discharge) on day three and everyone debusses ready for action.

Once you've reached the forward base area, proceed to isolate the town. You can ask Theron Venter to innovate by using his 106 mm in long-range mode[57] every time an aircraft approaches the town.

You can help stop the retaliation party from the town by supporting Unita in ground-role patrols. If required, demonstrate the use of the 81 mm mortar in a fire-and-movement type attack until the mortar is so hot it actually cooks off. Be mindful of the enemy's 82 mm rockets; they are deadly accurate when used in reactive bombardments.

The eggs will last about 14 days, so take them out when you need a treat. This meal serves one buddy pair.

Make a fire in a small hole in the sand (to prevent the glow being spotted from the air).

In your dixie, sauté thinly diced slices of onion in a mixture of water and cooking oil.

Break two eggs in a plastic ratpack bag. Add a dash of water, salt, self-raising flour and spices. If you still have biltong left, add it too. Shake to mix all the ingredients.

Pour over onions and cover with the dixie lid. Cook for about 20 minutes.

Serve with the tinned tomatoes.

Onions, diced
Water
Cooking oil
Eggs
Salt
Self-raising flour
Spices
Biltong (or tinned viennas), diced
1 tin of tomatoes

TIPS
The flies can be a real bother, so rather make this meal at last light.

Also, some other members may not have packed enough food; this is another reason to eat in the dark. Cook downwind of them to avoid a surprise visit.

When you act as an instructor for Unita you have the rare privilege of a small table to eat and work at.

---

57 The 106 mm recoilless gun is designed as an anti-tank weapon and is hardly ever used over more than 1 200 m. In this application, the barrel is elevated just like an artillery piece and is used like artillery. The 106 mm projectile has a range of just over 6 km when used in this way. It is not recommended but it works as a deterrent to scare off the approaching aircraft.

KAVANGO LAMB SHANK

à la Oom Koos

by Koos Moorcroft, Koos Loots, John Heyns and Chris Oosthuizen

4 lamb shanks
Cooking oil
Water
Garlic
3 large onions, diced
15 baby potatoes
Cherry tomatoes
1 red pepper
Cabbage, diced
Chillies
Barbecue spice
Steak and chop spice
Italian herbs
1 packet of mushrooms
Butternut
Rice
Turmeric
Bisto
Corn flour (Maizena)

After 30-plus years in the army you deserve to do something different during your retirement. Start a professional training company with old comrades to train and teach in beautiful Namibia. Get together on the banks of the Okavango River on a Sunday to cook a MasterChef version of a lamb shank potjie.

Set up your site so you'll have a decent view of the elephant and buffalo that come to drink at the river. This recipe was last cooked on 6 March 2016. The master bush chef in attendance was Koos Loots. The support group consisted of Koos Moorcroft, John Heyns and Chris Oosthuizen.

Heat the potjie and then brown the meat in some oil. Add a half cup of water and let it simmer for an hour.

Add the garlic and vegetables and let them simmer for an additional four hours. Flavour with your favourite spices.

After three hours, add the diced mushrooms (no, not a vegetable!) as well as the butternut pieces.

Cook the rice in a separate pot and add two to three teaspoons of turmeric.

Thicken the gravy by adding two teaspoons of Bisto and one teaspoon of corn flour to 100 ml of cold water. Stir well before adding this to the potjie.

Simmer for 30 minutes.

Open some chilled wine and enjoy the meal.

EDITORS' NOTE

This recipe is published as it was received. However, some variation on the timing of the chilled wine is allowed. No self-respecting Recce will wait six and a half hours before having a glass of wine with a potjie. Even if you started the pot at 06h00, this would be too much to ask. The editors have also been made aware that the huge amount of beer that was consumed before the wine was purposefully omitted.

The legendary Koos Moorcroft still lives out his passion for the bush by doing regular tours up the Angolan West Coast, as well as to Namibia, Botswana and Zambia.

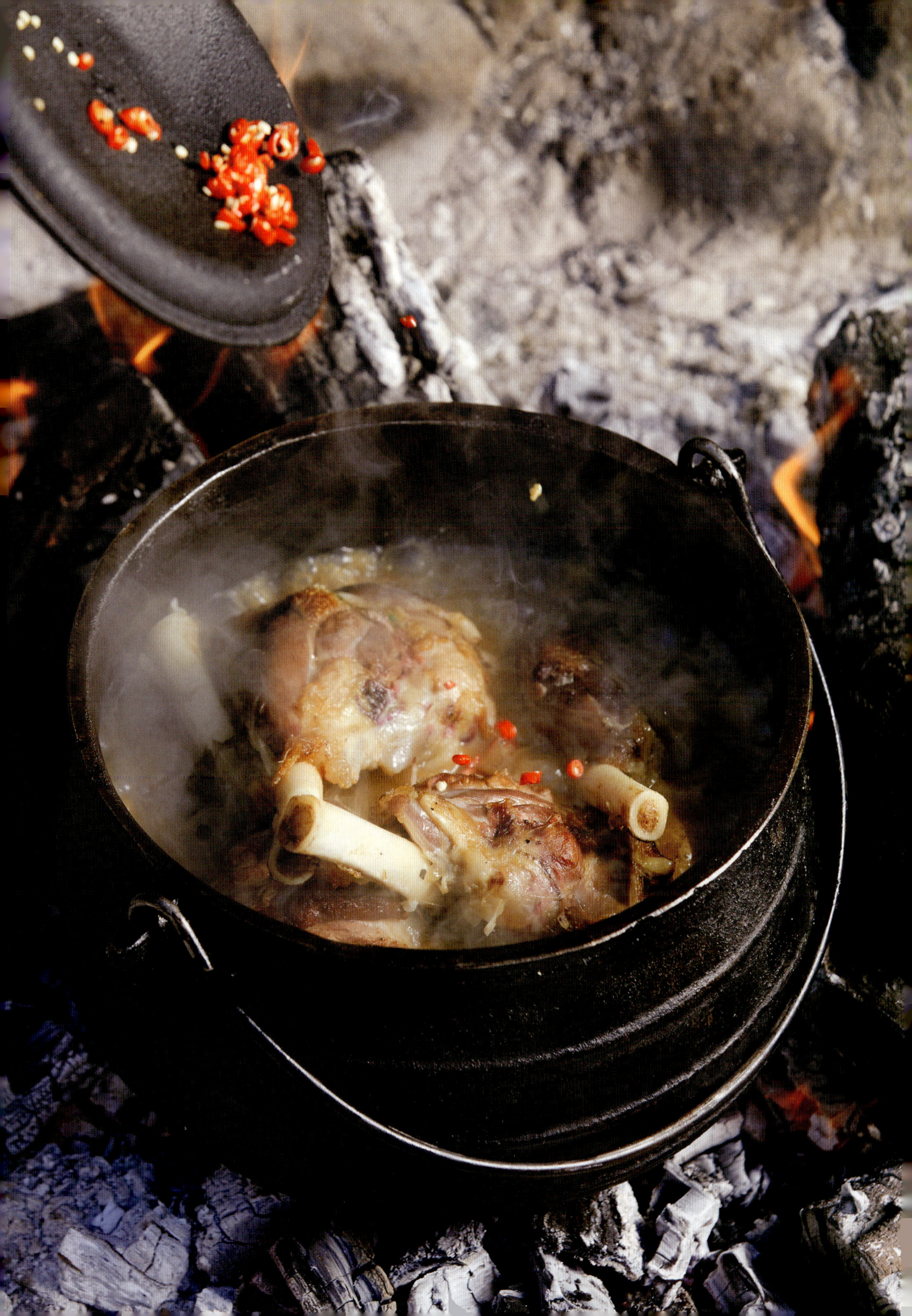

The Caprivi Strip

The Caprivi Strip became German territory in 1890 as part of an exchange with Great Britain in which Germany gave up its claim to the island of Zanzibar. At the time, the Germans wanted to link German South West Africa (Namibia) to German East Africa (Tanzania). The strip, originally named after German chancellor Leo von Caprivi, who negotiated the deal with Great Britain, was renamed the Zambezi Region in 2013.

Four rivers flow through or along the borders of the Caprivi: the Okavango, Kwando, Chobe and Zambezi. This strip of land contains a diversity of local tribes, including the San. In the east, at Katima Mulilo and Mpacha, the Caprivi is quite densely populated, since these towns lie on the main road to Zambia. With so much water and wildlife, meat is a staple food in the region.

Four international borders – Zambia, Namibia, Botswana and Zimbabwe – meet at Impalile Island, in the Zambezi floodplain at the far eastern end of the Caprivi. Today, the area is in reality one large national reserve with the Bwabwata, Mudumu and Nkasa Rupara national parks all contained within it. The region is very flat but interspersed with dry river beds called *omirambas* (singular: *omuramba*).

Fort Doppies

(also see p. 47)

Fort Doppies was situated on the high banks of the Kwando River at Kongola. During the Border War, this base was in many ways the heart and soul of the Recces. It served as the training ground for the selection, survival and minor tactics courses, and retraining was also done here. In addition, it acted as a staging post for numerous operations. When required, it also hosted politicians and negotiators for discreet meetings with Unita leader Jonas Savimbi and others.

The demarcated Doppies training area covered 33 km by 31 km – just about 100 000 ha. Beyond that, in all directions lay a further 100 km of bush with little or no local population and no fences. It was a true wilderness covered with miombo woodland interspersed with *omirambas* and dunes.

Training here was done in the most natural environment that existed. Even though we knew our own lion's name, it didn't help. There were many more lions and other wild animals in the area. It was not uncommon for operators and Recce hopefuls to be attacked by hippos, charged by buffaloes or chased by elephants.

Still, this was where we learned two very important lessons that are dear to all Recce soldiers: to respect nature, and that the bush is neutral.

A group of the 'ou manne' at Fort Doppies probably in 1976. Their long hair indicates how much time they had spent in the bush.

162 SPECIALISED COOKING – THE RECCE WAY

PUTU AND COKE

Unita soldiers on the urban course at the St Michelle base in the Caprivi Strip in 1986. No matter how deep into the bush you are, soldiers will find a way to play soccer.

In the 1980s, specialist training for Unita troops often took place at the St Michelle training area in the north of Fort Doppies. If you were sent there to present the specialist urban operations course, you could expect to meet guys like Captain Derek (Vossie) Vorster, James Teitge, André Cloete and Dirk Steenkamp.

Training the Unita soldiers presented a number of unique challenges, so once again you had to be able to adjust, adapt and move on to plan B if plan A didn't work. If you were chief instructor on the urban operations course, the first few lectures to the select group of 30 students would be on how to pass through roadblocks with their 'specialised tools'.

You would start by showing them the adapted PE4 explosives, which look exactly like putu pap (a product supplied courtesy of EMLC).[58] You would demonstrate how this special PE4 can be packed in a normal lunch container to look like food. You could also show them how to use liquid Semtex, which was adapted to look like Coke.

This is the easy part. The difficult part starts when you explain to them how to place the putu in a flush toilet at the target and activate the trigger mechanism. You will notice the *donkiepoepol* frowns (ask your Afrikaans friend to explain) all around. Stop the lecture to inquire. You'll soon learn that none of your Unita students has ever been to a major city nor has even seen a flush toilet! Stop the lecture.

Load them on a truck the next day and drive the 120 km to Katima Mulilo. There they will experience the town of Katima and the airport at Mpacha with the same amazement as a child on his first visit to Disneyland. Katima then had a population of only 15 000 people, but they won't stop gawking at this 'modern city'.

Use this opportunity to show how you can think on your feet. While the men eat (real) putu and Coke you ordered for them at the restaurant overlooking the Zambezi, go to the local building supply store to buy a flush toilet. Jan van der Merwe of MI will look after the men while you are gone. Take the toilet back for them to practise on.

---

[58] 'EMLC' refers to a subsidiary of Armscor that provided specialised weaponry to the Special Forces and accessed the services of specialists such as Dr Vernon Joynt. In Afrikaans, EMLC stands for Elektriese, meganiese, landboukundige en chemiese ingenieurskonsultante (electrical, mechanical, agricultural and chemical engineering consultants).

REGIONAL FLAVOURS

Buffalo Steaks

Bushman style

The Border War required Special Forces operators to have pretty serious bushcraft skills. To learn these skills, lengthy courses on survival, tracking and food augmentation in the field were presented.

The Doppies camp had a full complement of Bushmen, who lived close to the base and were integral to the training in the base area. If a survival course was in progress, the city boys would soon get their first lesson from the Bushmen in how to hunt and skin a buck. (Buffalo was seen as the prize meat. These animals not only provide a huge quantity of meat but also taste amazingly similar to beef but with less fat.)

Hunting with the Bushmen teaches you about having respect for nature and wildlife. Once you have tracked an animal with your Bushman guide, you make the shot by staying calm and fighting *bokkoors*. If you killed it, it's important to pay respect to the animal before you start cutting it up. The Bushmen normally say a small prayer thanking the animal for sacrificing its life for you.

A big challenge is cutting up an animal on its skin without getting any sand on the meat. Old Ben the Bushman will

Ian Strange risks his life as he tries to place a rope around a buffalo stuck in the mud. Today it needs help to get out; tomorrow the relationship between man and animal will be neutral again.

show you how to do this and where to find the softest steak right at the bottom of the fillet.

Make a fire – just like he taught you – and braai the meat right there in the middle of the bush. All you'll hear are the sounds of the bush and the clicking sounds of the Bushmen instructors. Smell the bush and the grass and breathe in deeply! It's clean and it's beautiful.

The meat will taste like nothing you've tasted before. Savour the moment and let it etch into your memory and your soul. You have just been accepted into the bush.

Survival Biltong

When you come upon food in the bush (read: game), you should make the most of it. While you won't have any refrigeration facilities and can't stay in one area for too long, you can always make biltong. Think long, wide pieces of rump with that perfect strip of fat on the side. But you better be quick about it.

You need your meat dry in 48 hours, so cut little strips as thick as your fingers. Find an appropriate tree with enough branches; a thorn bush or jackalberry will do. Within two days the meat should be dry enough to pack away in a backpack bag. When you have a chance, air the biltong to keep the mould away.

If you have just shot your first buffalo, take your time to make proper biltong. Cut a front quarter into normal biltong-sized strips. Find some dried coriander, vinegar, salt and pepper and marinate the meat in big pots for at least a day. Turn it once. Then hang the pieces in the drying room at Fort Doppies. (If you're out in the Doppies area, you'll need strong wire mesh covered with mosquito net gauze to keep out flies as well as Terry the Lion, the hyenas and the monkeys.

A week later, your biltong should be good to go – dry on the outside, with the inside still soft but not raw. You will get to eat it only after you finish work on Saturday – meaning after 13h00. Go and have a shower, then select ten pieces and cut them into thin strips. Serve as snacks as you listen to the rugby on a Syncal 30 radio in the pub.

Don't shout for Province; it's a mortal sin. Also be mindful of Joe the Parrot, the pub thief, who is equally keen on biltong and cigarette lighters.

SPECIALISED COOKING – THE RECCE WAY

Nature Provides

Once you learn that the bush is neutral, you can survive and live in it and it will provide for you. The Bushmen live and breathe this truth. The stately baobab tree is one of nature's best gifts. It offers water in its hollows, food from its fruits, rope from its trunk and shade from its leaves, as well as a sense of stability. Rest under it and you will get up refreshed. Then there is the simple lala palm (left), which gets tapped for its juice to make a kind of beer. Mopane worms (top left) are very nutritious!

REGIONAL FLAVOURS 165

Angola

Angola is the land of plenty. It even has an abundance of different climates: the north is tropical; in the southwest you'll find jagged desert mountains; the southeast is savanna; and the central and northern parts are the sources of many of Africa's great rivers.

Today the capital city of Luanda is one of the most expensive cities in the world. It is incredible to look at photos and see how Luanda's main strip has developed over the past decade. However, when you leave the city and its 7 million inhabitants, you will realise that things change much more slowly for the rural masses.

The long civil war has left its mark on the landscape, with pockmarked buildings and signposts warning of mines. Still, Angolans are generous with their smiles.

While meals are often meagre and based on whatever subsistence farming can produce, you stand a strong chance of finding excellent seafood at the coast or freshwater fish from any one of the country's massive rivers. Whenever you can lay your hands on fresh fish, simply fry it in a pan and serve with cassava and okra.

If local beans are available, you can also add them to your now very traditional meal.

TRAIN FOOD
Benguela Railway style

The Orient Express, the Blue Train and the Trans-Siberian Railway. These iconic names in train travel (all three are still operational) conjure up images of exotic adventures. While the Orient Express suggests images of fine dining and elegance, the Blue Train and the Trans-Siberian Railway make you think of vast distances, wide-open spaces and rugged landscapes. In this regard, they have much in common with the Benguela Railway, which also travels through seriously harsh terrain.

The Benguela Railway was built by the Portuguese to connect the port city of Lobito with the Copperbelt in the Congo. During the Border War, it was used to transport military equipment and supplies from the coast. Another line, the Moçâmedes Railway, ran from the port of Namibe to the strategically important town of Menongue. Looked at from a purely military point of view, there was ample reason to want to disable these lines.

While bridges and crossings present better points at which to blow up a railway line, causing an explosion in a big tunnel running through a mountain would disable the line for many years. Of course both parties were aware of this, so there were constant and committed efforts from both sides each year to either protect or attack the tunnel. All you needed was a ticket to the show.

If you were a Recce, quite a few tickets would've been issued to you during the war to get to the railway lines in Angola. Unfortunately, you weren't allowed on the train.

Many options were available. You could blow up the locomotives in Lobito, blow up the bridge over the Gural River or blow up the line before Menongue. Last but not least, you could blow up the tunnel in the pass before Lubango. All of these options bring a unique set of challenges, but blowing up the locomotives in Lobito would at least ensure you of a decent meal or two.

For this one, you'd be served regular meals in the comfort of the SAS *Tafelberg*'s mess while the ship made its way up the coast of South Africa, Namibia and Angola.

LEFT A team lays demolition charges at a culvert on the Benguela railway line to cut the supply line to the Angolan army in the east.

OPPOSITE Lubango Pass, in southern Angola – a key point on the Benguela railway line from the coast to the interior.

SPECIALISED COOKING – THE RECCE WAY

167

Unita Country

Unita leader Dr Jonas Savimbi (third from left) and his officers address his fighters while explaining the significance of crossing the railway line.

Unita country might not be a real place but the geographical area played such a big role in the Border War that it deserves a mention. It refers to the southeastern part of Angola bordering Zambia in the east and the Caprivi Strip in the south. Unita's headquarters area, at Jamba, was the only place with a concentration of people.

Unita leader Jonas Savimbi and his allies were supported by the South African government in their fight against the communist MPLA government. Before the outbreak of the Angolan civil war, this area was almost unpopulated, with few roads or towns. The war displaced even more people, leaving the area almost totally depopulated.

A major part of the Recce history in Angola is interwoven with Unita, and many operations were completed with their assistance. When you work with a partisan force such as Unita, the first thing you need to do is to acknowledge that you come from different worlds. In Africa, and especially in the remote war arenas, foot soldiers have little exposure to modern military equipment and other things. Many soldiers will be underage and most will be uneducated, yet all will have been indoctrinated to believe in an elusive freedom. You might consider the conditions they grew up in tough but they are normal to them. These fighters are mere pawns of the war but they have all found personal relevance in fighting for a cause.

It is also important that you realise that they are fighting 'their' war and that you only present a certain opportunity to them – to help them win. Your arrival on the scene has to deliver tangible benefits to them and they look forward to working with you. Remind yourself that they are independent and entitled to their own ways – even if it frustrates you. Remember that they will still be there long after you have left and they will need the local support. Act and behave like a guest.

BROWN MUSHROOMS
à la Ops Cloud recipe

The Luena region is in the centre of Angola and consists of extensive, almost tropical, miombo woodland, interspersed with rivulets, that stretches all the way to the horizon. Flying to the area in a chopper, it looks like a carpeted forest with only the grassy stretches on the flood lines to indicate where the rivers are.

In the rainy season, you'll find the most amazing mushrooms here; they are big and tasty. To get to the area and its mushrooms is quite a mission, though, as Luena is exactly 678 km north of Rundu.

If you joined Operation Cloud to place some specially designed shaped charges at the Luena airfield, you would get to know the area well. You would get a good look from the air, from the trucks and by foot. The helicopters would do the first leg into Angola. This is about an hour and a half of flying.

Then you would drive on a truck – a Ural[59] or GAZ – crowded with Unita soldiers, ammo and basic foods. It takes a few days, as the route is not direct and goes past little groups dropping off ammo and food. Once you reach Sangombe – the last outpost controlled by Unita – you get off the trucks, and from then it is by foot – all 260 km of it.

At Sangombe, you will meet the Unita teams who will accompany you to the target. This will take about 30 days in all. To really enjoy the walk in such beautiful countryside, forget about the distance that you still have to cover and focus on the fact that you don't have to carry all of your equipment personally.

The Unita soldiers used porters to carry their goods between bases. These skinny-legged youths were paid to carry things around on their heads. They carried ammo and rations to the most forward troops in the field, then walked straight back for the next batch. For them, the shoulder straps of the rucksack were a novelty as everything went onto their heads. This amazing 'service' was available up to a few days from the target area.

Do your quota of about 22 km a day[60] for the first ten days.

Every day the clouds start building around midday – like it does in the tropics – and by late afternoon it will rain. Use this time to leave the single-file formation you are walking in and gather a few mushrooms from the forest floor. Two of them should be enough for you and your buddy pair, as they are big. By 17h00 you will start to look for a place to sleep for the night and to have your main meal of the day.

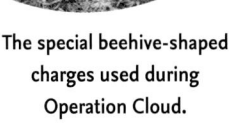

The special beehive-shaped charges used during Operation Cloud.

Beehive-shaped charges
Water
Imana soya mince
Mushrooms, chopped
Salt and pepper

When the light starts to fade, get out your little gas stove and fire bucket. It will probably still be rainy and dripping, so you can catch water from the edge of your bivvy.

Boil the water and add the Imana soya mince to one container.

Ask your buddy to peel and then chop up the mushrooms.

He will cook them in his fire bucket. They are very big, so he will have to repeat this exercise at least three times for a single mushroom to get cooked.

Share the mushrooms and mince equally.

Silently eat the food with the steam coming off your backs and the buckets as the last light welcomes the night.

VARIATION

By day 20 you will have limited food and be mostly dependent on the Unita-supplied rations, meaning you will live off mostly maize/cassava meal for the last 15 days. The one meal of the day will be a big pot of pap or cassava. Nobody said it was going to be easy, so now is the time to excel. As a true specialised chef, you can use the mushrooms with everything. After you dish your portion of pap, go back to your bivvy and make the meal an occasion. Stretch that freeze-dried packet into four meals instead of one. When you use that last half of a stock cube from your backpack to mix a broth for the pap, just smile. This is why you are different.

---

[59] A Ural is a utility truck of Russian origin that was widely used by Unita. The GAZ company, which produces the Ural range of trucks, is one of Russia's largest truck manufacturers.

[60] Walking in the bush is done at about 5 km/h. A 25-km walk would consist of six 45-minute stretches of walking with a 15-minute rest in between and a longer rest at midday. This means being active for seven to eight hours a day. This was only possible in the sparsely populated areas of the country.

Zaire

During the Border War, the country we know today as the Democratic Republic of the Congo (DRC) was still called Zaire. This tropical giant straddles the equator with vast areas of tropical forest. It is the largest country on the continent after Sudan. Everything in the DRC is oversized – the Congo River, the forests and the challenges the country faces.

The distances are so vast and the infrastructure so poor that areas to the east, bordering Lake Tanganyika, lack road connections to the Copperbelt region around Lubumbashi and neither region is connected by road to the capital, Kinshasa. While there are many different ethnic groups in the DRC, French is the lingua franca even if Swahili becomes more dominant towards the east.

The Democratic Republic of Congo received its independence from Belgium in 1960, but the country almost immediately fell into civil war when the democratically elected government of Patrice Lumumba was deposed in a mercenary-assisted coup. Dictatorial rule followed when Mobutu Sese Seko seized power in 1965. Once in power, Mobutu established an authoritarian regime, amassed great personal wealth and attempted to purge the country of all colonial cultural influences. He became notorious for widespread human rights violations, corruption, nepotism and extravagances such as shopping trips to Paris on the Concorde.

One of the markets in Kinshasa, capital of the DRC, where you can buy anything from chimpanzees to bats on a string.

Still, Mobutu's anti-communist stance – and of course the country's vast mineral wealth – won him considerable support from both the United States and the South African government, particularly during the crisis around Angolan independence. It was a matter of the enemy of my enemy is my friend.

Mobutu was eventually deposed by Laurent Kabila in 1997, whereafter a new dictatorship was put in place and even more people died in a civil war without explanation. The more things change, they more they stay the same.

BAKED FISH WITH FRIED PLANTAIN AND FUFU

Fresh fish
Rice or fufu
Palm oil

For real Congolese food, you can't go wrong by stopping at an *nganda* (roadside café), where you'll find affordable and well-prepared food. With the mighty Congo River close by, expect to find fish with a wide array of accompaniments on nearly any local menu.

The fish is baked and served whole with either rice or fufu, a light sticky porridge made from cassava and plantain (the unsweetened version of banana). For such a meal, the plantain pieces are usually cut in slices and fried in palm oil. If you get a chance, visit the local presses where the palm fruit is cooked in drums to release the oil from the meat.

CROCODILE STEAK
Congo River style

Crocodile tastes like something in between fish and chicken. As with chicken, you can therefore build a variety of tastes around its natural flavour. When baking crocodile in the oven, allow at least one hour per kilogram of meat.

Crocodile steak fries well in a pan, and a good rule of thumb is to treat it like chicken breast. It has a delicate taste and little fat, so don't overcook it as it will dry out quickly. Ideally, crocodile should be cooked in foil like fish.

Marinate the crocodile fillets for an hour.

Season with basil, crushed garlic, fresh ginger, curry, chilli, salt and pepper.

Fry in olive oil over slow heat until brown.

Serve with fresh tomatoes and onion.

VARIATIONS

Travel to Kinshasa to train Mobutu Sese Seko's personal guard on higher instruction. Go with associates, such as Taffy Pelser, Struis Strydom and a few MI staff (from the Navy, *nogal*), as the trip will last almost three months.

On arrival at the airport, you will be met by your local associate, one 'Mr M Kinghorn', and by local dignitaries who will ensure you don't end up in prison. You'll then check into the Intercontinental Hotel in the city centre, ostensibly as German businessmen.

After working through the limited menu of the Intercontinental a few times, you'll be dying to try out the local dishes. When you sit on the wide veranda overlooking the Congo River, you can just about make out Brazzaville on the other side. The sheer size of the river will overwhelm you every time. It is just the most incredible and powerful mass of water to see.

The crocodile skewers here are wonderfully juicy. Add lime when available, as the tangy taste enhances the croc's flavour. Order G&Ts to fight off malaria and to help you cope with the tropical heat. Drinking Red Heart and Coke will only blow your cover.

We wouldn't recommend the rest of the bush cuisine on offer in Kinshasa. It will keep you in bed for days. If you were visiting in the 1980s, it was also advisable to stay clear of the Casino.

Unless you are a serious shopper, it is advisable not visit the live market, where chimps, parrots, bats on sticks, bush meat, dogs and heaven knows what else is on offer. However, if you do end up there and feel sorry for one of the poor chimps, make sure you have a plan for him for when you leave.

While you can hand over your chimp to the team that replaces you when your deployment comes to an end, you will need to put the 40 African grey parrots you have acquired into steel army trunks. Ensure that the trunks are properly ventilated before putting them on the C-130 that comes to fetch you.

Plead innocence when the parrots start screeching at Waterkloof Air Force Base, and offer five of them to the pilot as a gift. It's too late now to send them back.

Crocodile fillets (300 g each at rump steak sizes; thinner is better)

Basil, fresh

Garlic, crushed

Ginger, fresh

Curry spice mix

Chilli

Salt and pepper

Olive oil

Tomatoes

Onion

MARINADE

Use any one of lime, mandarin, orange or carrot juice.

Mango chutney can also be added.

The Congo River

Zambia

Zambia is probably one of the most peaceful countries in Africa. That might be because it has never experienced a civil war. Zambia gained independence from Britain in October 1964 and Kenneth Kaunda became its inaugural president. His socialist party remained in power until 1991.

Kaunda played a key role in regional diplomacy, especially in the 1970s and 1980s. He cooperated closely with the United States in the search for solutions to the conflicts in then Rhodesia (Zimbabwe), Angola and Namibia. For this he is widely respected.

The mighty Zambezi River originates in the far north of the country and runs through Angola where it collects the summer rains before flowing eastward along the northern border of the Caprivi. There it joins the Chobe River before this mass of water cascades into the abyss at Victoria Falls, one of the prime destinations in Zambia, alongside Lake Kariba.

The best way to see Zambia is by 4x4 since that gives you access to its many beautiful game parks. During the Border War, you could also visit the country by bicycle or motorbike. If you are on a bicycle and carrying lots of military equipment, it is best to travel at night when no one will see you.[61] You also won't see much of the country apart from the target you're heading to.

Kazungula to Livingstone is a nice stretch of road; it is about 60 km and can be covered in four hours if you have a normal thick-wheeled bicycle. To cross the Zambezi at Kazungula, you will need a small boat. Having a 4 Recce team there with an inflatable Zodiac allows the four two-man teams to focus on their part. The Zodiac will collect you on the river bank and ferry you across to a hidden drop-off in the reeds. You will walk the last 30 m through the reeds with the bicycle and kit on your shoulders, but you will arrive unseen.

Once on the other side, cycle until 04h00, then move into

Two of the two-man reconnaissance teams who took part in Operation Rolio, on their bicycles.

the bush to hide for the day. For the next few nights finish your reconnaissance on the targets. Take the photos and sketches you need, then leave after the roads get quiet. The roadblock at Kazungula closes at 22h00, meaning no traffic will be allowed to pass there, so you can peddle as hard as you need.

By 02h00 you will be close. In the dark you may misjudge exactly where the two drums are that demarcate the roadblock and you will cycle straight through it. When you hear an AK-47 being cocked, it is time to put more power on the pedals, arch your back as you wait for the shots to start and get down the hill at best speed and straight into the river.

Be very grateful when your 4 Recce colleagues come to fetch you in the Zodiac hidden in the reeds at the agreed collection point. They will bring you to safety on the Caprivi side of the river.

---

61 Operation Rolio took place in 1986. The reconnaissance was done by ordinary bicycle and the raid executed by a team of Special Forces operators on off-road motorcycles. It is a good example of how different units and parts of the Defence Force could work together in a coordinated manner.

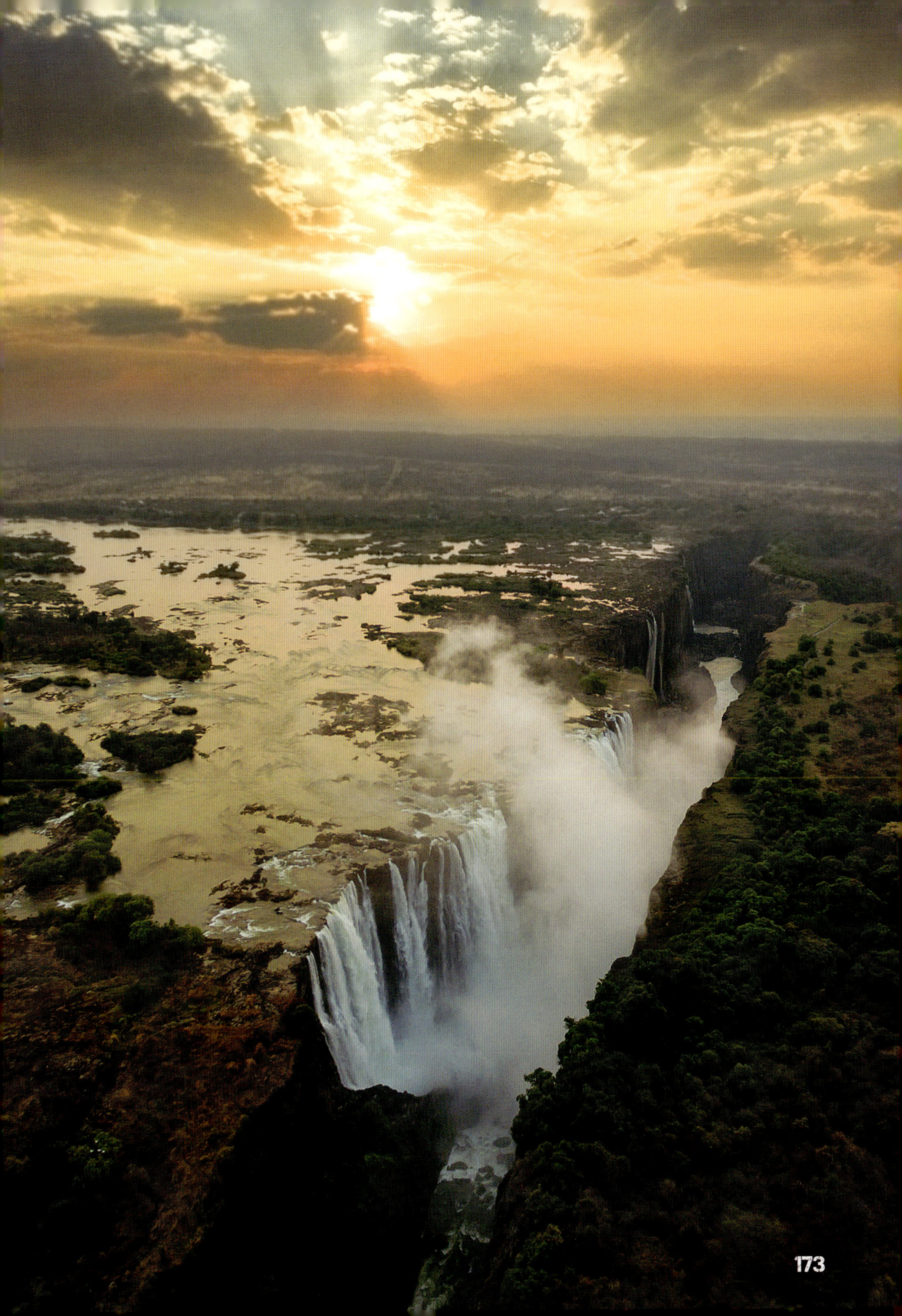

Zimbabwe

Zimbabwe, the former British colony of Rhodesia, is a landlocked country bordering South Africa, Mozambique, Zambia and Botswana. For many years, it was known for its agricultural expertise, especially in maize and tobacco, as well as its excellent education system. Its fertile soils made it the bread basket of Africa.

As far as food goes, you'll find excellent meat there. Zimbabwe is renowned for its steaks; simply eat with a sprinkling of salt.

Zimbabweans are a tolerant and friendly people who always make you feel welcome in their country. Despite its political woes and the economic stagnation of the past 15 years, Zimbabwe remains a beautiful country in which to travel.

The Rhodesian SAS

('D' Squadron)

In the 1960s and 1970s in Rhodesia, as in South Africa, a white minority government was trying to hold on to power in the face of an increasingly restless black majority. As a consequence, Rhodesia ended up fighting a war on its borders and in Mozambique for an extended period. In this, Rhodesia was supported by the South African government, even if it was never publicly acknowledged for political reasons. All operations were done covertly.

The Recce interaction with the Rhodesian Special Air Service (SAS) started early. In the early 1970s, when the Reconnaissance Commandos were started, most of the founding members did the SAS selection in Rhodesia.

This relationship lasted until 1980, when black majority rule arrived in Zimbabwe. In between, the Recces deployed regularly in Zimbabwe but under the cover of being SAS soldiers.

As with all top-end performers, there is often a strong professional rivalry, and the SAS versus the Recces was no exception. In the case of the SAS, the British connection bred a specific style of soldier and officer. They were highly skilled in their efforts during the war. However, the capacity and ability of the South African Army grew tremendously as a result of the conflict in Angola, and the Recces performed a very similar role to the SAS.

Members of the Rhodesian SAS get ready for a training jump. Note the light machine gun carried by the jumper in the foreground.

SPECIALISED COOKING – THE RECCE WAY

Recipes for Rivalry

When you deploy in another country with their Special Forces, it is best you study the local conditions before you deploy. You also need to find out what you'll have to do to fit in if you want your deployment there to go unnoticed.

If nobody briefs you about this, just know the following:
- South Africans drink coffee, Oros, Clover milk and Castle Lager. We eat boerewors and pap. Your ratpacks will contain hard dog biscuits and canned bully beef. During a smoke break, the aroma will be from Gunston or Chesterfield cigarettes.
- Your SAS counterparts will drink tea, Mazoe orange juice and cold Vungu milk, while Zambezis are their beer of choice. Their ratpacks will have amazing canned chicken with gourmet-type crackers and tubes of butter. They will also have those amazing steaks and the smokers will light up the high-quality Madisons.

In addition, you will notice that the Rhodesian officers have batmen who iron their clothes and present them folded. These are placed neatly next to the officer's folding chair with matching canvas hand basin. When you see this, you can be forgiven for reacting to the north/south rivalry and look to get even; they can't have it all.

There is not much you can do about the rations, so take your revenge by starting to teach their batmen how to speak 'proper Afrikaans', for example 'Môre Majoor, jy lyk pragtig' (Morning, Major, you look pretty), or 'Môre Majoor, jy maak my lus' (Morning, Major, you turn me on). After these basics are mastered and you feel you are holding your own, you can get a bit more adventurous. Stop lessons immediately when Corrie Meerholz – the OC on the deployment – realises what you are doing and threatens you with death.

This is a good time to stop fretting about the fact that the SAS have such a better work setup than the Recces. Be grateful that you have the better equipment; this is probably more important. Get on with the job.

Build enough goodwill to receive them as full counterparts when they close down the SAS in January 1980. Establish a unit for them called 6 Reconnaissance Regiment and keep it like that until the end of 1980 when these quality soldiers can be transferred into the regular units of 1, 4 and 5 Recce.

Enkeldoorn Hamburgers

Driving from Salisbury (today Harare) to the Masvingo front in the late 1970s, one would pass a little place called Enkeldoorn – even today the name hasn't changed. There you'd find a shop called the Troopies canteen. This is where all the army conscripts could get really good meals at affordable prices.

If your money is low, send in Charles Wolstenholmer to go and buy the hamburgers. He will walk in and ask for 'free' hamburgers, much to the disgust of the ladies behind the counter, who'll explain to him in the Queen's English that he must be dreaming. At this point your cover of being a troepie will be blown, so go ahead and pay the full price.

In future, learn to speak English so you don't stand out like a sore thumb.

Members of Bravo group of 1 Recce, including Gus Davidson, Rocky van Blerk and Kwartel Kruger, at Lake Kariba in late 1978, in their Rhodesian camouflage.

REGIONAL FLAVOURS

Mozambique

With an abundance of dazzling beaches, great seafood and beer, Mozambique has always been a premier holiday destination. It was a Portuguese colony for more than 400 years before it became independent in 1975. In addition to the Portuguese colonial influence, the heritage of Somali and Arab traders is still evident in the cuisine and along the Indian Ocean coast.

Mozambique is mostly populated along the coast and to the adjacent interior. The main highway stretches some 1 400 km from Maputo in the south to Mtwara on the Tanzanian border in the north. When travelling on this highway you'll see large tracts of coconut plantations, especially at the turnoffs to coastal towns such as Bilene, Inhambane, Vilankulos, Nacala and Pemba. With such a long and beautiful coastline, it is to be expected that seafood plays a big role in the local cuisine. Mozambique is also renowned for its peri-peri dishes.

The country's main economic centre is Maputo (formerly Lourenço Marques), with Beira and Nampula being the other major cities. Today most Mozambicans speak Portuguese and at least one native language.

Portugal's withdrawal in 1975 left a power vacuum in the country, and the communist-backed Frelimo[62] government struggled to establish itself. From 1975 to 1992 it was engaged in a civil war with Renamo (an acronym for Mozambique National Resistance), led by Afonso Dhlakama. Renamo operated from its stronghold, commonly known as Fort Renamo, in the central Gorongosa region. Renamo was at first supported by the Rhodesian government and later by the South African government.

Even today the Gorongosa area is still the heartland of Renamo, which transformed into a political party after the end of the civil war. There are occasional flare-ups between its supporters and those of rival parties. This is not an area to visit without prior investigation into the security situation, as the political divisions within the country have not fully healed.

CLAMS IN PEANUT SAUCE WITH PORT
aka Matata

Onions
Palm oil
Clams, chopped
Port wine
Roasted peanuts, chopped
Tomatoes
Red chillies, crushed into a paste
Salt and pepper
Fresh spinach, chopped
Rice

Apart from the wonderful fish and prawns on offer in Mozambique, this clam dish is unique and as traditional as it comes.

Dice and then sauté the onions in palm oil.

Add the chopped clams and port and bring to a boil, then immediately lower the heat to a simmer.

Add the peanuts, tomatoes, crushed red chillies, as well as salt and pepper to taste, and continue simmering.

Stir occasionally for 30 minutes.

Add chopped spinach and cover until the leaves have wilted.

Serve on a bed of rice.

---

[62] The Frente de Libertação de Moçambique (Frelimo) was the main liberation movement during the struggle against Portuguese colonial rule.

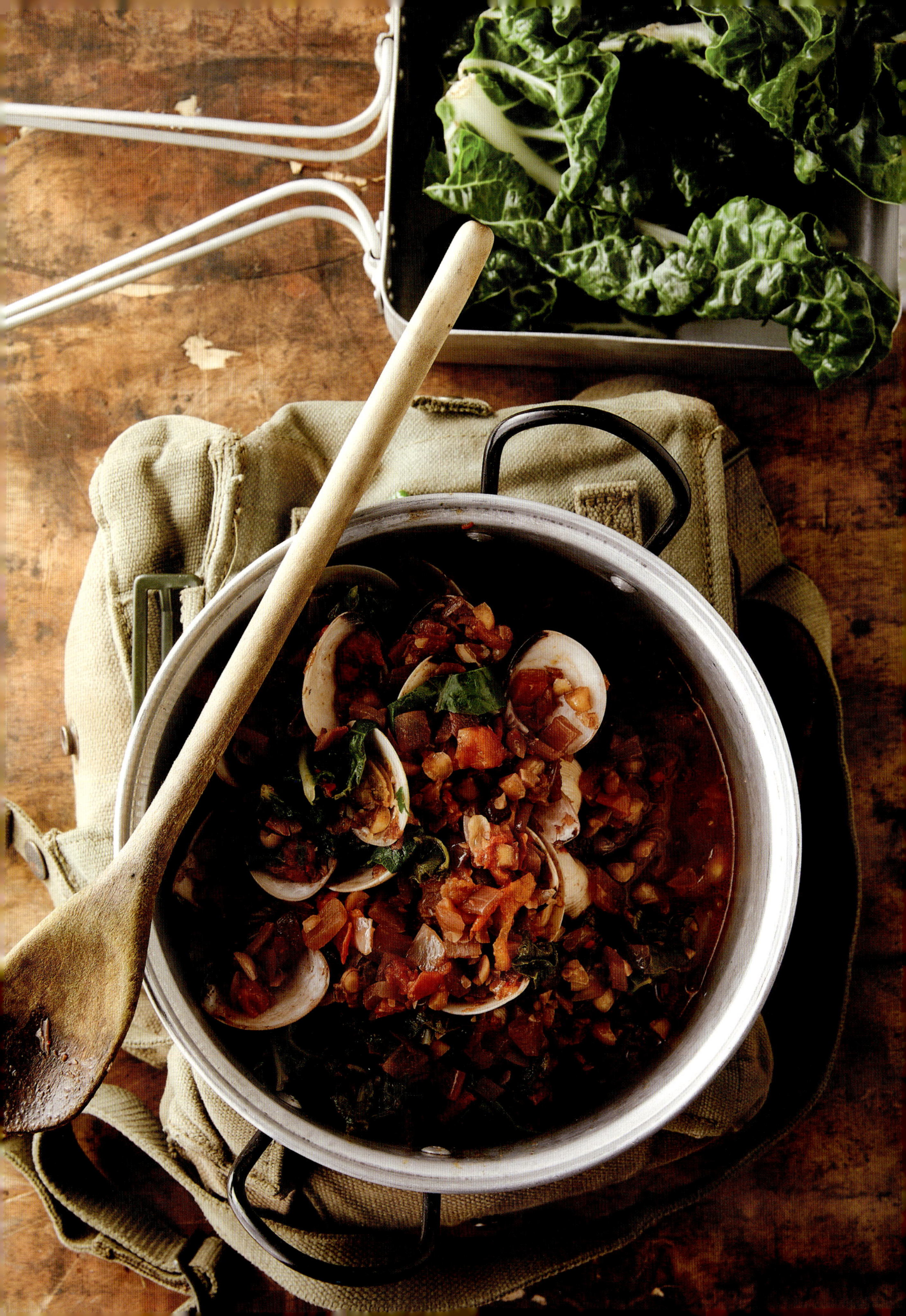

COCONUT WAFFLES WITH MANGO

Dry yeast (or baking powder)

Lemon juice (or vinegar)

Flour

Milk

Coconut oil

Dried coconut

Mangoes

OPPOSITE **Fishermen on the Mozambican coast.**

BELOW **An array of munitions, including landmines, laid out at a base in the bush. Long after soldiers leave, the landmines remain, silently waiting for their targets. When the war is long-forgotten, anyone will do.**

For the specialised chef, it is all about stirring things up and making the most of what you have available. In rural Mozambique, you'll find coconuts and mangoes galore. So, why not make a waffle batter using the local fruit?

If you find yourself deployed with Renamo in the late 1970s, in a team with Niek du Toit, Maquina, Mazanga, Pedro and others,[63] you and the team were probably sent there to build a runway for Renamo. You will also have assisted Sakkie Seegers, the operational commander, and the guys from 4 Recce to sneak in another 200 Renamo trainees there on a South African Navy boat.

These men will need something to eat and you will be the appointed cook. You definitely won't have a waffle maker, so adapt. This recipe works equally well for pancakes and flapjacks. There will be a pan at the base, but even a square dixie makes an excellent replacement for a waffle pan. If you want to escape the flies, cook this away from the central base area in the shade of your basher (grass hut).

Dissolve the dry yeast with some lemon juice or vinegar to take away that yeasty taste.

Make a batter with flour, the yeast mix, milk and some coconut oil.

Add some dried coconut to the batter and pour into the pan or waffle maker.

Once the waffles are done, drizzle a little coconut oil over them.

Cut up the mangoes and serve on top of the waffles.

---

[63] For security reasons, only their first names have been given.

SPECIALISED COOKING – THE RECCE WAY

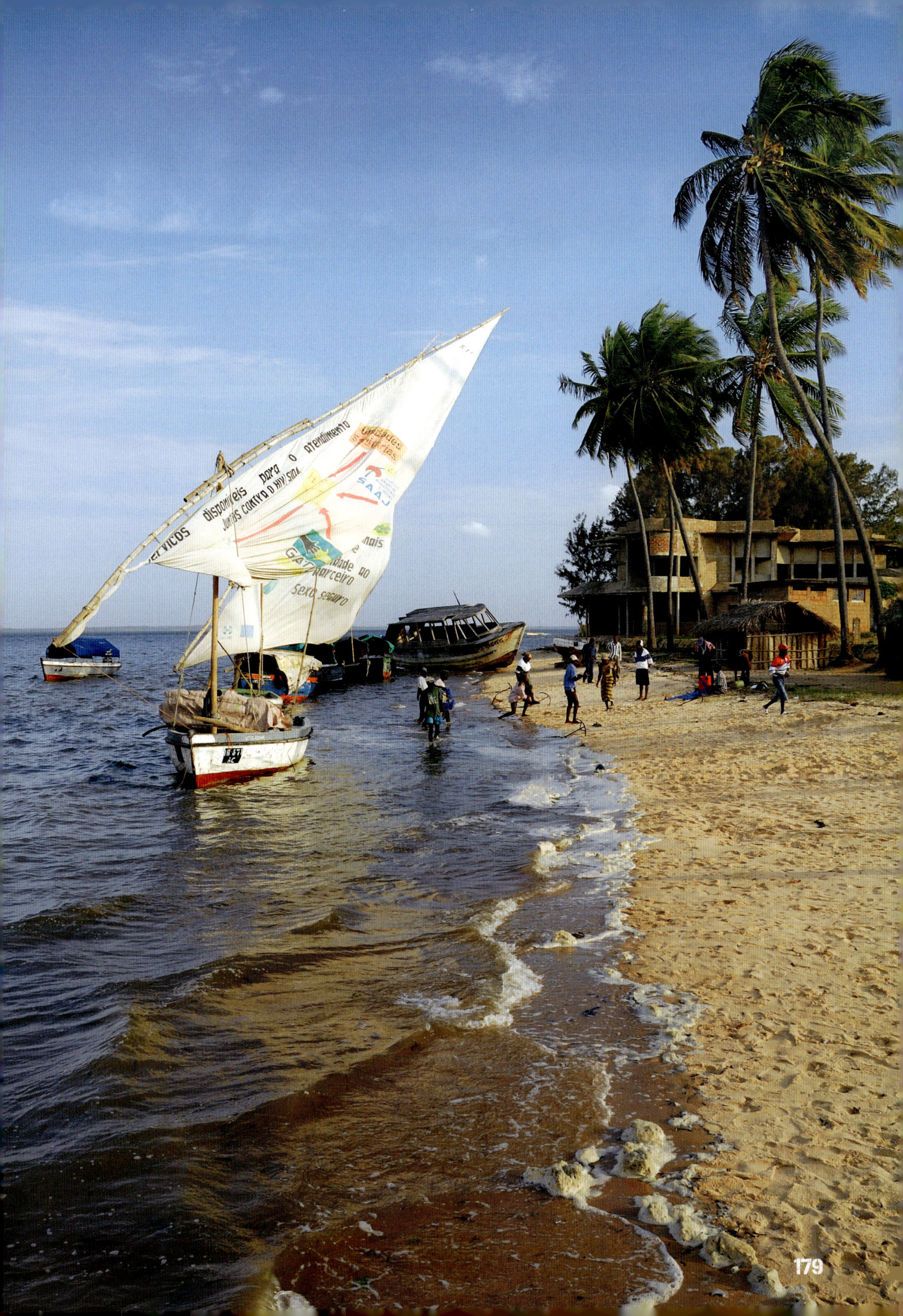
disponiveis para o atendimento
SAAJ
sexo seguro

Middle East

A wise old man once said, 'Just remember, you are never alone.' So it was that, even at the height of the international sanctions against South Africa in the late 1970s and 1980s, the apartheid government didn't find itself completely alone.

Even in the most trying times, people always find a way to trade, and in this the state of Israel was an indispensable ally. South Africa bought oil from countries in the Persian Gulf and also sold steel into the region. As part of the barter, the Navy got brand-new strike craft. The Israelis acted as the intermediary for most of these.

Of course, Israel has been involved in conflicts since its independence. Unlike southern Africa, Israel has no bush. Most of the country is desert-like, and so almost all their fighting is done in urban environments. They are probably the world's best urban army and have a well-established urban warfare capacity.

So, if you want to learn how to be a specialist urban assault team and what urban warfare requires, then the opportunity to learn from the best should be grabbed with open arms.

MANSAF (LAMB)

500 g deboned lamb
Onion
Bay leaves
Cardamom
Cumin
Salt and pepper
Fermented dried yoghurt (jameed), or plain Greek yoghurt
Rice
Almonds, crushed
2 tablespoons of butter
Saffron
Pine nuts

This Jordanian national dish is best eaten in Jordan. Since that country might not be your first choice as a holiday destination, you could always find a spot on Koos Loots's[64] team, that provided training to the King's elite troops.

As always, adapt and try to fit in. Learn the small things first. Start by joining the Jordanians when they buy jam and a newspaper on their way to the shooting range.

Once there, don't look surprised when they use the jam to stick the newspaper on to drums, which they will then use as targets. Stay professional and carry on with the training; you'll soon realise it actually works.

Next time, buy some pita bread as well so you can use the leftover jam on the pita for lunch.

On the way back, stop at one of the many restaurants and order *mansaf*; this tender lamb stew with pine nuts and almonds will blow you away. If you insist on cooking it yourself, then proceed as follows …

Cut the meat into cubes.

Brown the meat and onion in a pan.

Add the bay leaves and spices (except the saffron) and cover with water. Simmer for 90 minutes.

Add the *jameed* (or Greek yoghurt), stirring it in slowly to maintain an even consistency. Leave to simmer while you make the rice.

While the rice is cooking, add crushed almonds, two tablespoons of butter and a pinch of saffron.

Serve the lamb on the rice and sprinkle with pine nuts; it makes all the difference to the taste.

---

[64] Warrant Officer Koos Loots (Ret), ex-Rhodesian SAS. Joined 1 Recce in 1980. Became RSM at 4 Recce and WO Special Forces for many years.

A F**KING MENU

by Roy Vermaak

When you send four Recces and a few Takies (members of the Police Task Force) to Desertland in Israel on a training course for a few weeks in 1982, you've just created a lethal combination. The men will be used to their own food, that is, all kinds of meat and having regular braais. It won't come as a surprise that an overdose of falafel and kosher food will go down reluctantly, especially if there's no Red Heart rum to go down with it.

Just between us, the food was f**king boring.

However, we tried our best to make a good impression on our hosts. We dined with members of the Yamam specialist counter-terror support unit (part of the Israel Border Police), where we were being trained, as well as the female support staff and troops.

As time went by, the Israelis got to know a little more about us and our language, even if more inadvertently than on purpose. One day our liaison officer, David Tuser, asked me the meaning of a word we used frequently when we spoke in Afrikaans. Of course I knew exactly what word he was referring to, but I still asked politely, 'Umm, what does it sound like?'

'Something like "fiek" or "fohken"?'

I had to spill the beans and admit that it was the F-word. He started laughing uncontrollably before telling us that it sounded very much like a Hebrew word with a similar meaning, only with a more humorous connotation.

The next morning, at breakfast, everyone around us was f**king transformed: 'Good f**king morning, please pass me the f**king butter.'

And later, during our training, 'Run f**king faster, shoot f**king slower.'

We got f**kafied to the tenth degree.

The next day, the trip reached its supposed highlight when we were invited to the military attaché's house. General Constand Viljoen, then head of the Defence Force, was also there. The function was in the form of a garden party and we were asked to carry out the snacks and serve the guests. We couldn't really say no, so we obliged and helped to open packets and lay out trays.

At least we managed to down a few whiskies and rum and nab some biltong in between. One member, it could have been James Teitge or Japie Kloppers, also decided that our dog biscuits would go down very well with the cheeses and pickles. Believe me, all the guests enjoyed them.

As Frans Fourie, another colleague with us, said, 'We're only doing this in the f**king desert for f**king flag and f**king country.'

We adapted, stayed in the moment and did our jobs as waiters, but under duress. Let it be known across the desert: Recces aren't f**king waiters!

REGIONAL FLAVOURS

Mother Russia

In 1989 the Berlin Wall fell, heralding the end of the Cold War and the opening up of Russia and the so-called Eastern Bloc countries. By 1991, the Union of Soviet Socialist Republics (USSR) had dissolved. The fight against communism came to an abrupt end, including in Africa.

By 1990, the Border War had ended and Namibia had achieved its independence. We were no longer fighting the Red Peril. While the Russians were the enemy during the war, the new world order opened up opportunities to get to know each other better.

RUSSIAN ROADSIDE MEAL

by Roy Vermaak

In 1992, the Special Forces were invited to a parachute exercise in the newly formed Russian Federation. In retrospect, our knowledge of the Russian military – their achievements on the battlefield during the Second World War, particularly at Stalingrad, the development of tough and versatile vehicles such as the Ural truck and BRDM troop carrier, as well as the amazingly simple but efficient AK-47 assault rifle – should have prepared us for the Russian way of doing things. So be it.

We visited Red Square with the South African flag draped around our shoulders, and with Stroh rum mixed into our Cokes. From there we were taken to Ryazan, around 400 km southeast of Moscow, where we would stay for the duration of the two-week jumping exercise.

On the bus to Ryazan, our first discussion with our Russian counterparts was about social habits. It wasn't long before our natural competitiveness kicked in and we felt it necessary to test our respective alcohol consumption abilities. However, after the long flight and our extended sessions with Stroh and Coke on arrival, I realised we were going to lose this one hands down. We needed an ambush plan.

Using gestures, we nodded and toasted our little competition. Then we swapped our two bottles of Stroh rum (80 per cent alcohol) for their two bottles of Pushkin vodka (43 per cent alcohol).

As the Stroh flowed, the Russian airborne lads looked more and more like Bolshoi Circus clowns when they gestured and tried to speak English. On our side, the vodka slowed down our incessant questions about when we would stop for food. By now we were apparently halfway to the 'hotel' in Ryazan.

When the bus stopped for a food resupply, Clown No. 1 was out the door – head first. He stayed where he landed. A No. 2 was appointed after some oohs and aahs at the fate of No. 1. A short while later, he returned with a paper bag filled with stuff. No. 1 was bundled back into the bus – head first again – and onwards we steamed.

The Stroh versus Pushkin competition was expertly controlled by Gif Opperman, one of the 5 Recce jumpers in our team, who did a sterling job pouring shots and getting the Russians to drink everything he poured. He proved to be quite the psychological warfare expert. In the meantime, the

ABOVE **The jump delegation in good spirits shortly after arriving in Russia. Obviously, the Stroh rum had done its work by then.**

TOP RIGHT **A Russian ten-year good service medal.**

ABOVE The Mi-24 helicopter gunship was the most feared enemy aircraft during the Border War. Its weaponry commanded great respect. It was a rare privilege to enjoy a reversal of roles and jump out of one.

BELOW Headgear for the extreme Russian winter.

translator told us the intended stopping place (we thought it would be a picnic spot) was close by.

About 45 minutes later, with full bladders and very empty stomachs, we pulled off at an empty and dirty petrol station. It was nothing more than a potholed piece of tar where truckers pulled off to sleep. It also stank like hell.

We debussed and emptied our bladders before returning for lunch, which had been neatly laid out on a newspaper on the ground. The surroundings were beautiful ... vehicles speeding past only a few metres from us. On the menu was about three slices of rye bread and thick slices of horse polony. No cutlery in sight.

Never in my life have I missed Joe Hunter, the chef of 1 Recce, so much as at this moment. What I wouldn't have given for some of the snacks he served at RSM's parade or any of our functions. In fact, even the average contents of my *varkpan* from basics got elevated at that moment – and *sommer* quite a bit at that.

We were still staring dumbstruck at our lunch when one of the Stroh clowns managed to get up for a pee, with his back turned towards us. At one point, he turned round and invited us with a broad smile to start eating. You don't even want to know where the spatter went. Adapt and stay in the moment.

Someone had the presence of mind to start. The bread was broken into pieces and we started eating, only to be reminded that we should keep some out for the morning. We did so gladly, thinking hello hotel, here we come.

We arrived at their base with visions of how we would enjoy the clean bathrooms and have a decent mess, but then we were told that we were just changing drivers as our 'hotel' was still 30 minutes out of town. We got on the bus again.

When we turned into the 'hotel' parking area half an hour later, silence descended on the bus, and the effect of the vodka suddenly wore off. Our 'hotel' was a deserted old Soviet hostel with rotten beds, no water, no sanitation, just plain bugger-all.

The bus left – we stayed.

PS: After I contacted the Ambassador, things improved rapidly and they assisted us as much as possible. All in all, the rest of our trip was a pleasant experience, even if it was spent in quite a 'robust' environment. I've heard that things change fairly slowly in Russia, so I don't recommend venturing into the rural hinterland in search of quality cuisine.

REGIONAL FLAVOURS

FOR THE RECORD

OFFICIAL DATES OF UNIT DESIGNATIONS:

1 RECCE

1 Oct 1972–31 Dec 1980	1 Reconnaissance Commando
1 Jan 1981–31 Jul 1993	1 Reconnaissance Regiment
1 Aug 1993–31 Jul 1995	452 Parachute Battalion
1 Aug 1995–31 Mar 1997	1 Special Forces Regiment (closed down on last date)

2 RECCE

1 Jun 1974–31 Dec 1980	2 Reconnaissance Commando
1 Jan 1981–31 Jul 1992	2 Reconnaissance Regiment (closed down on last date)

4 RECCE

17 July 1978–31 Dec 1980	4 Reconnaissance Commando
1 Jan 1981–31 Jul 1993	4 Reconnaissance Regiment
1 Aug 1993–31 Jul 1995	453 Parachute Battalion
1 Aug 1995–to date	4 Special Forces Regiment

5 RECCE

5 Dec 1976–31 Dec 1980	5 Reconnaissance Commando
1 Jan 1981–31 Jul 1993	5 Reconnaissance Regiment
1 Aug 1993–31 Jul 1995	451 Parachute Battalion
1 Aug 1995–to date	5 Special Forces Regiment

6 RECCE

14 Mar 1980–31 Dec 1980	6 Reconnaissance Commando (closed down on last date)

Sergeant Sam Manyatela shows his PE4 charge on a steel object during a demolitions course.

The Class of 1972 after completing their free-fall course at the Parachute Battalion in Bloemfontein. Back, from left to right: Jimmy Oberholzer, Kenaas Conradie, Wannies Wannenberg and At Schoeman. Front: Johnny Kieser, Boytjie Viviers, Eric Lamprecht and Kevin Potgieter.

Bully beef saves the day – again!

Members of 1, 4 and 5 Recce on a joint training exercise where they honed their urban skills at the Whaling Station in Durban.

A set of old SADF medals, from left to right: Honoris Crux, Military Merit medal, Pro Patria, Southern African medal and the Good Service medal (bronze, 10 years).

Recce instructors and recruits shortly after a selection course (VK21, 12–30 August 1974) was completed in Oudtshoorn.

An urban team practise house clearing with full kit to protect them from flying objects.

REGIONAL FLAVOURS 185

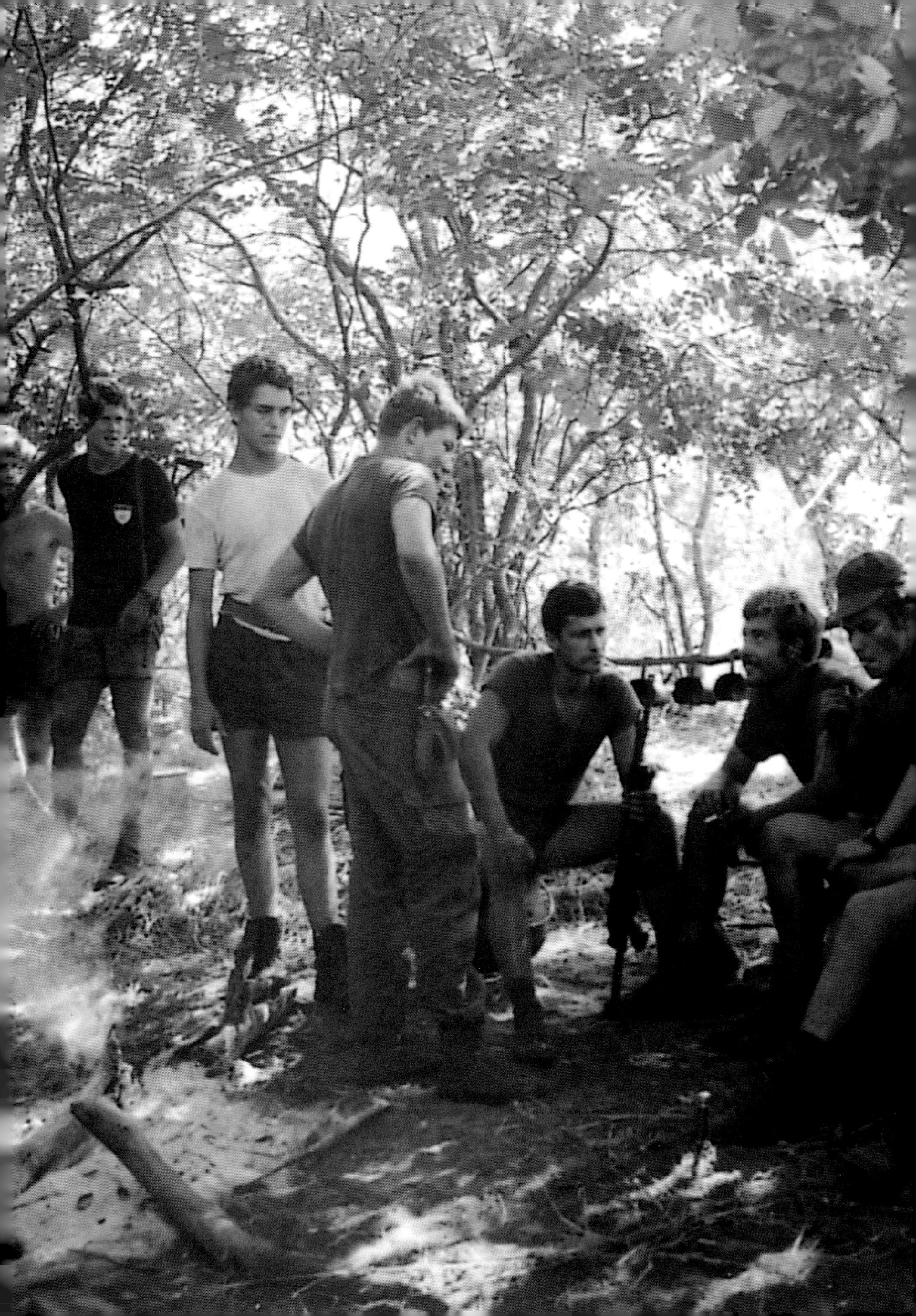

THE SWEETER SIDE

The only thing that makes things sweet is sugar. Full stop. In these days of healthy living, some turn sugar into the devil and try to replace it with artificial sweeteners. But that defeats the object. So, if you're on a diet or struggling with your weight, rather turn to the next chapter. Here we only work with the real deal.

A body that is busy burning a serious number of calories – such as a Special Forces operator out in the field – always welcomes the energy that comes from sugar. Besides, tasting any sweet flavours gives most people a proper psychological boost.

If you've never made a proper pudding in your life before, don't be intimidated. When it comes to the sweeter things in life, it's quite easy to get creative. Our recipes vary from the most basic to very elaborate.

Out in the bush on high-risk missions, a unique cameraderie develops among Special Forces operators.

ICE CREAM WITH AMARULA

Vanilla ice cream
Amarula cream liqueur
Canned oranges in light syrup
Chocolate, crumbled
Marula fruit, pips removed

During Zodiac training at Vetch's Pier in Durban in 1983, a group of guys were placing the Kleppers (folding canoes) back on the truck when an ice cream vendor drove past on his bicycle cart. It was a hot day, so they stopped him and bought a few ice creams.

Major Frans van Dyk, then commando sergeant major of 1 Recce,[65] was not impressed with this departure from the normal protocol, much to the surprise of the men. To Frans, it just didn't look right and he promptly admonished the group with the customary wagging finger.

'Think of our image,' he said. 'We aren't sissies – we don't eat ice cream in public!'

The story did the rounds, and soon everybody joked that 'Recces don't eat ice cream'.

However, we doubt whether Frans or anyone will object when you serve ice cream after hours, especially if you serve it with Amarula.

Ice cream is a really versatile dessert that goes with waffles, fresh fruit or on its own with chocolate sauce. Try to use the same type of cocktail glass as you would for a prawn cocktail or vodka martini. It will impress your guests more than a blob in a bowl. For the more discerning chef, the presentation style à la Dom Pedro rules supreme.

For those who are unafraid, mix the ice cream and Amarula 50/50. That way, you'll get the effect of the alcohol without eating too much. For everyone else, use the standard 50 ml tot or three caps per portion.

Blend in a food processor or mix well in a mixing bowl until smooth and runny.

Fill the glasses and add some canned oranges or crumbled chocolate. If it is marula season in Phalaborwa, you can take the flesh off the pip and place it on top. This will show you have class.

VARIATION

If you found yourself in South West Africa before 1989, you would have used Baileys (the Irish version of Amarula), which in those days ruled supreme in this part of the world. If it is not marula season, canned naartjies or oranges will also work.

> He will win whose army is animated by the same spirit throughout the ranks
>
> SUN TZU

---

[65] Frans van Dyk joined the Special Forces in 1974 and served until the disbanding of 1 Recce in 1997. He is one of the parachuting legends of the Special Forces.

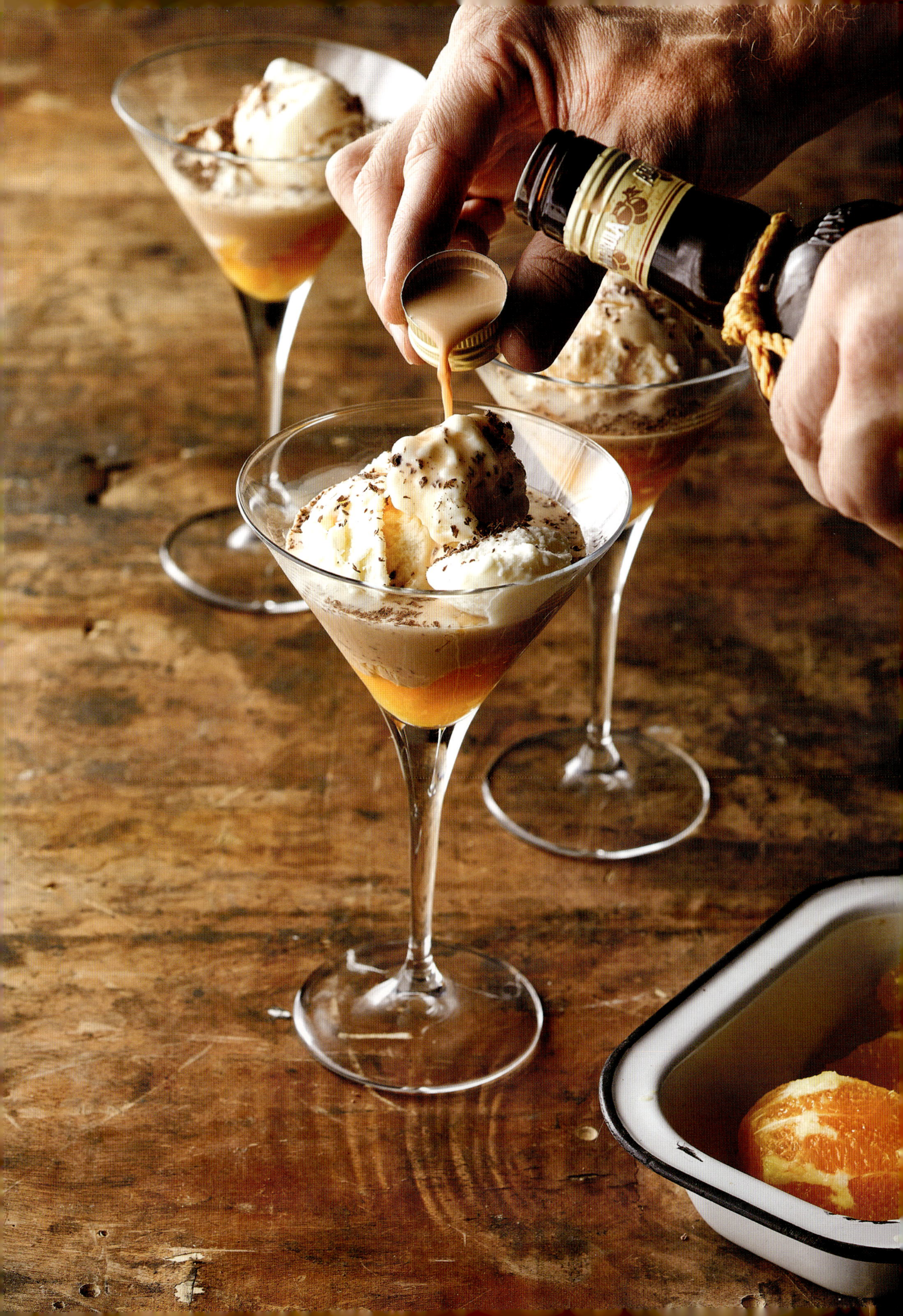

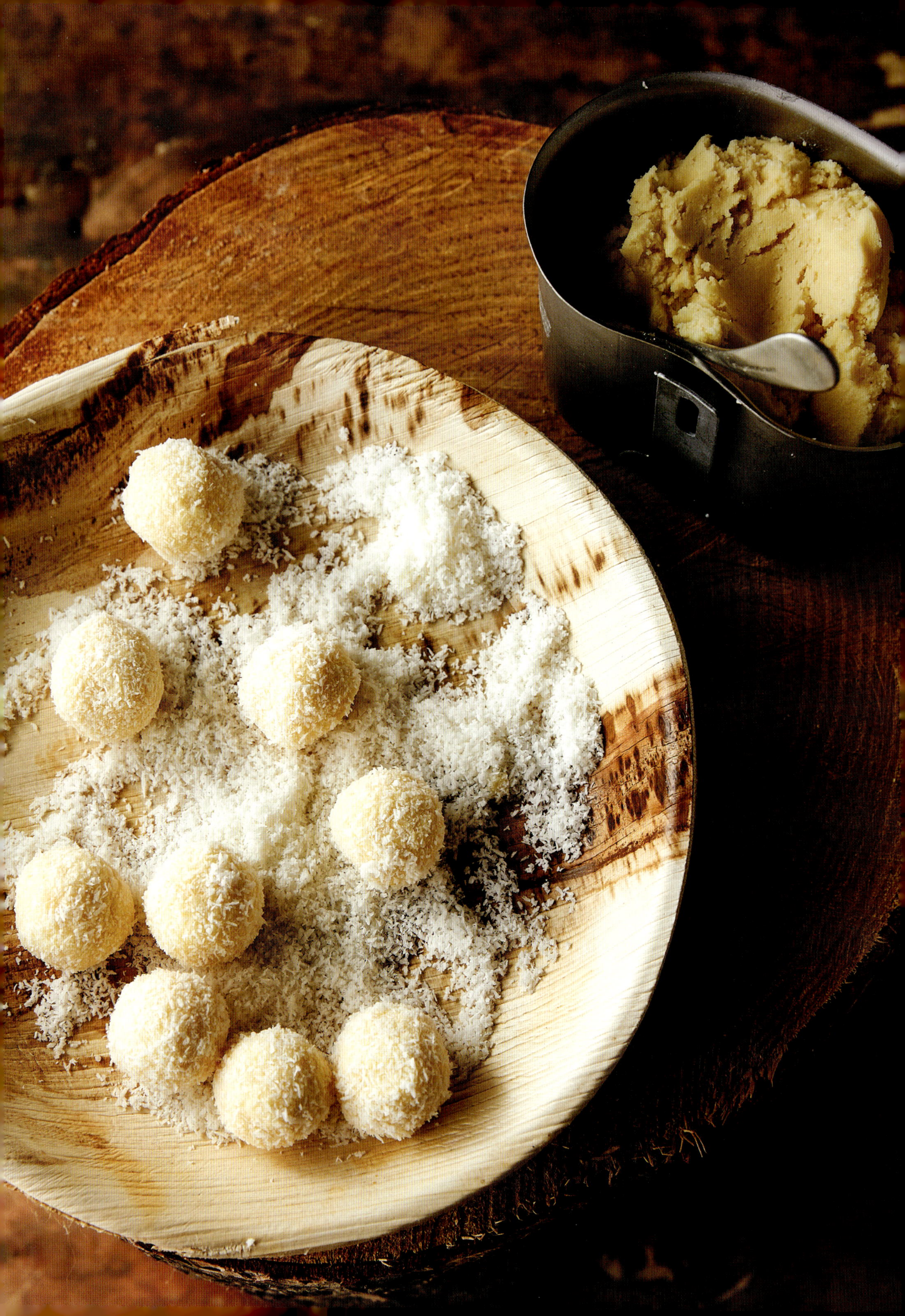

BUSH FERRERO ROCHER

If you had to ask me which recipe every soldier should know, it is this one. It is classy, super easy and you will easily find the ingredients from Bangui to Kampala or in the kitchens of the Ritz and the Hyatt. Imagine this on the Minister's menu? (See the last chapter.)

Mix the icing sugar, vanilla essence, milk powder and butter.
Add most of the desiccated coconut (or crumbled biscuits) and mix until doughy.
Put an almond in the middle and add dough around it.
Roll the dough into small meatball-sized balls.
Roll the balls in the remaining coconut powder.
This is one of those wow offerings, especially if you make it in the middle of the bush when it is least expected.

1 part icing sugar
Vanilla essence
1 part milk powder
1 part butter
½ part desiccated coconut (or crumbled biscuits)
Almonds
Coconut flakes

BAKED PANCAKE STRUDEL

Flapjacks and pancakes are easy and quick to make. The ingredients can be found nearly everywhere, and even if there are no eggs, this is not the end of the world. The key to baked pancake strudel is the filling. This one uses chopped nuts, apricot jam, stewed apple and ricotta cheese. The filling is Rosh Hashanah style, and you are likely to eat it when attending a training course in Israel.

Make the pancakes according to the table shown on page 130.
Chop the stewed apples, making sure there are no pieces of apple core left. There must be no skin on the apples.
Now mix the raisins, chopped nuts, ricotta cheese and apricot jam. Spoon some filling onto each pancake, then roll them up and lay them out on a baking tray.
Fill the tray with milk until the pancakes are just visible.
Bake until the milk has boiled down.
Serve with a dollop of sour cream, icing sugar and a sprinkle of cinnamon. Mmmmm.

Pancake dough
 (see basic bakes on page 130)
Stewed apples
Handful of raisins
1 cup of chopped nuts
1 cup of ricotta cheese
Apricot jam
Milk
Sour cream
Icing sugar
Cinnamon

After a long deployment during Operation Hunter, this 4 Recce Small Team under Rob Jennings look more than ready for a piece of strudel.

FLOUR BALLS

5 parts water
1 part brown sugar
1 part butter
2 parts self-raising flour
½ part golden syrup
1 part milk
Ice cream

Flour balls can be made anywhere and at any time. They don't even require oil. You can use cups or metric measures (100 g or ml).

Heat the water, brown sugar and half the butter in a large saucepan.

Stir over a low heat until all the ingredients are melted.

In the meantime, with your fingertips, rub the remaining butter into the flour.

Pour golden syrup into the milk. Stir into the flour mixture to make a dough.

Bring the sauce to the boil. Drop heaped spoonfuls of the dough into the sauce.

Reduce to a low heat and let the balls simmer, covered, for 15–20 minutes or until a skewer comes out clean when you stick it into one of the balls.

Serve with ice cream.

VERSATILE DOUGHNUTS

Vetkoek dough (see basic bakes, page 130)
100 g of castor sugar
Cooking oil
Butter
Jams
Grated cheese

VARIATION
When you are out in the bush, you can always improvise by adding energy bar shavings and milkshake mix to the dough. Raisins will also work, especially if you have just made raisin beer (see p. 200).

Every chef has a signature dish that he makes when he really needs to impress, and usually also when he has nothing else to offer. It is crucial for all specialised chefs to know how to make doughnuts (also known as vetkoek), since the ingredients are always readily available and they are more or less flop-proof.

Prepare the dough according to the instructions for vetkoek on page 131, but add castor sugar to it.

Heat the oil in a pot or a deep pan (the oil should be at least 1 cm deep if in a pan).

Spoon the dough into the hot oil to get round doughnuts and fry. Turn regularly to brown all over. Take out and drain on kitchen paper.

When the doughnuts are done, melt some butter and drizzle over.

Serve hot or cold with any kind of jam and grated cheese.

COOKED WHEAT AND CINNAMON

Whole wheat kernels
Water
Brown sugar
Salt
Cinnamon

Wheat is a raw food and delicious on top of it. It is commonly served in Eastern Europe where, after 50 years of communism, people really knew how to cook with everything that was available and had refined their cooking during the cold winter months.

Rinse the wheat kernels to remove dirt. You will need a cup per person.

Cover with water and boil until almost soft.

Stir in the brown sugar and boil for a further 15 minutes. A good guide is a tablespoon of sugar per cup of wheat.

Season with salt. Serve with cinnamon.

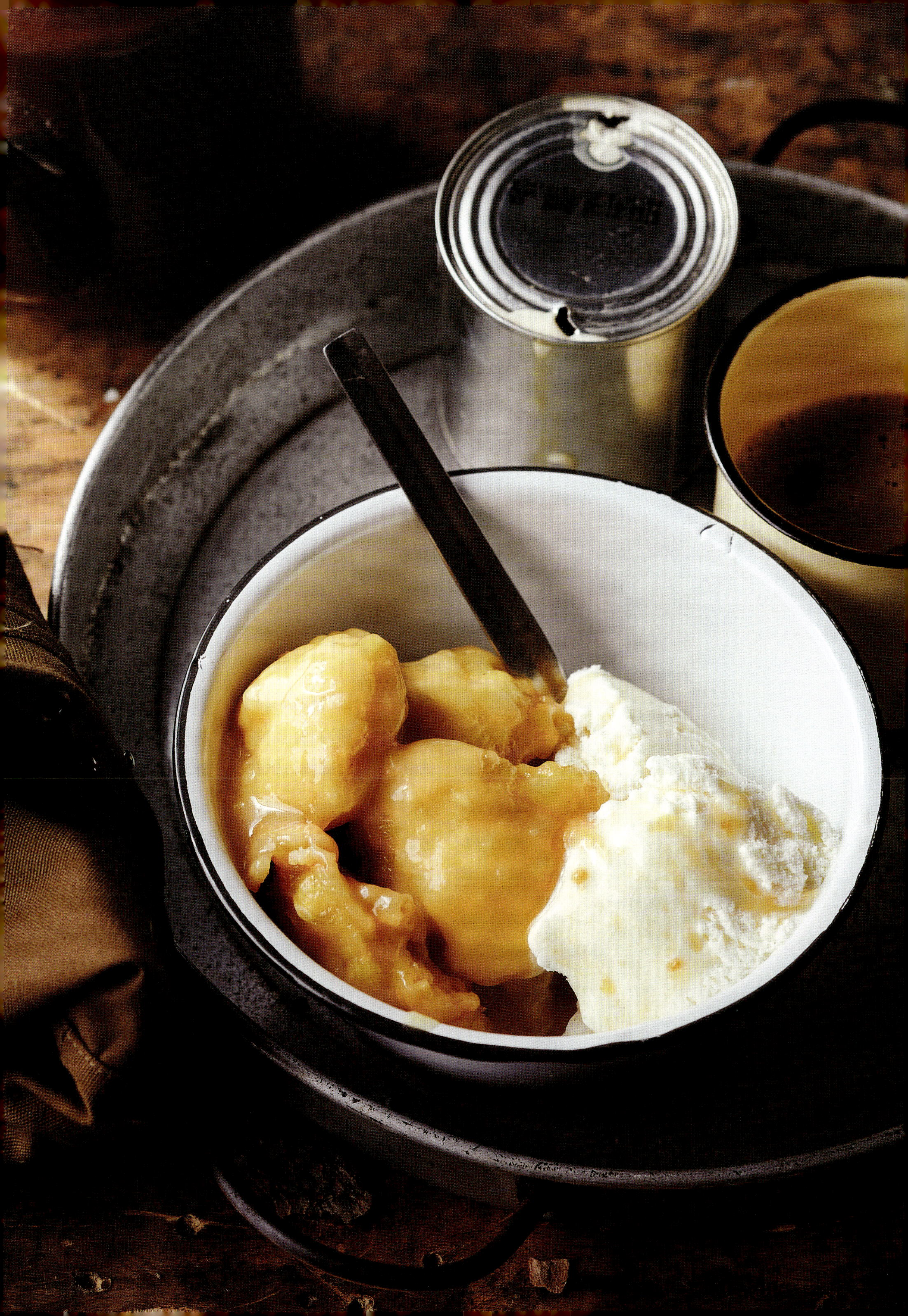

BROWN PUDDING

à la Doiby[66]

by Blikkies Blignaut

SYRUP
3 cups of water
2 cups of sugar

PUDDING
1 cup of soft butter
3 eggs
½ teaspoon of salt
1 teaspoon of baking soda
2 teaspoons of vinegar
2 cups of flour

As any member of the Special Forces will know, Brigadier General Doiby Coetzee – the only officer to have served 30 years in the Special Forces as an officer – is hooked on brown pudding with custard. When he was in charge of social functions at 5 Recce, brown pudding would for many years be the only dessert served.

When I took over as PMC (President of the Mess Committee) in 1989, I took the menu for a formal supper to him and informed him that the dessert would be chocolate mousse. He just glared at me. But since I stated it as a fact and didn't ask his permission, it was passed.

Then the bloody chef mixed up the icing sugar and the salt and we ended up with chocolate soot instead of mousse. Needless to say, I have never heard the last of it.

To make the syrup, bring the water to the boil and then melt the sugar in the water.

Mix the butter and eggs and some salt.

Add baking soda and vinegar.

Mix in the flour to form a dough.

Pour the dough mixture into the boiling syrup and cook for an hour.

When it turns golden brown the pudding is done.

Serve with cream, custard or, dare we say, ice cream. (See recipe on page 188. There is no consensus as to whether Recces are allowed to eat ice cream or not.)

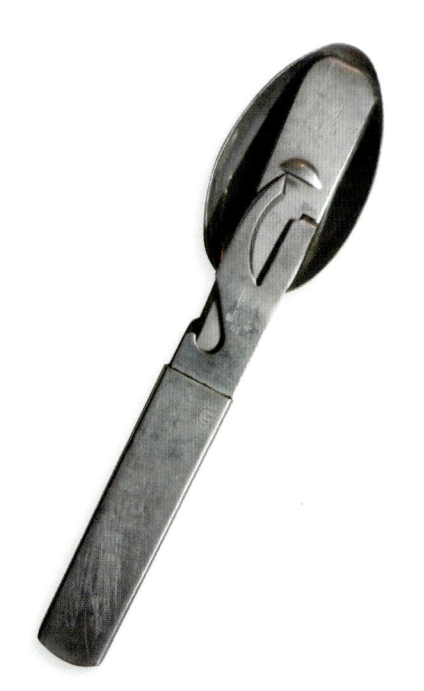

Brigadier General Doiby Coetzee.

---

[66] Doiby Coetzee joined the Special Forces in 1983 and was still a serving member in 2017. He has been awarded the 30-year operator's badge.

SPECIALISED COOKING – THE RECCE WAY

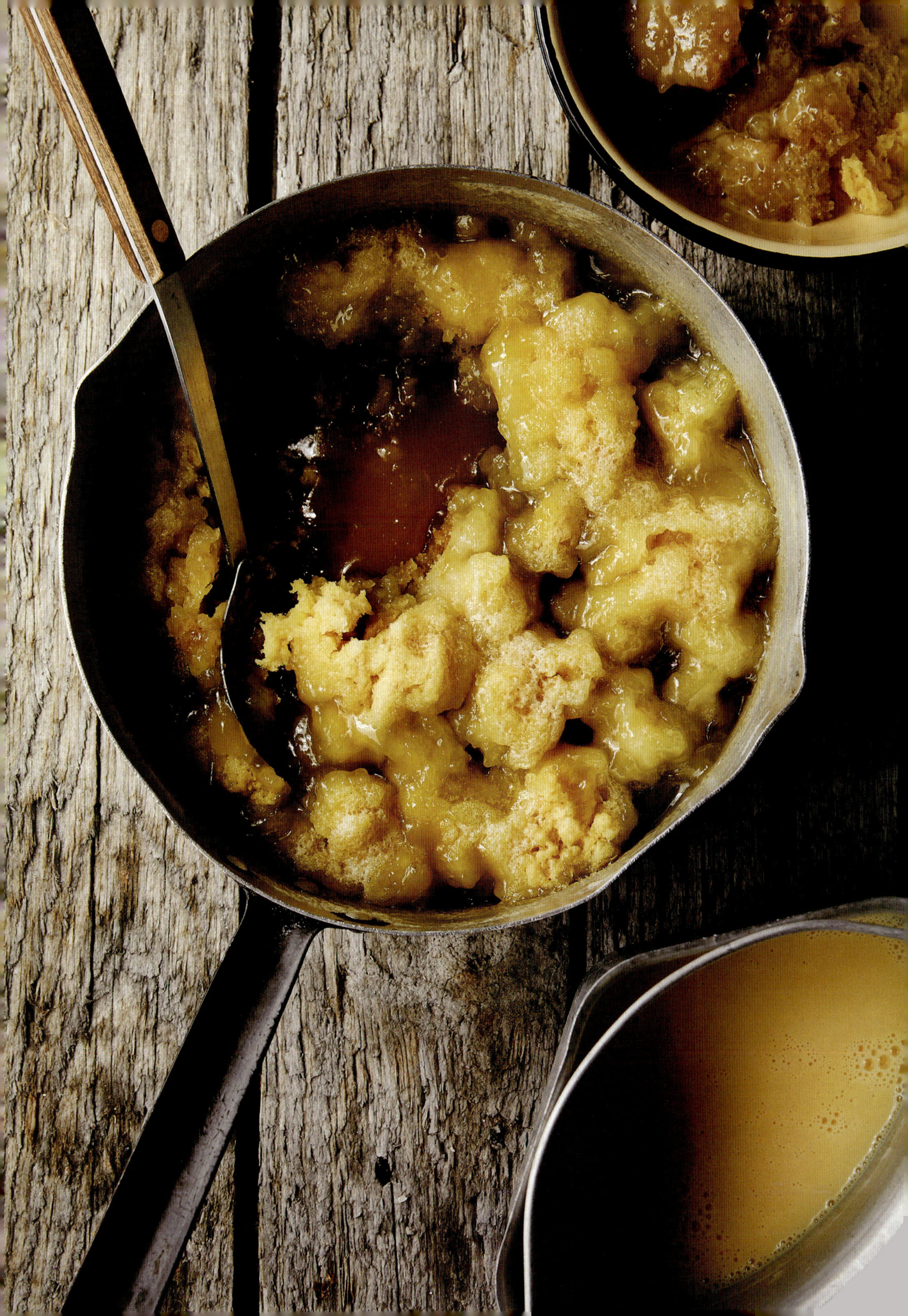

STRAWBERRIES AND CREAM

A freeze-dried treat

1 packet of freeze-dried strawberries
1 tin of cream

When we discussed the nutritional value of food earlier in the book, we noted that it is not so smart to carry around bags of vegetables because their kilojoule values are low. While the makers of freeze-dried foods also know the kilojoule value of dried strawberries is low, they still make them and we always packed them.

The thing is, they serve another purpose. When you go on longer deployments, mental fitness is crucial and you have to find ways to keep your spirits up. Making a dessert with freeze-dried strawberries will do exactly that. Sneak in a small tin of cream and hide it under your clothes so you'll forget about it until just the right moment.

Go on a long deployment such as Operation Hunter; you will get really, really hungry and this will make you count the days until you get back to your cache.

When you arrive at the cache, be grateful the hyenas only opened up some things. Search for the treats pack. Take out the packets of freeze-dried stroganoff as well as the freeze-dried strawberries and the tin of cream that you packed six weeks earlier.

Boil some water on the little gas stove for the stroganoff and empty the packet into the water.

You can open the freeze-dried strawberries and hydrate them so long by adding water.

Open the tin of cream.

Add the cream to the strawberries and use the leftover cream to really escalate the freeze-dried stroganoff into a serious meal.

If this was any other cookbook, we would have said it was to die for, but we'd rather not!

> I love cooking with wine, sometimes I even put it in the food . . .

ONION JAM

Sweet onion
Salt
Brown sugar
Vinegar
White wine

VARIATIONS

If onions aren't available, you can use sour litchis, figs, apples, guavas or watermelon skins. Experiment by adding cloves and cinnamon, but use these ingredients sparingly.

When operating in remote areas, there will usually be onions and sugar around. You can use these ingredients to make an unusual sweet treat – onion jam. This goes well with pork and game dishes or in a vetkoek/*roosterkoek*. If stored properly in a jar, it keeps for months.

Cut up the onion finely, as you would to make a sambal.

Sprinkle over salt, sugar and vinegar and let it slowly dissolve in the onion juice for an hour.

Add the ingredients to a pot and pour in a dash of white wine. Simmer until all the alcohol is boiled down and/or the syrup has thickened (it usually takes around 15 minutes).

SPECIALISED COOKING – THE RECCE WAY

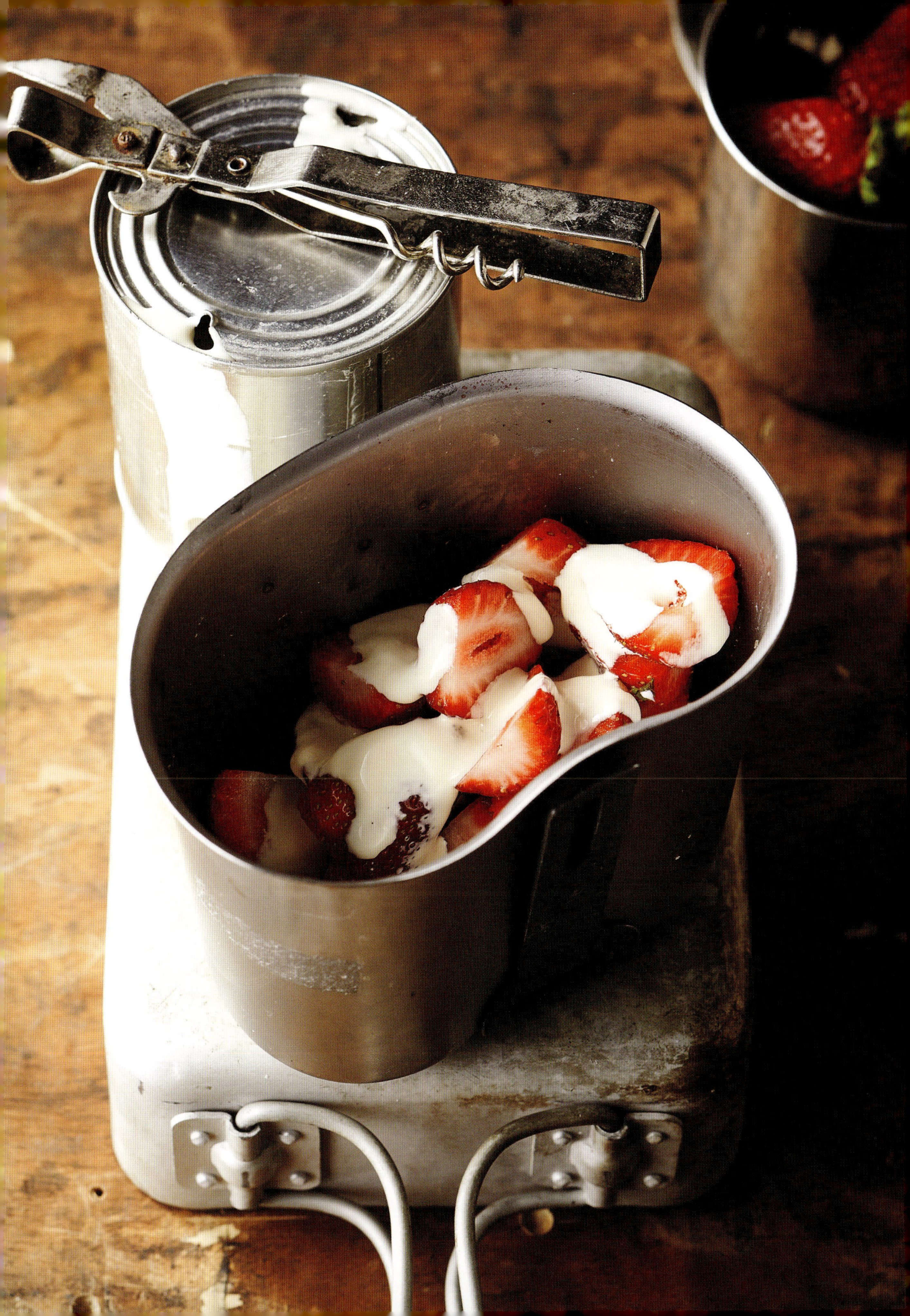

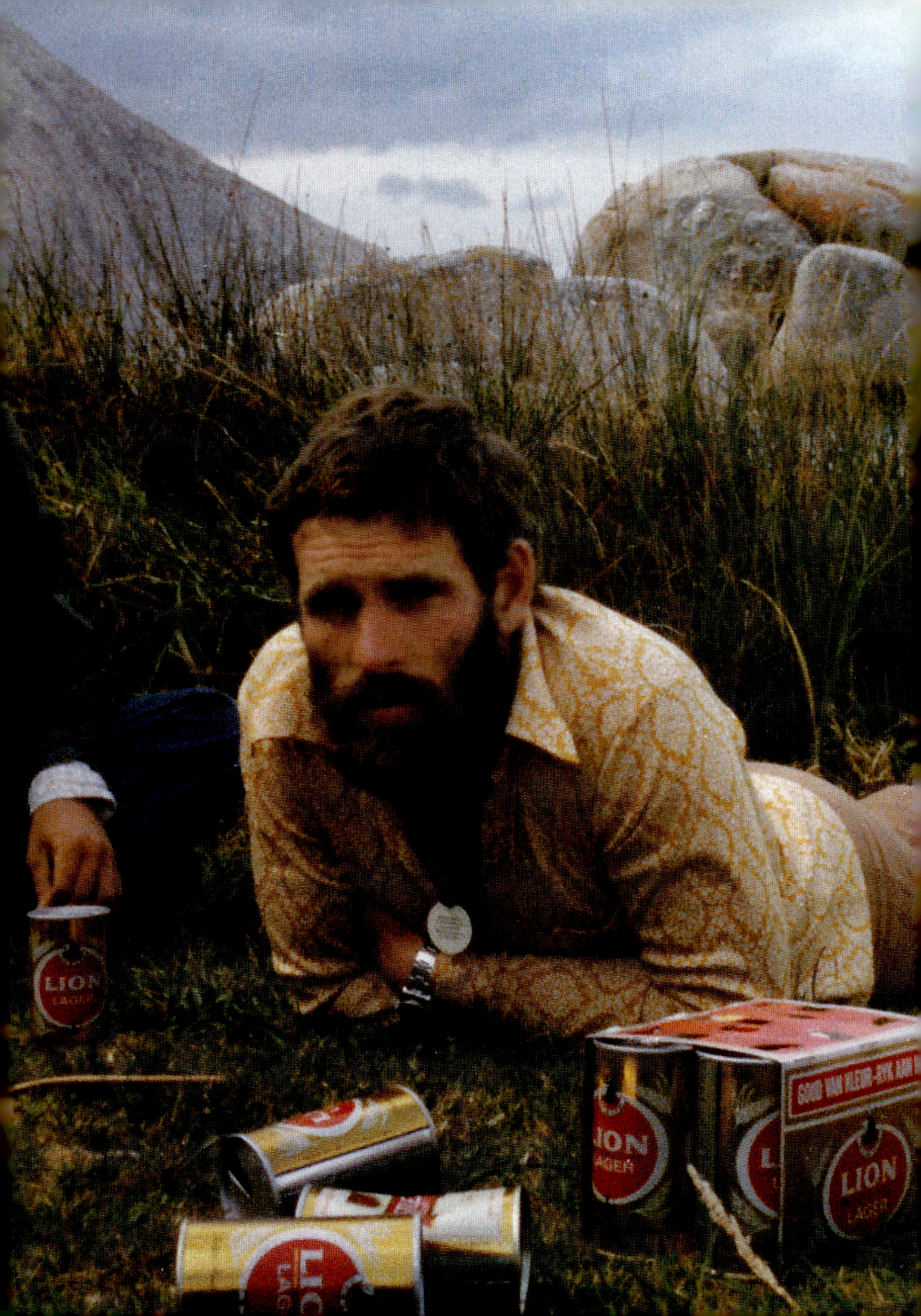
LION
LAGER

8

THE DRINKS TROLLEY

We will be forever grateful to Adalhard the Elder, the monk who first worked out how to make beer in AD 822 and shared that knowledge with the rest of us. We thank him and of course also Charles Glass for their valuable inputs.

We also bow in recognition to all the premier wine estates of South Africa that stretch from the Cape winelands to the Gariep River and the Drakensberg in KwaZulu-Natal. They continue to push the boundaries of winemaking in our country.

A glass of good wine will turn a pasta dish into a feel-good meal and ensure that it becomes an occasion. Similarly, Amarula liqueur can turn a modest scoop of ice cream into a dessert fit for kings, while an ice-cold G&T on a deck overlooking a river will turn the sunset into a spectacle. Just beware of good *skuimkoppie*,[67] which can turn the night into chaos.

Sam Fourie relaxes with a few Lions near Hugo's Pos, Langebaan. Fourie, a recipient of the Honoris Crux, became a game ranger after service. He died when an elephant trampled him to death.

---

[67] Dark rum, such as Red Heart or Captain Morgan.

RAISIN BEER

Raisins from a ratpack
Sugar
Water

Open a ratpack that has raisins inside. Empty the raisins with the sugar from the ratpack into a water bottle. Close the lid to stop flies from getting in, but open from time to time to allow the gas to escape.

Leave for about five to eight days – depending on the heat.

Strain and add more sugar before you serve. This softens the sourness.

The raisins can be replaced with pineapple, mango, litchi, apricot or plum. Leave the starch-based beers made from sorghum, millet and maize for the local professionals.

TIP

Do not seal the bottle too tightly, and especially not if you are going to leave it at the Tac HQ during Operation Moduler while you are gone for three weeks doing forward fire observation. The bottle will swell and eventually pop just at last light, leaving everyone wondering about where the 'shot' came from.

> Parade ground inspections are to combat readiness as mess hall food is to cuisine.

Passing Out

Parrot style

Newton's third law of motion says that for every action there is an equal and opposite reaction. Like all laws, there are exceptions to the rule, but this doesn't apply to the drinks trolley – even if you are a parrot.

Many people passed through the pub at Doppies, but, as can be expected from a place in which Dewald de Beer (the base warrant officer) had a big part to play, it was the animals that were the most recognisable. As Terry the Lion was banned from the pub, it was left to Joe the Parrot to prey on unsuspecting guests.

Joe was a master at dissecting lighters and could lift a can of Coke on his own – which he frequently did (we frequently added rum). Once he'd had enough he would pass out graciously, meaning he wouldn't fall off his perch – as corporals do. Someone would simply turn him on his back and place him on the Coke can. He would lie there motionless until the earth stabilised.

So, here is a lesson for all the youngsters: know when you reach your limits and just bow out gracefully – or someone will mix you a *skokkejaan*.

Joe the Parrot lies on his back in the pub at Doppies while Obie Oberholzer and BC Greyling can't stop laughing at the resident pub thief.

SPECIALISED COOKING – THE RECCE WAY

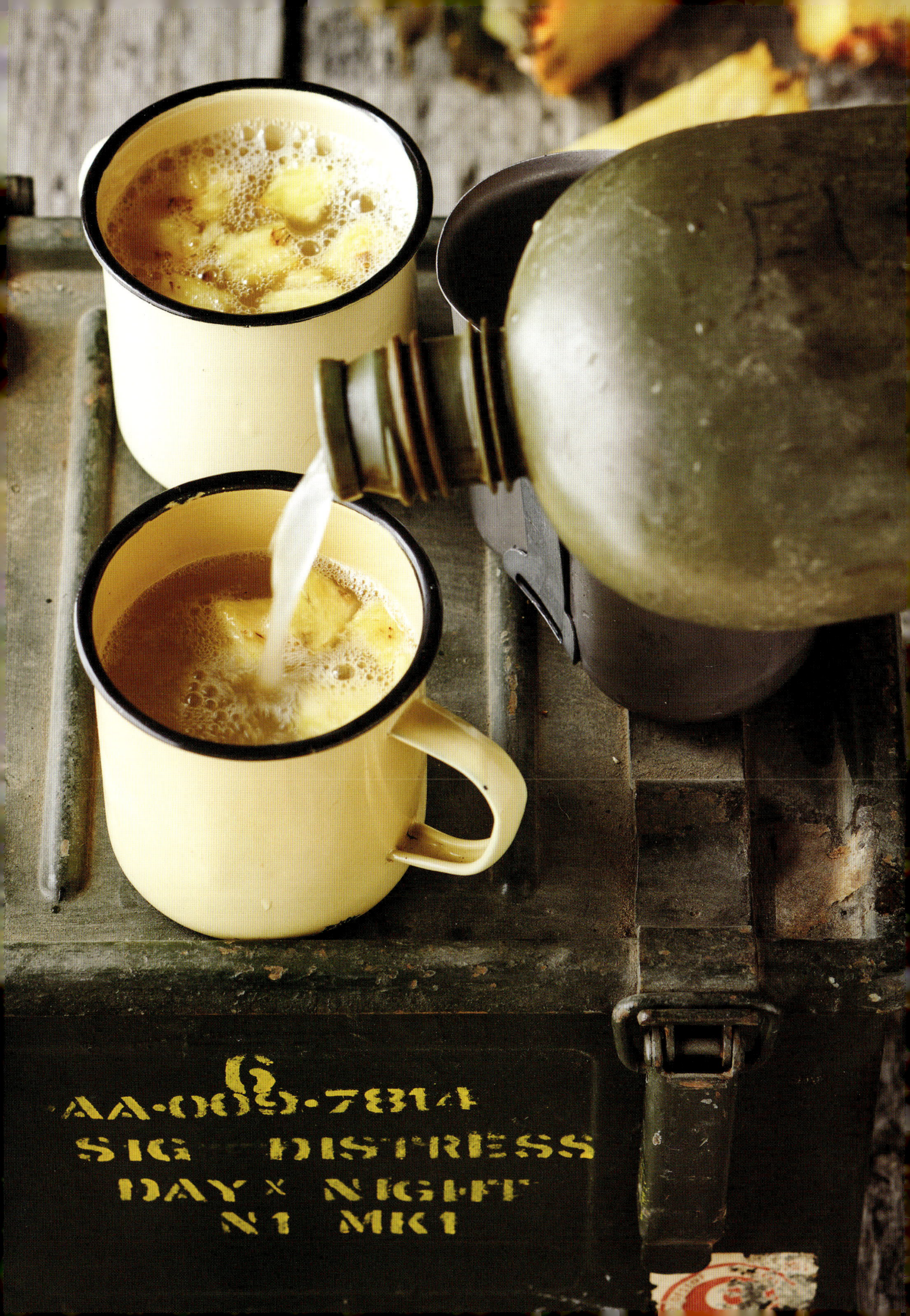
6
AA-009-7814
SIG DISTRESS
DAY × NIGHT
N1 MK1

Coffee and Tiger's Milk

à la Wally

While some of us wake up screaming for coffee, it takes a lot to beat the smell of smoke from a fire mingling with the aroma of strong dark-roast coffee gently bubbling away in a black kettle on low coals as the evening hours drag on. Especially if you are doing a very late-night stint waiting for Special Forces recruits to pass a checkpoint.

The kettle is called the *Keuringsketel* (selection kettle) and is part of the history of the Special Forces. Between 1985 and 1991, it was present at every selection course presented by 1 Recce. It was a permanent feature in the *Keuringstrommel* (selection trunk).[68]

During the selection course, the evaluators would be placed at certain points and would wait for the recruits to arrive, in order to evaluate them. The *Keuringsketel* has seen many try and fail to become Recces, but has also witnessed all of those who passed. Those who did make it include individuals like Chris Spanneberg, Doiby Coetzee and Div Lamprecht, all of whom later became unit commanders.

Koos Moorcroft and André (Diedies) Diedericks

Over the years, many doing duty as evaluators have drunk from the *Keuringsketel*, including Koos Moorcroft, Norman Power, Julius Kratz, André Diedericks, Jack Greeff and of course Bruce Laing, with his unique brand of humour. On more than one occasion, Bruce helped a struggling wannabe out of his misery and off the course. In his reports he would make comments such as the following: 'The student set a very low standard which he failed to maintain.' Another favourite was: 'You need to be a really special person to like this guy …'

When the last students passed the checkpoint it was usually close to midnight, meaning it was time to add some tiger's milk to the coffee. At these times the universal favourite was whisky. However, based on years of experience, a tot of witblits/grappa proved to offer a more integrated taste experience. When your nose catches the blend of sweet and bitter, the goodness spreads to every part of the palate. The extra warmth it gives as it goes down makes the stretcher you sleep on softer, the sleeping bag warmer and the short night longer.

---

[68] A metal trunk that held the essentials for the course leader and his evaluators, who would observe the mental fitness of the men on the course.

Kwando Cocktail

aka RHR with jelly

You might shake your head when you read the recipe, but, believe me, this drink has been served to both troops and prime ministers. It rose to notoriety in 1976 during a Cabinet visit to Fort Doppies and has become a tradition ever since.

If you happened to be at Doppies when the Kwando River is in flood, it means that no rations can be delivered, and soon the rations become scarce. What to do?

It is inconceivable to spend a weekend at Doppies without Red Heart rum (RHR). Here are some tips to get you out of your predicament:

Jelly works well as a mixer.

Dissolve, using more water than specified on the packet.

Pick any flavour or colour, assuming you can still see colour.

SKOKKEJAAN VIR BOBBEJAAN

by Johan Raath

I get a cold sweat when I recall the degree of destructive energy a 21-year-old unmarried soldier can muster when he has a full Saturday on the veranda of the Malibu in Durban or in the Father's Moustache, not to mention Smugglers Inn, London Town Pub or the Lonsdale. Barry Visser and I worked out the following cocktail for when the energy levels required to prevent such a member from inflicting self-induced damage became too much.

Double tot gin (for effect)
Double tot vodka (for effect)
Double tot tequila (for effect)
Double tot lemon juice (for colour)

When you see the member is about to disintegrate, attack is the best method of defence.

Mix all the ingredients and offer it to him.

Wait 5 minutes, then offer another one.

Wait 15 minutes, then accompany him to the car and leave him there. That way, you won't forget to take him back to the base when the rest of you are finally ready to go home.

No amount of logic can explain the levels of energy and creativity that flow from mixing alcohol and young corporals with spare time.

THE DRINKS TROLLEY

A Formal Supper

with Jack Dippenaar[69]

The formal supper is the pinnacle of military meals. These black-tie events present ample opportunity for wives and girlfriends to see the military at its best. A formal supper involves getting into mess dress and evening wear, with all the ceremony and traditions that an army can muster. It is a grand occasion, much like an evening ball but without the dancing. From a food point of view, the seven-course event will bring out the finest in the chefs that run the kitchen, and the food on display will be of the highest order.

The drinks list is equally impressive. It starts with the finest of canapés and cocktails served on arrival. These are served continuously until all the guests are seated The wines served with the various courses are top-notch, and the meal ends with Port, together with a dazzling assortment of cheese and biscuits. At this time the bar is also open for those predisposed to RHR, and it is here that these events normally take a different course. The following story serves as a bold reminder that alcohol affects corporals and captains equally.

This particular formal supper took place in Durban in the late 1980s, when Colonel Gert Keulder was the OC there. As was normal, the mess hall was 'dickeyed up', with plants and decorations creating a ball-type atmosphere. The members arrived in smartly pressed mess dress, accompanied by their wives or girlfriends. Everything was ever so smart. After assembling in the bar, everyone moved to the anteroom, where the customary glass of OBS (Old Brown Sherry) was presented. After the announcement to take seats, everyone moved to their places at the long tables according to the seating plan. This was formal, with protocol observed, including alternating male-female seating. Major Jack Dippenaar – as his seniority dictated – always sat near the head of the table with his peer group, whom he knew before he became blind.

Once everyone had taken their seats you would notice a section where there were no females – meaning the 'living in' section, where the young bloods sat. The movements and discussion here suggested a very different sense of expectation and contained way too much energy for a classy formal supper. This seemed more of a licence to drink as opposed to a grand affair.

As was tradition, the meal was planned more or less like this:

Welcoming – speech and a toast to the President
Soup – toast to the members
Starter – toast to the OC
Fish – toast to the unit
Main meal – speech and a toast to
    the country
Dessert
Stand up
Cheese and biscuits – final toast, to
    the fallen.

As usual, the procession kicked off with the food being served by a crowd of servicemen. The speeches and toasts came and went. The dishes were emptied; new courses came and with them more wine. When it was time for decanters, everyone observed the protocol of take with the right hand, pour and place, and then pass on with the left.

Senior NCOs attend a formal supper at 1 Recce in Durban. From left to right, Koos Loots, Joe Hunter, Pep van Zyl, Gellie Geldenhuys and Bruce Laing.

[69] Jack Dippenaar was an early operator in 1 Recce, who spent a lifetime in the military. In the mid-1970s, he lost his sight in a detonator accident and thereafter wore two glass eyes. After his rehabilitation he was transferred to support and became the personnel officer at 1 Recce.

SPECIALISED COOKING – THE RECCE WAY

Throughout all this, Jack Dippenaar, although blind, managed to observe protocol and made sure he didn't get caught out. He didn't ask for favours. The 'living ins' saw this differently and 'made mistakes' on purpose, for which they would be handed a spot fine – a double drink. So it was that, after dessert, everyone rose from the table and began to mingle more informally.

With the supper and formalities over, the members all went to the bar. The seniors stood together in a group with Jack, while the 'living ins' built up their courage at the other end of the bar. It was at this point that things went wrong, as they normally do.

On this particular occasion, there had been a few challenges at the 'living ins' section of the table. One of these required that some officers (names withheld) had to launch an 'attack' on the OC and his group. They prepared and positioned themselves and then brought the hall to silence to propose a toast. As the hall quietened, they raised their hands and toasted: 'We toast to … fire extinguishers!' Then they attacked.

The extinguishers were the dry powder type, and produced massive clouds of white powder as the 'living ins' changed towards the OC. The hall cleared in an instant. As the powdery mist settled, the lone, fully white 'statue' of Jack Dippenaar stood upright in the silence. During the hasty retreat, he had been abandoned by all and had taken the full force of the attack. Needless to say, the humour of the situation wasn't immediately recognised by Jack or anybody in the OC's entourage.

If you ever wondered how commanding officers decide which officers get the best assignments and the worst assignments, then this may provide a helpful clue.

Disciplinary Hearing

Kinghorn style

This story took place some time in 1976. The Special Forces recruits had just finished their pre-selection period and were ready to go on course. That night, one student ended up in the city (Durban) and, even worse, in a fight. The duty driver collected him and brought him back to base.

By the next morning the vehicles were ready to leave and he needed to get on – except he still had to face a disciplinary hearing. Trevor Floyd brought him to Major Malcolm Kinghorn, who at the time was the only officer on the base and was thus qualified to conduct a disciplinary hearing.

Before the troop was marched in double time, the situation was discussed. With the need for suitable people in the Recces, they discussed the charge and what the consequence should be. The hearing went more or less as follows:

Floyd: He broke the rules by going out and into town.
Kinghorn: We need people with initiative.
Floyd: He had drinks and got drunk.
Kinghorn: Do you guys not drink on a regular basis?

Flip Marx and Sam Fourie the day after they got into a fight with each other. As the boss said: natural aggression combined with an ability to control yourself is a good thing.

Floyd: He got into a fight with other people.
Kinghorn: We need people with natural aggression.
Floyd: He got beaten up.
Kinghorn: We can't have our troops losing fights. Charge him with bringing the unit into disrepute and fine him R50. Then load him on the truck.

THE DRINKS TROLLEY 205

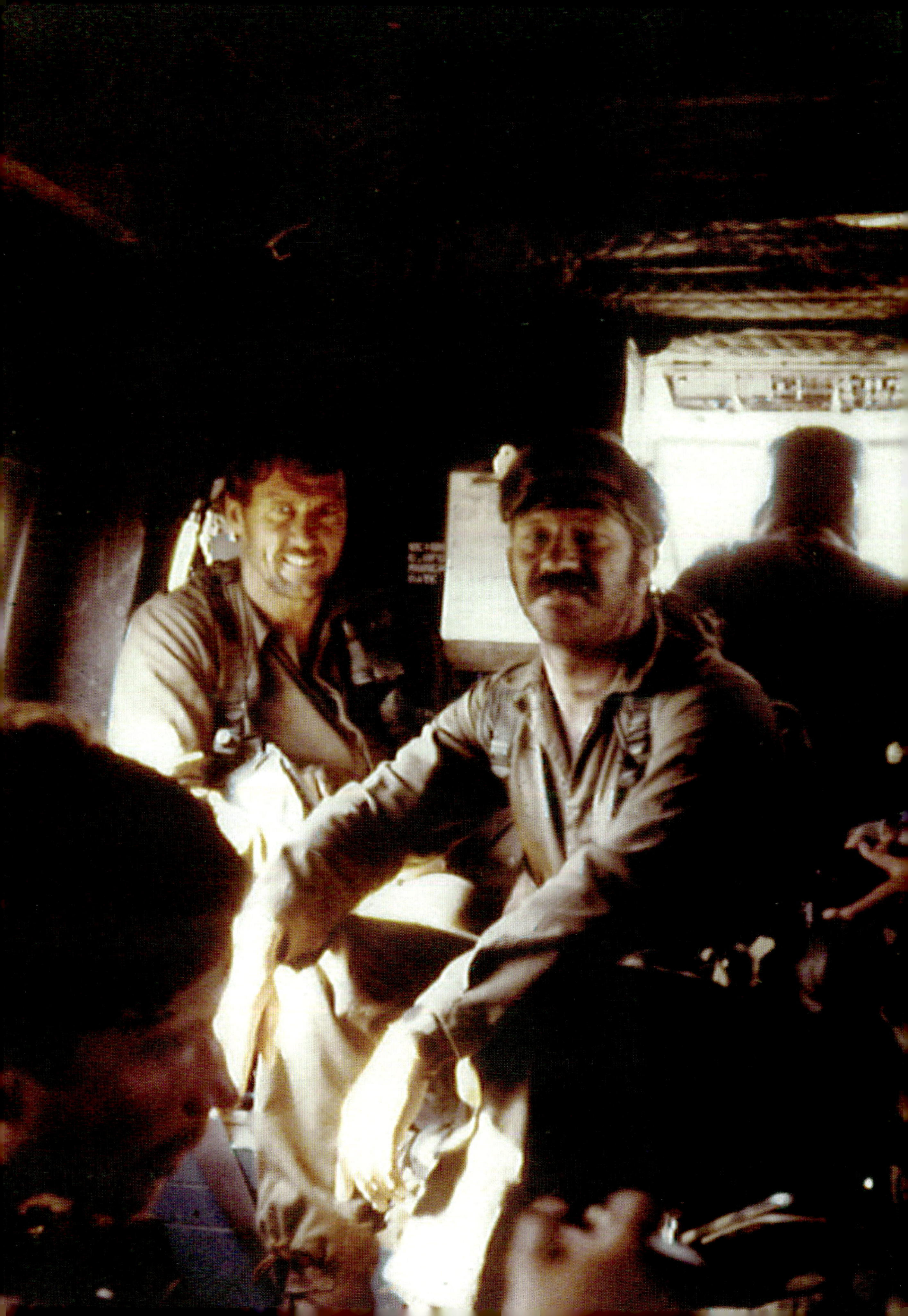

KILLER MEALS

The meals and recipes that have been included in this chapter are aimed at highlighting the very essence of being a member of the Special Forces. The Recce way of living is inspired by a strong sense of belonging and enduring camaraderie. The ever-present sense of humour among members of the Special Forces helps them to deal with challenges and promotes personal excellence.

> The enemy invariably attacks on one of two occasions: When you're ready for them. When you're not ready for them.

Special Forces operators after being picked up by a Puma helicopter north of Calueque, in southern Angola. From left to right: Mugger Swanepoel, Mike West, Anton Benade and Wayne Ross-Smith.

Ministerial Menu

with 'Palanca negra'
by Hannes Venter[70]

One day in 1976, when we were at Fort Doppies preparing to deploy with Unita, Commandant Jakes Swart informed me that Prime Minister BJ Vorster, the Cabinet, the Chief of the Defence Force, as well as the chiefs of the Army, Air Force and Navy would be staying at Fort Doppies for two nights for a *bosberaad*.

A chef from the Military Academy who had plenty of catering experience at the Prime Minister's Cape Town residence was on his way to prepare the food. After he arrived, I had a planning session with the late Kenaas Conradie, then the group warrant officer.[71] By then I had already decided that we would braai *palanca negra* (sable antelope) steaks and pork chops on the first night. After all, a special occasion requires a special meal.

Before I continue, some background: after the original Fort Doppies was destroyed by a fire in late 1974, a temporary tented camp we called Seekoei was built at the Horseshoe. When the Portuguese forces withdrew from Angola and Mozambique towards the end of 1974, a number of Portuguese soldiers who were intelligence operatives could not return to Portugal or stay on in Angola and Mozambique. They were given special asylum by the South African government and stayed at Seekoei for safety reasons until the situation had stabilised.

---

[70] Hannes Venter was the long-standing OC of 4 Recce as well as Acting GOC Special Forces.

[71] Conradie was also a founding member of the Special Forces.

Late in 1974, approximately ten of these Portuguese soldiers joined us at Seekoei Camp under a blanket of secrecy. Among them were Marou da Costa, Danny Roxo, Ribeiro, Souarez, Manual and José da Silva. These men all did excellent work with the South African Defence Force during Operation Savannah and afterwards. (Sadly, the majority of them were killed in action during the Border War.)

When I established Bravo Group,[72] I spent a long time at Seekoei Camp with the Portuguese soldiers. One morning in early 1975, Marou da Costa came up to me and told me that it was his birthday in a few days' time. It was difficult for us to communicate with the Portuguese, but he went on and on about how *he* wanted to prepare the food for *his* party.

I finally realised that he needed a special venison for the celebrations – 'palanca', which *he* wanted to hunt. A few days later, WO PW van Heerden and I found ourselves accompanying the hunting party. Close to old Doppies, a fair-sized herd of sables usually lived in peace, but on that day they were disturbed because of Marou's birthday preparations.

He shot a young calf and explained with a broad smile that the 'palanca' calf's meat is the best there is. Only then did I realise that in Portuguese sable is 'palanca'. The meat was even better than how Marou and his cronies had described it. It was definitely fit for a king, or in our case, a prime minister.

Back to the Cabinet visit to Fort Doppies in 1976. Kenaas was a demolitions boffin. Now, you can only be a demolitions expert if you are very responsible, disciplined and accurate. Given these characteristics, I tasked him with hunting a *palanca negra* a day before the arrival of our eminent guests.

So Kenaas, a few Bushmen and one or two operators departed in a flatbed Unimog on their very important mission. I started to worry when they had still not returned by lunchtime. The chef and I started considering a plan B.

Late in the afternoon Kenaas and his hunters arrived with great fanfare. Through the kitchen window I saw how the smiling hunters slapped each other on the back (those were the days before high fives) and delivered their booty. I could not believe my eyes … On the back of the vehicle was

---

[72] At that time there was only 1 Reconnaissance Commando and the operators were divided into two groups, Alpha and Bravo.

Sable antelope rush to drink from the Chobe River in Botswana.

not only a young *palanca* but also a young buffalo, a lechwe, a tsessebe and a warthog!

From that moment I dubbed Kenaas the last of the great white hunters and banned him from any further hunting. We slaughtered the carcasses and kept the *palanca* and warthog (as replacement for the pork chops). All the nice cuts from the remaining meat were hidden in the walk-in cooler and the rest was taken to the Bushman village. This was perhaps not the best idea, because that night they had a mother of a feast and weren't really presentable when the heavies visited.

On D-day everything was in place, including 50 *palanca* steaks and a succulent warthog. After the visitors arrived, we took them on a drive along the Kwando. On their return the chef announced that he would be ready to braai in an hour's time.

I went over to take a look at his preparations. He proudly opened one of the big pots … disaster! To my disgust, I saw our 50 *palanca* steaks boiling in water. I almost had a hearty. With a broad smile, he told me how, whenever he had to braai a large number of steaks, he always first boiled the steaks and then only warmed them up on the grill.

I could not believe my eyes and my ears. I had to restrain myself from not dunking his head in the pot. To make matters worse, he had cut up the warthog (we had wanted to spitbraai it) and had also boiled the potatoes that were supposed to be cooked in the coals. After I recovered from the shock, I realised there was nothing we could do except get the heavies as drunk as the chef.

In the meantime, our guests, under the leadership of Minister of Foreign Affairs Pik Botha, had gone straight to the bar. By the time they gathered at Freedom Square for supper, most of them were up to speed.

I was asked to tell them more about the Recces. After I said a few words, I informed them that Recce tradition called for overnight visitors to drink a Doppies cocktail (rum with a 'secret mixture'). We had filled jugs with this cocktail and they drank it like water.

The chef was called forward to explain the menu. I chipped in to explain that, due to the unreliable supply chain to our remote location, we had to shoot for the pot and hinted that the meat might be on the tough side. Supper was then served, but hardly anyone ate the leathery meat. The pudding and digestives were offered almost immediately afterwards.

While the meal was over quickly, 'dinner' carried on until late into the night. In the end the politicians and generals enjoyed their visit so much that they visited Fort Doppies three more times between 1976 and 1980. But it was only the class of 1976 that were privileged to be served *palanca* steaks and the Kwando Cocktail.

Menu

Turn back the clock to 1976.

Appoint the chief hunter, but make sure he is not a dems boffin.

Ensure hunters do not get *bokkoors*.

Invest in a good chef and double check that he has never cooked for the prime minister before.

KWANDO COCKTAIL

Dissolve jelly (red is better than the green, which gives the cocktail a funny colour) in water from the Kwando River.

Note that this jelly is served as a liquid. For a container, you can choose between a fire bucket, a rigel glass or mortar tubes.

Pour a six thousand-count tot of Red Heart rum into the container.

Serve while you remind your guests this cocktail is true Recce tradition.

Good news: after this cocktail, anything you serve will taste good.

Programme and Menu for Cabinet Palanca Braai

1. Afternoon arrival and game drive
2. Welcome cocktail – Kwando style
3. Starters
   Dog biscuits with sardines
4. Main meal
   Boiled sable steaks
   Warthog chunks
5. Side dish
   Boiled potatoes
   Braaibroodjies with gut
6. Dessert
   Caramel condensed milk
7. Digestives
   Rum, brandy and witblits

STARTER AND SNACKS

Raid a few ratpacks for dog biscuits, Provita, tinned viennas and Melrose cheese.

Mix sardines with Worcestershire sauce, some vinegar and chopped onions.

Serve on dog biscuits.

MAINS

Skin the *palanca*, taking great care not to damage the skin (the latter will be used in the Ops room and the horns in the bar).

Keep the prime steaks under armed guard to prevent the chef from laying his hands on them.

If necessary, use force to keep the Tabasco and chilli junkies away from the marinade.

Braai over *hardekool* coals and serve rare or medium. Definitely not well done and definitely not boiled.

When preparing the warthog, control the alcohol intake of the braaier to avoid him being *gaar* before the warthog. Start your spit two hours before dinner must be served (and do not cut up the warthog!)

SIDE DISHES

Place the potatoes directly in the coals; foil is for sissies.

Make the *braaibroodjies* with cheese, chutney and tomato. To keep

Recce recruits on the initial training cycle in the pub at Doppies. By the looks of it, this photo was taken during the 1982–1983 cycle. The water jug and cheers suggest a course winner and a down-down of Kwando cocktails à la ministerial style.

the *broodjies* from flopping open when turned, tie them up with medical gut. This has the added benefit of providing a few laughs when you see the dignitaries struggling to pull the gut from their teeth.

PUDDING

Caramel condensed milk from a tin.

DIGESTIVE DRINKS

Offer a choice between rum and Kwando water, Limosin brandy and coffee or witblits from the late Johan Oltoff (presented in Tarzan shoes or Waxies).

EDITORS' NOTE: The writers wish to place it on record that if corporals were responsible for such a flop they would have gotten a dirty for it. If this was the example set by senior commanders and founding members of the Special Forces, what would you expect the corporals to do? Clearly, all Recces – from top to bottom – more or less feel *f**kol*.

KILLER MEALS

Savimbi Marching Pot

by Douw Steyn

From 1981 the war effort in Angola intensified and the interaction with Unita became more frequent, structured and formal. By then, 1 Recce already had some experience in working with Unita, but over time all the Recce units became involved with training (lots and lots of training) for Unita and supported them on more specialised operations.

Operations with Unita were mostly done from Fort Foot at Rundu. The fort got its name from an expression often used by Unita leader Jonas Savimbi before a big operation that required walking over long distances for two weeks or more: 'Let's go footing.' It was on one of these 'let's go footing' operations that I acquired the skills to make a Savimbi marching pot.

As usual, we prepared methodically for the trip and packed our rucksacks with great care. From Rundu we were taken in Puma helicopters to the Unita positions. Directly after take-off you cross the Okavango River and Calai on the Angolan side. On this occasion we flew some two hours into Huambo province (the Pumas were fitted with ferry tanks).

Needless to say, a footing exercise with a commander in attendance does not go down like the normal tactical working exercise. The walking party consisted of close to 400 people, with Savimbi and a small guard of soldiers in the centre and us close to them. The rest of the convoy/crowd was made up of children and women and more soldiers. The logistics teams were right at the back carrying all the equipment on their heads, including tents, some empty 210-litre metal drums, food, vehicle spares, tables, water, ammunition, firearms and whatever else was needed.

On a journey like this, you normally walk for between three and four hours and then rest for 30 minutes to allow the logistics convoy with bearers to catch up. We ate from our rations that we carried while we were on the move. The rest of the convoy had to eat whatever the bush offered; food for them was cooked only every three to four days, so people had to leave the convoy from time to time and wander off into the bush to dig out roots and hunt. This meant quite a chaotic 'march' routine.

When we arrived at the place Savimbi thought was safe and where training could be done, he ordered that a camp be built. This included sleeping huts made of grass and sticks and a parade ground on which a few chairs for the most senior officers were placed looking out on the grounds. This all took less than two days.

While the camp was being built, preparations began for the first meal, a gesture of goodwill on the part of Savimbi

OPPOSITE This is a good example of a permanent structure at a permanent Unita base. The Unita command did all their planning, training and operations from such bases.

ABOVE Oil drums filled with all kinds of meat provide food for an army – quite literally!

himself. It was to be potkos (I can't call it a potjie because the food was prepared in six of the 210-litre drums on big fires). The chefs assembled all the food the logistics teams had collected for the feast, which was to be served on long tables put together right there in the bush.

The meal included an array of wild animals, rabbits, buck, and field food that had been gathered, killed and carried on people's heads for the past two days, as well as two cows that had been herded along. These were slaughtered and laid out on the tables with the rest of the bush ensemble.

As meat was not often on the menu, it gathered quite a bit of interest from the convoy, and also became the centre of attraction for all the flies in southern Angola. In fact, with all the flies covering the ingredients it was impossible to work out what made it into the pot and what didn't, so I'm unsure if the ingredients listed below are accurate.

It was quite a sight, but, as you observed it all, you knew you were part of a special occasion and that you wouldn't hesitate to enjoy the meal with your fellow soldiers.

INGREDIENTS

10 big wild animals, on the bone

2 cows on the bone

Small wild animals, such as rabbits, birds and wild pig, on the bone

Several drums of pap

Gravy

For this dish use only natural ingredients, no preservatives, cold storage or pre-packed foods – only naturally well-matured meats. You are not allowed any sideshows such as wine …

Watch as the chefs make the fires, then place the drums next to the fires and add water to them – without even washing the drums.

The drums are then filled to the brim with meat pieces (anything from the tail to the nose). Initially, about a third of the meat will stick out above the water, so the flies just carry on eating. I'm sure this is their secret ingredient.

Then the cooking starts, with the drums working almost like slow cookers because of their size and the amount of ingredients that have to be cooked.

SERVING INSTRUCTIONS

The soldiers stood in long queues at each pot, so we joined them with our fire buckets in hand. The Unita soldiers used anything that was hollow to receive their share of the special food that had been made with so much love.

The dishing-up took about an hour or two. By then the flies had descended on everyone and everything – the pots, the pans, the people. A mere wave of your hand or a branch did not bother them at all, because they were as eager as us to get something hot in their mouths.

Once you got to the front, things became rather unceremonious. First came the heap of pap and then an unidentifiable piece of meat. If you were lucky, you got a bone to suck on. With your bucket filled with delicacies, you then moved to the nearest tree to sit and enjoy your first Savimbi six-meat marching pot.

We stared at each other to see who would be brave enough to dip into the concoction first. We furiously waved away the flies that immediately descended to claim their share. Each time they flew off, you gobbled down a portion.

Much to our surprise, the meat was very tasty, and the gravy, which was made from all the leftover stuff, was just as good. There was enough food for seconds, and my friends Greg Ashton, Valie, Paul Courtney and I were quickly standing in line again, hoping to get a bigger bone this time around.

As they say, what doesn't kill you will feed you!

KILLER MEALS

Frozen Chicken and Killer Sauce

by the Wife of an operator[73]

When the young and unmarried Recces exited the gates of 1 Recce on the Bluff in Durban on weekends, the little garden of our duplex flat in the Bisley Close complex fell in their direct line of sight. At that moment many of the guys would impulsively decide to invite themselves for a braai. In fact, in time it became a weekend pit-stop. It was open season at our house!

Their mothers must've taught them some manners. Parts of it stuck, even if very far at the back of their minds. At the moment they decided to invite themselves over, a distant memory must have surfaced: 'Just take something along. Anything, as long as you don't go empty-handed.'

Now, the Greek café on the corner of Marine Drive down the road had a small freezer with horribly old and skinny frozen chickens. Convenience being the operative word, this became the guys' standard offering at these weekend braais.

To many of them, I became a confidante in matters of the heart. Once, one of the guys had a rude awakening when he discovered that the girl with whom he had fallen in love was not a girl after all. She had seduced him at the strip club near the harbour, nogal. It was quite a blow to him and I had to comfort him.

The guys were also avid card players, and the games usually started during the braai or after we'd eaten. You had to watch them closely; I once caught Struis Strydom cheating. *Die bliksem!*

It's been a while now, but this was sort of what I did to try and salvage those dismal frozen chickens.

1 frozen chicken
Water
Lemon juice
Spices

FOR THE KILLER SAUCE

2 onions
Cooking oil
Mushrooms
Salt and pepper
Milk
Flour (or Maizena)
Cream
Old Brown Sherry

METHOD FOR CHICKEN

Steam the damn pieces of old and blue chicken in water with lemon juice added.
Spice the thing.
Braai.
Finished!

[73] We salute all Recce wives who had to run things at home while their husbands were away for long periods. On top of that they put up with their mischief. They are definitely more adaptable and focused than the men.

METHOD FOR KILLER SAUCE

My secret was the sauce in which I smothered the chicken (or any other suspect meat brought by guests).

Fry lots of onions in oil.

Add tons of mushrooms.

Season with salt and pepper.

Add any other ingredients you like, but no tomatoes or acidic stuff, though.

Add milk.

Thicken the sauce with flour (or Maizena).

Add cream by the bucketful.

Stir in OBS (Old Brown Sherry). If you want to pretend you are not a Recce, and that you know the meaning of the word 'sophistication', use a really good white wine instead of OBS.

Finally, grind some black pepper and mix it into the sauce.

This sauce transformed those old, skinny chickens into gourmet chicken à la Bluff. In those days women were expected to be 'goeie, gehoorsame vroue' (dutiful wives). My frozen chicken story is evidence that there was a time in my life when we actually tried.

Many good times were had around *potjies* at 1 Recce's E Block in Durban.

The boom gate at the entrance to 1 Recce base within the Bluff military area in Durban.

The only problem with the transformed chicken was that our uninvited guests now got rather proud of their contribution. They actually believed this way of serving chicken was normal. So, the next weekend, they would just pop in at the Greek café again!

Ah, I remember those braais fondly.

PS: I still miss our games of bridge. And poker!

KILLER MEALS 215

Christmas Lunch at Cuito

by Justin Vermaak

The face of the battle for Cuito Cuanavale.

Being entrenched in the Tumpo Triangle, close to Cuito Cuanavale, during Operation Moduler over the festive season in 1987 is not a first-choice setting for Christmas lunch. If, however, you are a seasoned Recce working for the first time with a large-scale conventional force it can be quite an eye-opener.

If you are used to operating in smaller groups of two to twelve people, then seeing 3 000 soldiers assembled in battle formation is quite a new experience. Here you get see real tanks, large pieces of artillery, mechanised infantry and vast numbers of really young soldiers.

Everything you ever learned and trained for comes into play. You get to be the soldier you are needed to be – the eyes and ears of the Army.

Your entire unit will deploy, some as SA-7 teams, others to set up ambushes on the road north of town, while others will do night missions into the enemy encampments to establish the exact positions. This is true specialised work. You will go off for a few weeks at a time on a mission.

Should you leave on such a mission just before Christmas, stay true to tradition and start planning your Christmas lunch early.

If your tradition is about serving *frikkadelle* and potato salad, make sure you have the ingredients.

If your tradition is about decorating your house, make a few decorations.

If your tradition is about giving gifts, make sure you can do so.

If your tradition is about having a beer or a glass of wine, then you better have some ready.

So, as you pack for the forward observation deployment you should select your Christmas meal from the ratpacks you were given. Meatballs will serve as substitute for *frikkadelle*, and the little cans of potato salad are really good, so all you now need are the ingredients for the beer.

For beer, rely on your experience and fill a two-litre water bottle with all the raisins from four of the ratpacks. You can then empty all the sugar from these few ratpacks into the bottle. Shake the bottle and close. You will drink bitter coffee for a few days but you will have beer when you return to the camp. In the meantime, you can now start thinking about how to decorate your basher/hut.

The next day you will join up with your Unita party and the vehicles at the assembly place at the back of the

SPECIALISED COOKING – THE RECCE WAY

encampment. Normally, driving by vehicle is better than walking, but in these conditions walking is almost a better alternative. The Ural is piled so high with ammunition and bombs that you and your team have to sit on top of this pile of boxes and share the space with about 50 Unita soldiers. Remind yourself to stay in the moment. Find a spot close to the front – it will be less bouncy there.

When the vehicle lumbers in the soft sandy soil, a few ammo boxes and soldiers will fall onto your shins and remain there. The thought of these unwashed soldiers being spread all over you is quite overwhelming. Now is the time to dig deep and recall that incredible sense of humour Recces are known for.

At this moment, my fellow operator Dave Hall looked at me and Gary Yaffe, the other member of our team and said, 'Now I know why they call it the log route …'. He was, of course, referring to the logs we were driving over instead of the log(istics) route we were following. We just laughed at how ridiculous the situation was.

By 22 December your mission will have been completed. By now you have studied the enemy positions for eight days and have made careful notes of everything in your pigskin diary.[74] You will come back in this position for the final assault, which will take place later. You will also have had time to carve out one or two wooden pipes as gifts. The route is only 28 km, so it is a day's walk.

On arrival at the camp later in the evening, report to the officers in charge, who will be poring over their maps at their command vehicles (Casspirs covered with camouflage nets). The following day, there will be a full debrief when all the teams have returned. You will now be able to build a composite view of the enemy positions.

After the morning briefings, you will have some free time to rest, wash and check on your beer. The beer might be slightly bitter, so add more sugar, shake and close. After doing kit maintenance and weapon cleaning, you can give your undivided attention to decorating your basher. Grab this opportunity to display your resourcefulness.

The cheese wrappers you used (and set aside) during deployment can be cut into long, thin streamers. You have enough time to kill and your knife is sharp. The lids from tins can be bent to make festive twirlies. Punch a hole in them and hang them up all over. The medical bag contains good surgical scissors that you can use to cut long paper strips to make bunting. Add a few balloons (condoms from the medical bag) and your basher will look a treat.

By now it is only one day before Christmas, so better you find a way to wrap your presents and find a Christmas tree.

Attend the late afternoon briefing and do the last light stand-to. At least the bed of grass and the sleeping bag ensures a good night's rest. However, at about 23h00 you will be awoken by a loud bang that sounds very close. Is it a bomb or a shot? The sound of muffled voices floats over from the bashers around you. You peer into the darkness with every sense alert, trying to understand the nature of the threat.

Then, slowly, the smell of beer gets into your nose.
Oh dear!

Word spreads quickly in the dark as to the true nature of the 'explosion'. A few f**ks are heard but things calm down soon enough. You go back to sleep knowing you will now have to share your beer, even if it's a mere two litres.

On Christmas Day, stay true to tradition and first open the gifts. Be very grateful for the can of fruit salad from your buddy. A wonderful surprise will be the Lion Lagers the team in Rundu have packed and your Tac HQ have kept for you. Enjoy the beer with your leader group; these are good men.

When everyone returns to their own quarters, it's time to have your Christmas meal and share the home-brewed beer with some of your brothers in arms. Take a moment to take everything in and reflect on the fact that you should never have a Christmas like this ever again. Tomorrow the war will continue … one more push to Cuito, then this war is over.

Christmas lunch in a suitably decorated observation post (OP) north of 21 Brigade's positions near Cuito Cuanavale. From left to right: Barry Visser, Gary Yaffe, PJ Johns, Robert Trautman and Justin Vermaak.

---

[74] These diaries were made from special material, so that once written the text would not come off, however wet the diary became.

From time to time old soldiers meet - this photo was taken at the Recce Bash in September 2016 and shows 94 former operators and 24 serving members. The photo is remarkable because it includes four founding members of the organisation, four generals (serving and retired) and a group of students then on the Special Forces training cycle.

Call for submissions for Volume 2

We trust you have enjoyed this book. The stories are many and the space is limited.

This volume purposely covers only the first 25 years of the Recces' history and ends with the disbanding of 1 Recce in 1997. We will publish a second volume in the near future that will cover the period up to 2007.

Volume 2 will focus much more on the remaining units (4 and 5 Recce). While it will also revisit the history of the Recces, it will focus more on the involvement of South African Special Forces in the expanded African operating arena. The book will include new types of stories, with much more of an African dynamic within a global framework. In this expanded arena, current serving Special Forces members are doing a great job under rapidly changing and challenging conditions.

Any submissions received for Volume 2 will be stored in an electronic archive. If you are a former or serving member, contact the South African Special Forces Association on the email address or link below to find out more about how you can get involved. Use the same contact details if you are a member of the public and you want to contribute to Sasfa or order a copy of this book online:

www.recce.co.za
info@recce.co.za

INDEX

Page numbers in *italics* indicate photographs.

1 Reconnaissance Commando 9, 72, 74, 209
1 Reconnaissance Regiment (1 Recce) 6, 21, 37, 38, 40, 50, 55, 62, 67, 71, 72, 81, 86, 94, 95, 102, 103, 107, 126, 137, 152, 158, *175*, 175, 180, 183, 185, 188, 202, 204, 212, 214
31 Battalion 158
32 Battalion 158
4 Reconnaissance Regiment (4 Recce) 37, 40, 42, 44, 48, 52, 53, 56, 57, 58, 59, 66, 67, 95, 158, 172, 175, 178, 180, 185, 191, 208
5 Reconnaissance Regiment (5 Recce) 22, 40, 48, 77, 92, 95, 106, 115, 116, 120, 121, 158, 175, 185, 194
51 Commando 116, 120
54 Commando 92
6 Reconnaissance Regiment 175
61 Mechanised Battalion 104, 112

A
Adam, GD (Maddies) 44, 94, 120, 148
Amanzimtoti 86
Angola 37, 46, 76, 78, 81, 82, 84, 97, 106, 113, 115, 121, 145, 152, 153, 158, 160, 166, 167, 168, 169, 172, 207, 208, 212, 213
Aristotle 49
Armscor 163
Ashton, Greg 213

B
Batter 15
Beef
    Beef ribs in the oven 114, *115*
    Oxtail 118, *119*
    Resupply pot roast 113
    Stroganoff in Blaauw cheese 116
    Underdone steak, E Block 102
Beira 53, 176
Benade, Anton 84, 158, 206
Benguela Railway 166, *166*, 167
Berger, Klein Ian 25
Bestbier, André 8, 86, 94

Beverages
    Kwando cocktail 203, 210, 211
    Raisin beer 200
    Skokkejaan vir bobbejaan 203
Bezuidenhout, Ertjies 92
Bezuidenhout, Neil (Bez) 102, *102*
Bhangazi 21
Bilene 176
Biltong 164
Blaauw, Hennie 116, 120
Blignaut, Blikkies 8, 194
Boonzaaier, Marius (Bone) 8, 21, 101, 113
Border War 6, 18, 32, 33, 35, 47, 53, 78, 97, 126, 152, 158, 162, 164, 166, 168, 170, 172, 183, 209
Borman, CJ (Borries) 148
Botes, JMJ (Boats) 94, 148
Botha, Pik 210
Botha, Spik 8, 41, 73, 103, 110
Botswana 21, 29, 30, 49, 101, 160, 162, 174, 209
Brazzaville 171
Bread
    Beer bread 131
    Braaibroodjies 132, *132*
    French toast 133
    Pizza bread 133
    Pot bread 130, *131*
    Stick bread 130, *130*
Breytenbach, JD (Jan) 72, 94, 148
Britz, Hannes 91
Brokaar, John 92
Buffalo base 158
Buffalo steaks 164
Bully beef and beans 33
Burger, Beyers 92
Burger, Rupert (Civvie) 22
Burr-Dixon, Johan 77
Buys, Buks 157
Bwabwata National Park 47, 162

C
Cabinda 6
Calai 212
Calueque 152, 207
Camel's Inn 121
Caprivi Strip (Zambezi Region) 7, 21, 22, 46, 47, 49, 137, 158, 162, 163, 168, 172
    Map 46
Cassava 127
Central African Republic 151
Chicken
    Blitz chicken 91
    Bunny chow 90, *91*
    Chicken livers 89, *89*
    Chicken sandwich 78, *79*
    Chicken schnitzel 86, *87*
    Frozen chicken and killer sauce 214–215
    Roadrunner curry 82, *83*
Christie, Gavin 52
Cloete, André 163
Clube Naval 53
Coconut waffles with mango 178
Coetzee, Doiby 8, 194, *194*, 202
Coetzee, Peet (Oom Pote) 41, 115
Compass Rose 37, 67
Conradie, Kenaas 22, 77, 120, 148, 184, 208, 209
Cooking basics 15
Courtney, Paul 213
Crocodile
    Crocodile steak 171
    Crocodile stew 48
Croucamp, K (Crokes) 102, 158
Crust mix 130
Cuba 78
Cuban Hat 95
Cuito Cuanavale 48, 82, 216, 217

D
Da Costa, José 84, 147
Da Costa, Marou 209
Da Silva, José 209
Dalla Pria, Rose 38
Dar es Salaam 6, 37
Davidson, Gus 85, 175
De Beer, Dewald (Dewies) 8, 22, 25, 26, 29, 77, 95, 148, *149*, 200
De Gouveia, Johnny 8, 102, 127
De Jager, Rieme 8, 32, 76
De Kock, K 99
De Vries, Roland 8, 104, 112
Dednam, John 147

Delport, Hans 113
Democratic Republic of the Congo 37, 133, 151, 170
Desserts and sweet treats
　Baked pancake strudel 191
　Brown pudding 194, 195
　Bush Ferrero Rocher 190, 191
　Cooked wheat and cinnamon 192
　Dog biscuit treat 35
　Flour balls 192, 193
　Ice cream with Amarula 188, 189
　Milkshake doughnuts 34
　Strawberries and cream 196, 197
　Versatile doughnuts 192
Dhlakama, Afonso 176
Diedericks, André (Diedies) 12, 94, 202
Dietriech, Paul 92
Dippenaar, Jack 204
Divundu 158
Donkergat 42, 44, 44, 56, 58, 59, 66
Dos Santos, Fernando 127
Du Plessis, JWA (Chilli) 66
Du Plooy, Roelf 8, 22
Du Toit, Niek 84, 178
Du Toit, Renier 8
Dukuduku 21, 98, 106, 106, 107
Dunkley, Stephen 8
Durban 21, 37, 38, 50, 62, 71, 71, 72, 74, 81, 91, 94, 95, 102, 107, 115, 188, 203, 204, 214, 215

E
Eenhana 158
Eggs
　Biltong and egg soufflé 159
　Eggs Benedict 70, 71
Els, Paul 8
Energy guide 12
Engelbrecht, Julius 120
Enkeldoorn 175
Epupa Falls 153
Erasmus, Abel 41
Erasmus, JC 50
Eshowe 81

F
Faber, Carel 21, 101
Fapla see People's Armed Forces of Liberation of Angola

Father's Moustache 94, 102, 203
Faul, Billy 40
Fish and seafood
　Baked barbel 60
　Baked fish with fried plantain and fufu 170
　Barnacle stew 62
　Calamari in curry yoghurt 58
　Calamari pieces 58
　Clams in peanut sauce with port 176, 177
　Crayfish 44, 45
　Crusted fish fingers 55
　Deep-fried flying fish 62, 62
　Dorado fillets 38, 39
　Fish curry on the beach 50, 51
　Fish head soup 59
　Freshwater mussels 46
　LM prawns 53
　Pan-seared tuna/marlin 50
　Perlemoen 59
　Prawn cocktail 52
　Seafood paella with pasta 60, 61
　Shanghai prawns 52
　Smoked snoek 42, 43
　Survival seafood ensemble with beach spices 40
　Sushi 41
　Tiger fish curry 49
　Trout salad 54, 55
Fitzsimons Snake Park 107
Flamingo Hotel 42
Flapjacks 130
Floyd, Trevor 22, 94, 148, 205
Forts
　Doppies 7, 7, 21, 22, 25, 26, 46, 46, 47, 49, 74, 137, 158, 162, 163, 164, 200, 203, 208, 209, 210
　Foot 115, 158, 158, 212
　KZN 88
　Nomad 153, 153
　Renamo 176
　Rev 82, 115, 120
Fourie, Dawie 106
Fourie, Frans 94, 181
Fourie, JJP (Hopkop/Hoppie) 148
Fourie, Sam 198, 205
Fourie, SW 8, 113, 127
Frelimo see Frente de Libertação de Moçambique
French Foreign Legion 133
Frente de Libertação de Moçambique (Frelimo) 76, 176
Fruit, Mixed 35

G
Geldenhuys, Gellie 204
Geyer, Eugene 8
Goat in strips, Late-night 157
Godbeer, Ray 7, 29, 30
Golden Highway 21
Greeff, Jack 32, 95, 202
Greyling, BC 21, 101, 200
Greyling, Jan 21

H
Hall, Dave 217
Harare 175
Harrismith 55
Hartbeespoort Dam 110
Havana 78, 78
Heigers, Albie 158
Heiliger, Leon 25
Hell's Gate 147
Heydenrych, GJ (Gerrie) 66
Heyns, John 160
Hills, James 92, 120, 149
Holiday Inn 73
Hugo's Pos 44, 199
Human, Kobus (Kragvarkie) 107
Hunter, Joe 126, 183, 204

I
Impalile Island 162
Infantry School 72, 73
Inhambane 53, 176
Israel 151, 180, 181, 181

J
Jamba 82, 168
Jenkins, Dave 101
Jennings, Rob 29, 191
Joe the Parrot 164, 200, 200
Johannesburg 81
Johns, PJ 102, 217
Jordan 180
Joubert, AJM (Joep) 148, 149
Joubert, IJ (Tuffy) 8, 66, 74

Joynt, Vernon 163

K
Kabila, Laurent 170
Kaokoland 152, 152, 153, 154–155
Katima Mulilo 162, 163
Kaunda, Kenneth 172
Kavango region 158
Kazungula 172
Keulder, Gert 94, 149, 204
Kinghorn, Malcolm 56, 56, 58, 148, 171, 205
Kinshasa 6, 37, 133, 170, 170
Kitching, GJ (Kitcha) 92, 120
Kloppers, Japie (Kloppies) 38, 149, 181
Kongola 46, 162
Kratz, Julius 44, 202
Kruger National Park 80
Kruger, Kriek 103
Kruger, Kwartel 175
Kruger, Ouboet 106
KwaMbonambi 81
KwaZulu-Natal 107

L
Laing, Bruce 94, 202, 204
Lakes
    Bhangazi 76
    Kariba 37, 60, 172, 175
    Sibaya 76
    St Lucia 106
    Tanganyika 170
Lamb
    Kavango lamb shank 160, 161
    Lamb chops with tzatziki 104, 105
    Lamb knuckle pot 104
    Mansaf 180
Lamberti, Peter 7, 21, 80
Lamprecht, Div 8, 202
Lamprecht, DP (Dan) 148
Lamprecht, Eric 184
Langebaan 37, 40, 42, 44, 44, 52, 56, 57, 58, 66, 66, 199
LBJ stew recipe 156
Liebenberg, AJ (Kat) 38, 57, 148
Liebenberg, Basil 25, 110
Liebenberg, Henk 40
Linyanti swamps 46
Livingstone 172

Lobito 166
London Town Pub 203
Longa 82
Lonsdale 203
Loots, FW (Fritz) 148, 148
Loots, WJ (Koos) 66, 148, 148, 160, 180, 204
Lourenço Marques *see* Maputo
Lourens, Dirk 17
Luanda 99, 166
Lubango Pass 167
Luena 113, 127, 169
Luiting, Lafras 82
Lubumbashi 170
Lumumba, Patrice 170
Lundberg, Pierre 8

M
Maass, Johnny 118, 118
Malan, Jan 112
Malan, Magnus 149
Maleta, Ivan 21
Malibu Hotel 94, 102, 203
Mango atjar 144
Maputo 53, 53, 176
Marais, Frans 101
Maritz, Dap 8, 56
Marx, Flip 8, 21, 205
Marx, Wentzel 107, 107
Masvingo 175
Matias, Neves 147
McCabe, Mac 35
McIvor, Bruce 25, 29, 95
Meerholz, Corrie 120, 175
Meiers, André 84
Menongue 82, 166
Mince
    Chilli con carne 136, 137
    Giant frikkadelle 110, 111
    Mici 110
Mobutu Sese Seko 170
Moçâmedes Railway 166
Mongua 112
Moorcroft, Koos 8, 22, 22, 72, 92, 120, 148, 148, 160, 160, 202, 202
Mopane worms
    Braaied 153
    Dried 153
    Fried 153
    Roasted 7
More, John 77, 148
Moscow 182
Mozambican National Resistance (Renamo) 33, 106, 176, 178
Mozambique 53, 76, 106, 174, 176, 208
Mpacha 162, 163
Mtubatuba 106
Mtwara 176
Mudumu National Park 162
Muffins 130
    Energy bar and raisin muffins 34
Mullen, Sean 21, 158
Murphy, John 81
Mushrooms, Brown 169

N
Nacala 176
Namibe 166
Namibia 46, 104, 137, 152, 153, 160, 162, 172, 182
Nampula 176
Nando's 89
Napoleon 6
Nel, KE (Krubert) 66
Nico, Ric 147
Nkasa Rupara National Park 162
Nortjé, Gert 21, 48

O
Oberholzer, Jimmy 72, 73, 81, 95, 149, 184
Oberholzer, Obie 101, 200
Oetle, Johan 40
Official Secrets Act 6
Olckers, Ewald 94, 148
Olivier, Chris (Kolle) 38
Omega base 21, 158
Omuramba 101
Omuthiya 104
Ondangwa 82, 115, 153
Ongiva 112
Onions
    Creamy red onion 142, 143
    Onion jam 196
    Red onion and meatballs 142
    Sautéing 15
    Simply onion 142
Oosthuizen, Chris 160
Operations

Cloud 169
Coolidge 48
Hooper 104, 158
Hunter 191, 196
Kerslig 38, 67, 99
Kropduif 145
Meebos 104, 112, 158
Moduler 104, 158, 200, 216
Protea 104, 158
Rolio 172
Savannah 209
Sea Warrior 113
Vine 53
Operators Kop 66
Opperman, Gif 82, 182
Oshakati 115, 156
Oshakati Guesthouse 115
Oshikoto 158
Oshikuku 153
Ostrich
    Scrambled ostrich egg and braised steak 74
    Swartberg carpaccio 74, 75
Otto, Otch 56
Oudtshoorn 72, 73, 74, 128
Outapi 153
Ovamboland 10, 156

P
Pancakes 130
Pap
    Pap three ways 128
    Porridge and sour milk 152
Pasta
    Spaghetti carbonara 138, 139
    Spicy chicken noodles 138
Pelser, Taffy 8, 88, 128, 171
Pemba 53, 176
People's Armed Forces of Liberation of Angola (Fapla) 78, 82
People's Liberation Army of Namibia (Plan) 152
Phalaborwa 26, 80, 92, 106, 115, 116, 120, 121
Pickles 147
Plato 58, 63, 67
Polana Hotel 53
Polenta 128, 129
Police Task Force 151, 181
Ponta Malongane 53

Popular Movement for the Liberation of Angola (MPLA) 78, 168
Pork
    Bush pig in sweet and sour sauce 108
    Eisbein 108, 109
    Pork roll 116, 117
Porthole Grill restaurant 52
Potatoes
    Cheesy jacket potato 124, 125
    Pep's hot potatoes 126
    Potato bake 124
    Potato rosti 124
    Spinach and potatoes 140
Potgieter, Kevin 184
Potgieter, MJ (Yogi) 74, 148
Powell, Gordon 92
Power, Norman 202
Pretoria 41, 115, 149
Prinsloo, Schalk (Swapo) 107, 157
Python, Fried 25

Q
Qualifications for Special Forces 11
Queiroz, Amilcar 76, 76

R
Raath, JJ (John) 102, 102
Raath, Johan 8, 102, 203
Raisins 144
Renamo see Mozambican National Resistance
Retief, Anton 77, 106
Rhodesia see Zimbabwe
Rhodesian Special Air Service (SAS) 174, 174
Rice
    Pumpkin and ham 'risotto' 134
    Yellow savoury rice 134, 135
Richter, Jakes 8
Rivers
    Chobe 46, 162, 172, 209
    Congo 170, 171
    Cuito 37, 48
    Cunene 37, 152
    Gural 166
    Hoanib 152
    Kuvelai 156
    Kwando 7, 21, 37, 46, 47, 49, 101, 162, 203, 210
    Mui 112
    Okavango 37, 49, 60, 158, 160, 162, 212
    Zambezi 37, 46, 49, 162, 163, 172
Romania 110
Roos, Callie 8
Roos, Olga 8
Roosterkoek 130, 131
Ross-Smith, Wayne 103
Roxo, Danny 209
Roza, Charl 126
Ruacana 153
Rudman, Les 8
Rundu 84, 126, 158, 169, 212, 217
Russia 151, 182
Ryazan 182

S
Sachse, AG (Burt) 120, 121, 149
SADF medals 185
Salads 146
Salisbury see Harare
Sangombe 169
SAS *Drakensberg* 67
SAS *Maria van Riebeeck* 37
SAS *Oswald Pirow* 37, 62
SAS *Tafelberg* 37, 38, 166
Sauces
    Killer sauce 214–215
    Red sauce 15
    White sauce 15
Savimbi, Jonas 162, 168, 212
Savong 92
Scales, Chris 92
Scales, Dave 92
Schoeman, At 184
Schofield, Peter 21, 55, 101
Schutte, Chris 74
Schlanders, Shane 30
Schweyer, Pierre 113
Second World War 21, 182
Seegers, Sakkie 92, 120, 178
Seekoei camp 208, 209
Selection food
    Blitz breakfast 22, 23
    Diesel-dipped dog biscuits 7, 18, 21
    Empty pot stew 18, 20
    Suurpap 18, 19
Seloane, Steve 147
Simon's Town 37, 57
Sinclair, Pat 107
Smit, EJ (Tilly) 66
Smith, Martin 8, 157

Smugglers Inn 91, 95, 203
Snyders, HW (Willie) 120
Snyman, Etienne (Snakes) 107
South African Air Force (SAAF) 41, 93, 145
South African Defence Force (SADF) 33, 85, 93, 112, 172, 181, 208, 209
South African Special Forces Association (Sasfa) 6, 8, 9, 88
South African Special Forces Heritage Foundation 9
South West Africa *see* Namibia
South West Africa People's Organization (Swapo) 101, 152, 153, 156
Spanneberg, Chris 202
Special Air Service (SAS) 18
Speskop 149
Spies, Wynand 21
St Michelle base 47, 163
Stadler, Koos 147
Steenkamp, Dirk 40, 59, 163
Sterkfontein 55
Sterzel, Steward 84
Steyn, Adriaan 82
Steyn, Douw 7, 66, 212
Strange, Ian 164
Strydom, Struis 50, 149, 171, 214
Sudan 170
Sugar, Caramelised 34
Sun Tzu 28, 46, 50, 154, 185, 188
Sunday Express 29
Survival food
    Dark phase baboon 18, 31
    Mince and sand 29
Swanepoel, Mugger 21, 206
Swanepoel, P 84
Swapo *see* South West Africa People's Organization
Swart, JC (Jakes) 8, 94, 148, 148, 149, 208
Swartberg 73

T
Taylor, John 149
Teachers' Training College 71
Teitge, James 7, 44, 120, 163, 181
Terry the Lion 25, 28–29, 28, 29, 164, 200

Timmerman, Tim 8, 92, 95
Tippet, Dave 73, 77, 106, 120, 148
Trauernicht, Uil 57
Trautman, Robert 217
Trout and Toad 55
Turkey, Forty-minute 88, 88
Tuser, David 181

U
Uganda 10
UmKhonto we Sizwe (MK) 53
Unita 6, 33, 47, 82, 145, 158, 159, 162, 163, 168, 168, 169, 208, 212, 216
Uys, Menno 92

V
Van Basson, Ursula 57
Van Blerk, Rocky 175
Van der Berg, Buks (Fala Merde) 106
Van der Merwe, Arno 147
Van der Merwe, Jan 163
Van der Merwe, Mac 82
Van der Merwe, Renier 158
Van der Spuy, Sybrand (Sybie) 32, 149
Van Deventer, Willie 8
Van Dyk, Frans 8, 77, 81, 127, 188
Van Heerden, Johan 8
Van Heerden, PW 22, 22, 72, 209
Van Huysteen, Theo 8
Van Niekerk, Herman 82
Van Vuuren, PJ (Fires) 148
Van Zyl, Daan 53, 108
Van Zyl, Frans 148
Van Zyl, HG 7
Van Zyl, Magda 126, 126
Van Zyl, Pep 22, 94, 95, 126, 148, 148, 149, 204
Vegetables *see also* Onions, Potatoes
    Brinjals on the fire 141, 141
    Oven-roasted vegetables 141
    Steam-fried stir-fry 140
Venter, JJ (Hannes) 8, 40, 57, 66, 148, 149, 208
Venter, Theron 21, 159
Vermaak, Justin (Totti) 101, 158, 216, 217
Vermaak, Roy 8, 26, 181, 182

Vermaak, Wally 8
Verster, Martiens 8, 76
Verster, PJ (Joe) 120
Verwey, Koos 11, 25
Vetkoek 130, 131, 131
Victoria Bay 73
Victoria Falls 173
Victorino, CC 147
Vilankulos 53, 176
Viljoen, Constand 181
Viljoen, MP 30
Villa Nova 159
Visser, Barry (Jr) 8, 102, 203, 217
Visser, Barry (Sr) 72
Viviers, Boytjie 184
Vorster, BJ 208
Vorster, Derek 163
Vosloo, Hein 8, 25
Vulture soup, omuramba 7, 26

W
Wannenburg, FG (Wannies) 148, 184
Webb, Eddie 121, 148
West, Mike 84, 206
West Coast 41, 42, 44, 160
Whaling Station 38, 95
Wilke, Fred 40, 56, 94
Wilson, Nick 38
Wolstenholmer, Charles 175

X
Xai-Xai 53
Xangongo 121

Y
Yaffe, Gary 8, 29, 113, 127, 217, 217
Ysterplaat 115

Z
Zaire *see* Democratic Republic of the Congo
Zaire Special Presidential Guard 133
Zambia 107, 145, 160, 162, 168, 172, 174
Zanzibar 37, 162
Zimbabwe 162, 172, 174
Zululand 17

Why Men Who Have Been to War Yearn to Reunite

I now know why men who have been to war yearn to reunite. It's not merely to tell stories or look at old pictures. Nor is it to weep or laugh.

Comrades gather because they long to be with the people who they once suffered and sacrificed with. Together they pushed themselves to the limits of mental and physical ability. Together they were stripped to their core.

I did not pick these men. They were delivered to me by fate and the military. But I know them in a way I know no other men. I have never trusted anyone as much.

They were willing to guard something more precious than my life. They would have protected my reputation … and the memory of me.

It was part of the bargain we all made. The reason we were all willing to die for one another. As long as I still have memory I will think of them all, every day.

I am sure that when I leave this world my last thoughts will be of my family, and of my comrades.

Such good men.

Photographic credits

Front cover: Sasfa archive (top); kofana12/Shutterstock (bottom)
Back cover: Sasfa archive

Africa Media Online: Cedric Nunn/Ind. contrib. p. 106; Anthony van Tonder p. 152; Ariadne van Zandbergen pp. 154-155; Paul Weinberg/South Photos p. 157; Jeremy Jowell/Moonshine Media p. 167; Felix Masi p. 170; Anthony van Tonder p. 179;
Ditsong National Museum of Military History/Daan Grobler p. 35;
Douw Steyn pp. 6, 37, 38, 66, 76, 94, 182, 183;
Henning de Beer p. 26;
Jakes Richter pp. 47, 100, 121, 163, 165;
Justin Vermaak pp. 32, 33, 34, 35, 40, 132, 141, 149;
Leisure Wheels p. 160;
Pete Bosman pp. 35, 214;
Rietjie Diedericks p. 12;
SAN Museum WO1 David Harrison p. 63;
SANDF Documentation Centre 216;
Shutterstock: Villiers Steyn p. 25; Artush p. 31; Andaman p. 48 (bottom); David Steele pp. 56-57; Hajakely pp. 72-73; Irgitpro p. 78 (middle); danm12 p. 78 (bottom); Elzbieta Sekowska pp. 98-99; 4Pond p. 153; Anders Stoustrup p. 158; Hannes Thirion p. 165 (top); Alexandra Tyukavina p. 171; Alexandra Tyukavina p. 173; Tobie Oosthuizen pp. 208-209.
Wikimedia Commons: Josh Berglund p. 62; Qwesy Qwesy p. 71.

All other photos supplied by members of Sasfa.